*The Life and Times of Lord Mountbatten*

*The Life and Times*

*of*

# LORD MOUNTBATTEN

*by*

## JOHN TERRAINE

*with a foreword by*

## LORD MOUNTBATTEN

ARROW BOOKS

Arrow Books Ltd
3 Fitzroy Square, London W1P 6JD

An imprint of the Hutchinson Publishing Group

London Melbourne Sydney Auckland
Wellington Johannesburg and agencies
throughout the world

First published by Hutchinson & Co. 1968
Arrow edition 1980
© Emberdove Limited and John Terraine 1968, 1980

Made and printed in the United States of America

ISBN 0 09 922630 8

# Acknowledgements

I should like to express thanks to Commander
Robin Bousfield, R.N. (rtd.), who did invaluable research for the television series on which this book
is based, and to Mr. Michael Nicholson, who was
also a researcher for the series, and in addition
selected the illustrations for the book.

The staff officer who wrote the verse appearing
on page 97 has been identified since the book was
written as Wing Commander Mervyn Horder (now
Lord Horder) whose permission to reprint the lines
is gratefully acknowledged.

The author and publishers also wish to record
their thanks to Rediffusion Television for freely
making available the material contained in this
book, and for helpful, friendly co-operation
throughout its making.

J.T.

# Contents

# *Illustrations*

---

# Foreword

How did this book come about? I suppose I ought to explain, because my friends know that I have refused to authorise any biography during my lifetime, and I certainly never intended to write any memoirs myself. So why did I agree to this book about my 'Life and Times'?

It all started because my daughters wanted my grandchildren—ten of them at present—to have some idea of what their grandfather had done. I have been involved in many historical events, but history, as taught in schools, very rarely deals with recent times, so the younger generation often knows least about the period closest to it. My son-in-law, Lord Brabourne, being a film and television producer, then came up with the suggestion that we should try to put the story of my life on film.

Ever since the end of the First World War, I had made a hobby of collecting film of personal interest. We knew that the archives of the Imperial War Museum and news-reel companies would contain much that could be useful. But obviously it would be a massive task, requiring a great deal of time, skill and money, to edit all this into a comprehensible story. John Brabourne, however, said that it should be possible to find a television company which would undertake the job and then screen the result.

This went far further than I had bargained for, and a long time passed before I was finally persuaded to agree. When I did, he found that Rediffusion Television would be prepared to do just that. So on my retirement from active duty in July 1965 the making of a television series was launched under the title of 'The Life and Times of Earl Mountbatten of Burma'. None of us then realised quite what we were taking on!

That television series has taken over three years to make. We were fortunate to enlist a brilliant producer, Peter Morley, with a fine record of documentaries for I.T.V. behind him. We then got hold of John Terraine, who has a high reputation as a military historian, and who also played a considerable part in the making of the B.B.C.'s excellent television series, 'The Great War'. These two formed the nucleus of a very hard-working and efficient team—and a very happy one, too.

The first thing they had to do was to find out just what the story was. All that took up a lot of time. Then they had to give it a shape, which eventually turned out to be twelve one-hour television programmes. And then, with the help of their indefatigable researchers, they had the monumental task of clothing the bones of the story with the flesh of actual film—archive material, and commentary by me, often filmed 'on location' where the events concerned took place. All this turned out to be one of the hardest jobs I have ever done, but out of it there slowly emerged a 'television history' of a type which has never been done before, because never before has a living participant taken part in this way.

It was encouraging for all of us to have our faith in the project warmly supported by Dr. Noble Frankland, the Director of the Imperial War Museum. He made all his facilities—thousands of feet of film, 'stills', the expertise of his staff, even his premises—available to us, and a print of the series will be permanently available in the Museum.

Other experts in their special fields also helped to ensure the authenticity of what we were doing. The team have had the privilege of consulting (and filming) Prime Ministers, Presidents, senior officers of the Services, as well as other ranks and ratings who had important contributions to make. We are very grateful to them all.

Out of this painstaking effort our 'television history' finally took shape. The team then felt that it was a perfectly logical next step to ensure that it should not be committed to the one, somewhat ephemeral, medium of television. They thought it deserved a more permanent record, and I finally agreed : hence this book.

*The Life and Times of Lord Mountbatten*

# 1

# The King's ships were at sea

---

*To Queen Victoria and Albert, Prince Consort, were born nine children: four boys and five girls. The second girl, Alice Maud Mary, was born on April 25th 1843; in 1862 she married Prince Louis of Hesse, who subsequently became the Grand Duke Louis IV of Hesse and the Rhine. They, in turn, had five children, the eldest of whom they named Victoria.*

This was my mother—Queen Victoria's grand-daughter; they were very fond of each other. She was born in 1863, in the Lancaster Tower at Windsor Castle. And I was born thirty-seven years later in Frogmore House, in Windsor Great Park, just a few hundred yards away.

I was born on June 25th 1900, the sixty-third year of Queen Victoria's reign. I was the youngest of four children: my sister Alice was already fifteen years old; my sister Louise was eleven; and my brother Georgie was nearly eight.

My great-grandmother was always very particular about the names of her descendants. When I was born she wrote to my mother, in the rather shaky handwriting of an octogenarian: 'There is one thing that would give me great pleasure if you and Louis approve of it, viz. if you would add the name Albert to the four others.' So I was christened Louis Francis Albert Victor Nicholas—but all my life people have called me Dickie.

My great-grandmother drove over from the Castle in her carriage for my christening, which took place in Frogmore House three weeks after I was born. I gather that I gave an early indication of obstreperousness by knocking her spectacles off her nose while she was holding me—but to everyone's relief she took that in good part.

It is a tremendous thing to be one of Queen Victoria's descendants. Roger Fulford, in his book *Hanover to Windsor*, wrote: 'They filled or were about to fill the thrones of Europe . . .' They did indeed. Queen Victoria's eldest daughter, Princess Victoria, married Prince Frederick of Prussia, and became Empress of Germany when he ascended the throne as Kaiser Frederick III. My mother's sister Alix married the Tsar Nicholas II of Russia. Another grand-daughter —my cousin Ena—married King Alfonso XIII of Spain. Another married King Ferdinand I of Rumania; another married King Gustav VI of Sweden, who later married my sister Louise; yet another married King Constantine I of Greece; and yet another one married King Haakon VII of Norway; one of Queen Victoria's great-grand-daughters married King Alexander I of Yugoslavia.

To me, this meant that from my earliest childhood I had close links with many countries. Later I visited a number of them, and began to take an interest in them. World affairs for us have always been very largely family affairs.

Six months after my christening my great-grandmother died, and the Victorian Age departed with her. It was the Age of Empire, and we British were proud to boast that ours was an Empire 'on which the sun never set'.

This Empire was founded on sea-power, and in the year 1900, when I was born, British sea-power was supreme.

*At Queen Victoria's Diamond Jubilee Review, in June 1897, the Royal Navy assembled 165 fighting ships. This was a deeply impressive spectacle of naval might. But its significance did not merely lie in the numbers displayed; it lay in the fact that 'not a single post abroad had been weakened to make the strong show at Spithead. Only the modern units in home waters were used.'[1] Nobody, it seemed, could compete with this.*

*Indeed, the Royal Navy had not been challenged in battle since Trafalgar; it had found no occasion to fight a major fleet action single-handed since 1805. Now it was taken for granted as the country's protection, the guardian of trade, and the sanction of the Empire. Behind the shield of the Navy, British democracy seemed secure to advance in whatever direction it pleased: towards further imperialism—or towards socialism; towards materialism—or to-*

[1] A. J. Marder: *The Anatomy of British Sea Power*, p. 281

*wards idealism; towards stability—or towards revolution. The*
*strength of the Navy permitted Britain the luxury of these options*

The year 1900 found Britain at war—at war in China, where an
international force was in the field against the Boxers, but above all
at war in South Africa. This war had begun badly: British garrisons
were besieged and threatened with capture in Ladysmith, Kimberley
and Mafeking; relieving columns suffered defeats at Colenso,
Magersfontein and Stormberg—a 'Black Week' which shook a com-
placent Empire to its foundations. Now the war was going better:
the garrisons were relieved; Bloemfontein, capital of the Orange Free
State, and Pretoria, capital of the Transvaal, were in British hands.
But the war showed no signs of ending. Disconcerting humiliations
continued to be inflicted on British arms. And world opinion, as
Britain grappled with these misfortunes, was almost unanimously
against her. There were even alarmist rumours of invasion by
continental rivals.

Against the disapproval and threats of other powers Britain had
only one shield—the Navy. In this critical turn of events significant
voices questioned whether the Navy was all it seemed to be. Was it
really supreme? Or was it largely a show-piece, which might prove
to have defects as grave as the Army's, if put to the test? Were the
great numbers displayed at Spithead in 1897 perhaps an illusion?

All these questions were prompted by the accelerating rate of
technological progress which had emerged as the chief feature of the
nineteenth century. Technology had already twice revolutionised
the nature of naval power: with the coming of steam, and with the
replacement of the paddle-wheel by the screw-propeller. As the
century ran through its last decades, naval construction was already
becoming a feverish race between the development of engine-power,
armour, guns and underwater weapons.

All this took some getting used to: the old Navy, the 'wooden
walls' which had protected Britain for centuries, had been built to
last. At Trafalgar H.M.S. Victory was already forty years old—and
in her prime. Now a ship could be obsolescent even before she was
completed. This meant that there was nothing constant, now, about
the balance of naval power: every year it changed. And it was
against this background that misgivings about the British Fleet were
conceived.

*In 1900 British warships had black hulls, gleaming white upper works, yellow funnels, and gilded scrolls at the bow and stern. It was the age of spit-and-polish, of spotless decks, well-kept paintwork and gleaming brass. But sceptics and naval reformers asked whether these imposing ships were really efficient fighting units.*

*The critics had a case. Gunnery, they said, was often neglected, because it spoilt the paintwork. Long-range gunnery was unknown—although the range of modern weapons was constantly increasing. In some ships the guns were still muzzle-loaders; old-fashioned black powder, a poor propellent which threw out heavy clouds of smoke, was still in use. There were not enough torpedoes, nor torpedo-craft. Submarines had already emerged as a potential threat to surface ships and commerce; in 1900 Britain had none. Telescopic sights and gyroscopes were in short supply; the development of wireless telegraphy required attention. Basic training was still founded on the departed age of sail.*

*These revelations caused a considerable stir. If the equanimity of the British public was shaken by the revelation of defects in the Army, the mere thought of such a state of affairs in the Navy almost destroyed it. It was clear that far-reaching naval reforms were in the air.*

I was born into a period of drastic change which was bound to affect me very closely. There was scarcely any doubt about what I was going to do when I grew up—it was taken for granted that I would go into the Navy. That was the family tradition

My father was Prince Louis of Battenberg. He had entered the Royal Navy as a cadet in 1868; now he was a captain, and quite obviously going to the top. He belonged to the 'progressive' school of naval officers—the school headed at that time by Admiral Sir John Fisher, who initiated the great naval reforms then impending, and which really created the Navy which fought the First World War.

Fisher once referred to my father as 'out and away the best man inside the Admiralty building'—but their first close association was at sea, in the Mediterranean Fleet. And it was in the Mediterranean—after Fisher had left—that my father marked himself out for high command. Fisher had begun the practice of holding joint annual manœuvres of the Mediterranean and Channel Fleets. In 1902 my father, who was then commanding the battleship *Implacable*, was made a commodore, and put in command of the 'X' Fleet for the manoeuvres.

This was a force of older, weaker and slower ships, which was 'blockaded' in the harbour of Argostoli by the combined might of the Mediterranean and Channel Fleets, with all their modern vessels. My father contrived to make a brilliant escape from the harbour under their very noses. This was not only a very skilful performance, which singled him out among his contemporaries; it also signed the death-warrant of the Navy's traditional strategy of close blockade, which had been handed down from the days of Nelson.

It was in that same year, 1902, that my father became Director of Naval Intelligence. As such, he was virtually the head of the very small Naval Staff of those days. He held this post until 1905—key years, during which British policy underwent fundamental changes. My father was closely concerned with the naval implications of these—and no less concerned with the reforms which Fisher, now Second Sea Lord, was beginning to carry out in the Fleet. In fact, one disgruntled officer, leaving the Admiralty in 1903, complained that it was 'practically run by Fisher, Battenberg and Tyrwhitt'.

In 1905 my brother Georgie carried on the family tradition by entering the Royal Naval College at Osborne. Two years later my father went to Malta, as Second-in-Command of the Mediterranean Fleet, and I went with him. I had been there before, as a baby, but my Malta memories really begin with this occasion.

Malta and the Mediterranean were not virgin ground for our family. One of our ancestors, Prince Frederick of Hesse-Darmstadt (1616–1682), entered the Order of St. John as a Knight of Malta. He became Captain-General of the Galleys—what we would call Naval C.-in-C. of the Order—and in 1640 he defeated the Turks in one of their attacks on Malta. A later ancestor was Prince George of Hesse-Darmstadt (1669–1705). He was a soldier from the age of three—when he was appointed honorary captain in a Dutch regiment commanded by his uncle, Duke Albert of Saxony. But his real claim to fame was his appointment in 1704 to command an Allied army which was assembled to fight the Bourbons in Spain. The British contributed a fleet, and this fleet, commanded by Admiral Rooke, attacked Gibraltar on August 5th 1704. Prince George commanded and led the Marines who captured the fortress. In fact, he was really responsible for the success of the enterprise, and as overall commander of the expedition assumed the office of Governor of Gibraltar.

I enjoyed Malta. It was very different in those days; there were no cars then—but there were carriages and donkeys to ride. And there were parties: for one party, my father and I wore costumes given us by my uncle, the Tsar of Russia. My father went as an Imperial Falconer, and I went dressed as a Cossack.

My mother took charge of my education—in fact, I didn't go to school until I was ten. This was a positive advantage, because she had a talent for teaching. She really was that often-spoken-of thing: a walking encyclopaedia. All through her life she stored up knowledge on all sorts of subjects, and she had the great gift of being able to make it all interesting when she taught it to me. She was completely methodical; we had time-tables for each subject, and I had to do preparation, and so forth. She taught me to enjoy working hard, and to be thorough. She was outspoken and open-minded to a degree quite unusual in members of the Royal Family. And she was also entirely free from prejudice about politics or colour and things of that kind. So I was brought up without prejudice too; I was taught to examine everything on its merits.

I really was most fortunate in my parents. My father's interests and talents extended well beyond his profession. He was a fine musician, and he could draw and paint well. Like my mother, he was very well informed, and both of them always talked quite freely on all subjects to all of us children. I travelled a good deal as a child—to Malta or Gibraltar with the Fleet, or to Germany for holidays at my parents' castle, Schloss Heiligenberg in Hesse, or to Russia to stay with our relations. What with all this, and my mother's teaching, by the time my turn came to enter the Navy I feel I was considerably better-equipped than most cadets.

*At the beginning of the twentieth century the German Empire possessed the most powerful military machine in the world. Backed by vigorous industry and an expanding population, proudly bearing the laurels of lightning victories over Denmark in 1864, Austria and the South German Confederation in 1866, and France in 1870–1, the German Army outshone all others in numbers and efficiency. At* the head of this formidable organisation stood the German Emperor, the Kaiser Wilhelm II, the Supreme War Lord.

It was a splendid position, but it did not satisfy this strange, talented but unstable man. This grandson of Queen Victoria and nephew of Edward VII envied his British relatives the source of their world-wide standing and prestige: the supremacy of the Royal Navy. Under Wilhelm II Germany began to build a navy; not just a force for coastal protection, or squadrons to dominate the Baltic, but a High Seas Fleet. By 1906, while remaining the world's leading military power, Germany had also become the world's second naval power. Her fleet was modern, its equipment first-class; construction, gunnery, training, personnel were excellent.

The meaning of this astonishing development was also clear: this was a direct threat to the Royal Navy, and thus to Britain herself. From its harbours and bases in north-west Germany— Emden, Wilhelmshaven, Bremerhaven, Cuxhaven, Kiel—the German Fleet faced due west across the North Sea, straight towards Britain. And Britain's naval bases, after 250 years of contest with Spain and Holland and France, were at Chatham, a long way south, Portsmouth and Devonport, far to the west and facing south themselves. Yet every year it became more evident that the future decisive battleground would be the North Sea.

Fortunately, the Royal Navy found a leader who grasped the situation.

It was in 1904, when my father was still Director of Naval Intelligence, that Lord Fisher (as he afterwards became) returned to the Admiralty as First Sea Lord. He had already embarked upon his tremendous work of Naval Reform as Second Sea Lord, responsible for Personnel. But there is no doubt that his main achievement took place during his five years as First Sea Lord.

What an extraordinary man Fisher was!

He had dynamic energy, he was full of ideas, and completely unconventional in his mode of expressing them. On one occasion King Edward VII had to say to him: 'Would you kindly leave off shaking your fists in my face?'

Fisher proclaimed that his 'Three R's' were: 'Ruthless, Relentless and Remorseless'. And with this slogan he set about giving the Navy a tremendous shake-up. My father used to tell me how much he admired Fisher's work, and he always supported him. But he could never approve of some of Fisher's methods—in particular, the intrigue which always surrounded him.

'Favouritism,' Fisher said, 'is the secret of efficiency.' But the effect of this doctrine was to split the Navy from top to bottom.

Yet the work that Fisher did at the Admiralty was vital. He tackled the question of naval entry—he insisted on a common entry for all officers, to overcome the absurd 'class distinction' between 'seamen' and technical experts, such as engineer officers. This reform was later abandoned, and had to be revived by me in 1957.

Fisher lowered the promotion ages for captains and admirals. He started a proper system of higher training. He stopped the traditional practice of training a steam navy on sailing ships.

But above all he prepared the Fleet for war—war against Germany, which he was sure was coming. He started long-range battle practice at last. He put Jellicoe in charge of gunnery, which improved out of all recognition. He put the Naval Reserve on a sound footing, and created the Reserve Fleet. He scrapped 154 obsolete ships, amid howls of execration—fifty years later I got some idea of what that means! And finally he concentrated the Fleet at strategic points, specifically to face the German threat.

But the thing that Fisher is most famous for—and it was his most controversial act at the time—concerned the ships themselves. In February 1906 he brought about a naval revolution: the launching of H.M.S. *Dreadnought*, the first all-big-gun, turbine-driven, fast capital ship. By modern standards she didn't amount to much— even twelve years later she was out-of-date, although she served throughout the First World War. But when she was launched, in 1906, the *Dreadnought* made every other battleship in the world obsolete.

*The launching of H.M.S.* Dreadnought *instantly wiped out Britain's large existing advantage in numbers of capital ships. (For this reason, above all, Fisher's critics attacked him with renewed violence.) Now all shipbuilding nations competed on practically level terms, and the naval race against Germany gained a fearful momentum. The powers of Europe, in the first decade of the twentieth century, talked much of disarmament, but everywhere arms were multiplying, and alignments were being formed.*

*In 1903 King Edward VII visited Paris and prepared the way for* friendship between Britain and France—the Entente Cordiale. The traditional enemies and rivals drew together under the growing shadow of German might. The first test of the new alliance was not long delayed: it came in 1905, and the Entente stood firm, to the astonishment of many, through the Moroccan crisis brought on by Germany in 1905–6.

In 1907 Britain reached agreement with France's chief ally, Russia; and now the alignments of Europe hardened into a dangerous pattern: the Triple Entente of Britain, France and Russia, against the Triple Alliance of Germany, Austria-Hungary and Italy.

The pace of crisis quickened. In 1909 Britain was swept by a scare of secret German naval construction which might give Germany equality or even superiority in dreadnoughts. The Admiralty demanded six new dreadnoughts; the economists in the Government, headed by Winston Churchill and Lloyd George, insisted that four would be ample. Then the slogan was heard:

'We want eight, and we won't wait!'

'Panic,' declared The Daily News, 'is spreading like the plague.'

The Observer urged its readers to insist on 'the eight, the whole eight, and nothing but the eight'.

And so the eight were laid down.

The 1909 scare had been largely based on fear and false information, but, wrote Churchill later, 'although Lloyd George and I were right in the narrow sense, we were absolutely wrong in relation to the deep tides of destiny'.

Neither pacific speeches nor friendly gestures could now halt these tides. At the funeral of King Edward VII in 1910 nine monarchs walked or rode in procession together—prominent among them the German Kaiser, following the coffin of the uncle whom he had detested, beside the new King George V. His presence was construed as a friendly sign; in Anglo-German relations it was practically the last.

In 1911 a new quarrel arose between France and Germany, once more over Morocco. This was the 'Agadir Crisis', which for a time seemed certain to drag Britain into war. And now a frightening gap in British preparations was perceived. There was no agreement— not even understanding—between the War Office and the Admiralty, over what should be done in case of war. Indeed, it appeared that Lord Fisher had retired leaving the Navy with no war plan at all. It was a habit of that strange genius to carry much vital *matter in his head, not trusting it to paper, and now, as far as could be discovered, the Fisher plan for the Navy would have been to force an entry into the Baltic, and land the Army on Germany's northern shores. The War Office, on the other hand, was well advanced with detailed arrangements, in agreement with France, to place the British Army on the left wing of the French, concentrating at Amiens.*

*When this appalling divergence became apparent those who understood were profoundly shocked. Drastic and immediate action was demanded.*

.    .    .    .    .

It was to clear up the mess which had been revealed during the Agadir Crisis that Winston Churchill first came to the Admiralty as First Lord in October 1911.

Two months later my father returned to the Admiralty as Second Sea Lord, and in that position initiated many of the new and overdue personnel reforms which were carried out during Churchill's period of office.

But Churchill's chief task was to set up something against which Fisher had always firmly set his face—a real Naval Staff, to prepare strategic plans and integrate them with War Office plans, so that we should never find ourselves in such a ridiculous position again. My father had always believed in this, and he was Churchill's strongest backer—against, I need hardly add, the usual stiff opposition which innovators encounter in Britain.

It was during this time—I was eleven years old—that I first came to know Winston Churchill. He would often walk home with my father after a day's work, and call at our house. He was very good with young people, very friendly, and would talk to me as though I was grown up. I wasn't sure what to make of him. My mother told me he was unreliable—because he had once borrowed a book and failed to return it. Later I formed the same conclusion myself, when I was a cadet at Osborne, and he came down to inspect us. He asked whether we had any complaints, and whether there was anything he could do. Rather boldly, I got up and said, yes, there was something; he could get us three sardines each for our Sunday supper, instead of two. This he promised to do, but the third sardine never materialised, so that I knew he was unreliable!

He certainly fluttered the dovecots as First Lord. During his first eighteen months he spent 182 days at sea—something no First Lord has done before or since.

He upset a great many people. There were complaints to the Admiralty that he undermined naval discipline by consulting lower ranks without reference to senior officers. He disgusted his Radical friends by no longer talking of 'bloated armaments', but, instead, backing the Navy's demands for money. And he made the King furious when he proposed to name a new battleship the *Oliver Cromwell*!

But his achievements were great. He improved Lower Deck conditions, increased the prospects of promotion to commissioned rank, and brought forward younger officers—among them Sir John Jellicoe and Sir David Beatty.

A significant step forward was his speeding up of work on the new North Sea bases—Rosyth and Cromarty and Scapa Flow. These were absolutely vital, in view of the German menace; but it takes time and money to build naval bases, and time was running short.

In December 1912 my father became First Sea Lord, and the most fruitful period of his association with Churchill then began. Together they started a Naval War Staff—but that again is a long job. You can't produce a large number of fully trained staff officers overnight.

Churchill and my father revised the war plans, this time taking the Army into account, and they decided on the strategy of distant blockade which was adopted from the moment war was declared.

But beyond a doubt the most important thing that they did together—with tremendous consequences—was their decision not to hold the normal annual manœuvres in 1914. At my father's suggestion they decided instead to have a Test Mobilisation of the Reserve Fleet, something that had not been done before, to find out just how effective our arrangements were for bringing the Navy quickly up to strength in time of war. This extraordinarily valuable exercise took place in July 1914, and the whole mobilisation worked without a hitch.

By this time I was in the Navy myself. I had entered the Royal Naval College at Osborne the year before, and to our intense excitement we cadets were also mobilised. I was sent to my brother's ship—the battle-cruiser *New Zealand*.

After the Test Mobilisation the whole Fleet assembled at Spithead for the Royal Review, and so I had a grandstand seat. It was a wonderful spectacle—a sort of grand climax of two hundred years of British naval supremacy.

King George V, in the Royal Yacht *Victoria and Albert*, passed in review 40 miles of ships, manned by 70,000 men. There were no less than 59 battleships and battle-cruisers, 24 of them dreadnoughts. There were 55 cruisers of various types, 78 destroyers, 16 submarines, and a large number of minor craft.

None of us could know that this whole tremendous organisation of naval might—the product, first of Fisher's reforms, then of Churchill's and my father's—was going to be put immediately to the ultimate test. Because all the time the King was reviewing his Fleet at Spithead the international situation was building up to the final crisis which produced the Great War.

My father, of course, was one of the first to know. It was on July 26th 1914 that he took the most momentous decision of his life. It was a Sunday. The First Lord, the Prime Minister, the Foreign Secretary—in fact, I believe, most of the Cabinet—had gone away for the weekend, a sacrosanct custom. The next day, all the men who had been called up for the Test Mobilisation were due to be paid off, most of them would then go off on holiday, and the Fleet would be dispersed. This meant that from a position of unparalleled naval strength and preparedness the country would pass overnight into a state of unpreparedness.

On the other hand, *not* to demobilise on the advertised date could well be construed as an act of war, and might make the international situation even worse.

It was a fearful decision to have to take, and I remember my father telling me that he had had to take it absolutely alone. But there was no mistaking the meaning of the information coming in, and he reached his decision not to demobilise. He wrote out in his own hand the telegrams ordering the Fleet to stand fast. Churchill, when he heard what had been done, gave his immediate approval.

Two days later the signal went out from the Admiralty: 'Tomorrow, Wednesday, the First Fleet is to leave Portland for Scapa Flow. Destination to be kept secret . . .'

So the Royal Navy went to its war-stations. Winston Churchill wrote: 'We may now picture this great Fleet, with its flotillas and cruisers, steaming slowly out of Portland Harbour, squadron by squadron, scores of gigantic castles of steel wending their way across the misty, shining sea, like giants bowed in anxious thought. . . . We may picture them again as darkness fell, eighteen miles of warships running at high speed and in absolute blackness through the narrow Straits, bearing with them into the broad waters of the North the safeguard of considerable affairs. The King's ships were at sea.'

And so, on August 4th 1914, when Britain found herself at war, my father was able to report to the King: 'We have the drawn sword in our hand.'

*The Grand Fleet, commanded by Admiral Jellicoe, and containing the modern battleships which were the hard core of the Navy's strength in 1914, assembled uneasily at Scapa Flow. The great anchorage was not yet fully protected, and constant submarine and mine scares kept the precious ships and their escorts constantly alert, frequently on the move. Only at sea and at speed could Jellicoe feel really safe.*

*Further south, at Rosyth, under Vice-Admiral Beatty, stood the Battle-cruiser Fleet, devised by Fisher as the fast wing or advance-guard of the Grand Fleet. The battle-cruisers had yet to be proved in action; for the time being, whatever their main rôle might be, they constituted a useful support to the light cruiser, destroyer and submarine flotillas concentrated at Harwich under Commodore Tyrwhitt.*

*The general belief in August 1914 was that the German High Seas Fleet would immediately spring out from its bases across the North Sea and attempt to inflict crippling damage on the Grand Fleet, with the aid of submarines and mine-fields. At the very least the German Navy was expected to make any reasonable sacrifice to prevent or hinder the transportation of the British Expeditionary Force to France.*

*To the astonishment of experts and laymen alike it did neither of these things. The young, proud German Navy, the apple of the Kaiser's eye, built specifically as a challenge to England, remained passively in harbour. As days of inaction, broken only by Beatty's foray in the Heligoland Bight, passed into weeks, then months, the Royal Navy and the country at large felt cheated. It was hard to understand this style of war.*

*Yet the truth—hard indeed for laymen to understand—was that*

*naval supremacy had already been emphatically asserted. British
trade, on all the oceans, was able to continue almost without interruption. Food, raw material, all the sinews of war needed by an
island Power, continued to pour into British ports—thanks to naval
supremacy. The German Merchant Marine had been swept silently
from the seas.*

*Even more remarkable, the British Expeditionary Force, under
Field-Marshal Sir John French, some 80,000 strong to begin with,
was conveyed to France, maintained and steadily increased without
the loss of a single man, horse or gun by enemy action at sea.*

*Not only that—the Empire, also, was mobilised. Indian troops
were brought to France; Australians and New Zealanders (partly
escorted by the Japanese Navy) arrived in the Middle East;
Canadians poured into Britain. This was naval supremacy at work,
almost unbelievably successfully; but the man in the street took
such matters for granted. The public expected action they could
recognise.*

*During the first weeks of war the country was full of alarms and
rumours. Sensational stories of disaster circulated from the battle-
front in France. There were invasion scares and innumerable spy-
panics. The public mood turned ugly. Anti-German feeling ran high,
and sought an outlet against Germans and Austrians living in
Britain. German shops were attacked and looted; even German
churches were stoned.*

*Attention turned to individuals. It was asked whether all was well
at the Admiralty. Why was the Navy not winning the expected
victories?*

All this was a form of hysteria which gripped people at that time.
They insulted German governesses; they wouldn't listen to German
music; they would even kick dachshunds in the streets; they saw
spies under every bed.

And the Press played this hysteria up and made it worse. Lord
Haldane, the great War Minister who had reformed the Army only
a few years earlier, was accused of being pro-German, and hounded
out of public life.

My father was attacked because of our German name. One paper
even carried an attack on my father on one page, and on another a
glowing report of the first death in action of a member of the Royal

Family—his nephew, Prince Maurice of Battenberg, killed at Ypres, fighting in the 6oth, the King's Royal Rifle Corps.

My father came to the conclusion that these attacks on him were damaging to the Navy. On October 29th 1914 he resigned from his post as First Sea Lord, and the Government, under duress, accepted his resignation.

*Sensible men were horrified at this outcome. The Times wrote: 'Gossip of this kind is, we suppose, an inevitable concomitant of democratic Government. It exhibits none the less its most contemptible side, and honest men will not care to remember its results in this case.'*

The news of my father's resignation came as a terrible shock to me —though it was probably even worse for my brother, who was in the Fleet.

I was still at Osborne. I remember having to go away and think about it alone. The other cadets were kind and decent about it (in fact, many of them were shocked too), but I didn't want to see them. I just wanted to be by myself.

It was all so stupid. My father had been in the Royal Navy for forty-six years. He was completely identified with England, and we always regarded ourselves as an English family.

Of course, we were well aware of our German connections; how could we not be? It certainly never occurred to any of us to be ashamed of them—rather the contrary. We are a very old family, and proud of it.

I have always been interested in genealogy—in fact, I became President of the Society of Genealogists—and it was one of my spare-time pleasures to work out our lineage. It proved to be a very considerable task, which took me years to complete. I believe I can trace us back through forty-four generations, to the sixth century A.D. I *know* I can trace our line back to the ninth century, to Charlemagne.

At that time our lands were in Brabant and Lorraine—an area which is now mostly Belgium and Holland. The German connection didn't begin until the thirteenth century, when one of my ancestors became Landgrave of Hesse. Hesse then became the family centre, and remained so.

My grandfather was Prince Alexander of Hesse and the Rhine.

(He was the uncle of the Grand Duke Louis IV, who married Queen Victoria's daughter, Princess Alice, my maternal grandmother.) Prince Alexander was a professional soldier, as so many members of my family have been. He had a distinguished career in the Russian Army, and became a general. He even had a regiment of Russian Lancers named after him. In 1850 he became commander of the Guards Cuirassier Division, the crack Household Cavalry of the Russian Empire.

But then he committed a breach of etiquette. His sister Marie had married the Grand Duke Tsarevitch who later became Tsar Alexander II. My grandfather fell in love with one of his sister's ladies-in-waiting, and eloped with her. As this was done without the Tsar's permission (indeed, entirely against the Tsar's own intentions for him) he was dismissed from the Russian Army, and deprived of his Russian general's rank.

The lady my grandfather married was the Countess Julie of Hauke; they were a Polish family. The marriage was morganatic, and after the wedding the Grand Duke Louis III of Hesse, my grandfather's brother, created her Countess of Battenberg, after a small town in the north of the Grand Duchy. Later she became Princess of Battenberg, and their four sons and one daughter carried the titles of Princes and Princess of Battenberg.

Since he could no longer serve Russia, my grandfather, who was already a general in the Hessian Army, transferred his services to Austria. In 1852 he was appointed major-general in the Austrian Army, and in 1859 he commanded an Austrian division at the Battle of Solferino, where he distinguished himself by preventing a rout and rallying his men. In 1862 he retired.

But four years later most of Germany was involved in war—what is often wrongly called the Austro-Prussian War. This was the decisive struggle for the leadership of Germany, which the Prussians were determined to seize from Austria. A Confederation was formed to oppose them, which included Bavaria, Saxony and Hesse. My grandfather was called out of retirement to command the VIII Confederate Army Corps.

But even in 1866 the Prussian Army was a most efficient military machine, well trained, well equipped and well led. The Prussians had planned this campaign thoroughly; the Confederation, on the other hand, was quite unprepared—and so it was beaten. The whole thing was over in seven weeks. Some parts of the Hessian lands were annexed to Prussia, and those that weren't annexed had to accept her overlordship. It was a bitter moment for a state which had for centuries been proud and independent.

My father was twelve years old when this happened, so he had good reason to detest the Prussians from a very early age. But that apart, he passionately wanted to be a sailor. There was no such thing as a German Navy at that time, so when he was fourteen he left Germany and came to England. He became a naturalised British subject, went to a naval crammer, and joined the Royal Navy in 1868.

He had then worked his way to the top by sheer ability and industry. And now his career was finished—all because of the ridiculous suspicion that he might be in secret sympathy with the very people he had come to England to avoid!

*On the day of Prince Louis's resignation a new act of aggression brought Germany a fresh ally in the war—Turkey. Two German warships, the* Goeben *and the* Breslau, *which had escaped through the Dardanelles Straits to Constantinople in August, on October 29th bombarded Sebastopol and other Russian Black Sea ports.*

*Turkey's entry into the war opened up new prospects for British sea-power to exploit. If Turkey could be knocked out quickly the Allies would be able to open, through the Dardanelles, a direct, ice-free line of communication with Russia. Western war-material could be poured in to sustain the hard-pressed Russian armies; Russian wheat could be exported to the Allies; a new joint front against Germany might even be established, and so the deadlock of the Western Front might be broken. Glittering prospects—coupled with romantic place-names: the Hellespont, Constantinople, the Golden Horn! To no one did they appeal more forcibly than to Winston Churchill, First Lord of the Admiralty. Churchill's mind conceived the Gallipoli Expedition.*

Gallipoli is one of the large 'ifs' of history.

It was the great Combined Operation of the First World War, and it profoundly affected the British war-effort, not just in 1915, but for many years after.

In 1915 I was still a naval cadet—now at Dartmouth. I was tremendously interested in this campaign, and I discussed it with my father, who now, alas! had more time to spare to answer my questions.

My father was a friend of the famous American Admiral Mahan, who had made probably the profoundest existing analysis of the nature and use of sea-power. My father had also studied this deeply. All along he questioned the wisdom of a naval power like Britain committing herself to a continental land-war. Sea-power, he told me, is far more than just winning naval battles. It is a flexible weapon: it enables one to strike where one wishes, and get away again if necessary. It can open up new fronts in places which are difficult for the enemy. It offers opportunities for surprise. All these things, my father believed, were potentially true of Gallipoli.

To his great dismay, all the advantages were thrown away. Early in January, for no good military reason, an Allied fleet bombarded the Turkish forts at the entrance to the Dardanelles—and so alerted the enemy. After that nothing happened until February 19th. By then Winston had persuaded the Government that the Navy could force the Dardanelles by itself, using our old, obsolete battleships against the forts. This, also, dismayed my father: he considered that ships were not meant to fight forts.

The Fleet didn't do badly on February 19th, but bad weather forced it to stop. When it returned a week later the Turks had strengthened their defences still further, and were making good use of mine-fields. These had to be swept, which took up more time.

The next big naval attack was on March 18th—nearly three months after the first alert. This time things went badly: four French and three big British ships were either sunk or seriously damaged by mines or gun-fire—among them a modern unit, the battle-cruiser *Inflexible*.

It now became perfectly clear to everyone that this would have to be a Combined Operation: the Army would have to occupy the shores of the Straits, to open the way for the Navy into the Sea of Marmora.

The Army had the greatest difficulty in finding troops, and those it found were quite unprepared for this work. Soldiers were sent out from England in ships which were not tactically loaded—so they had to be sent back to Alexandria to be reloaded. There were no assault craft, no specialised equipment of any description, and no amphibious training. All the rules of Combined Operations were broken.

We all know the result: severe losses on some of the beaches—

the sea stained red with blood for fifty yards out from the shore; then a long-drawn-out, costly campaign, ending in failure.

It ended the career of the Military Commander, General Sir Ian Hamilton, and it cost Winston Churchill his job as First Lord. Worse still, it lost British sea-power the chance to intervene decisively in the war, because nothing like this was ever tried again.

And twenty-five years later, when Churchill set up a Combined Operations Headquarters, of which I was to become Chief, the ghosts of Gallipoli still haunted us.

*After Gallipoli the strength of the British Empire was poured into France. The British Expeditionary Force, in August 1914, consisted of four infantry divisions; in 1916 it grew to fifty-eight divisions. Australians, New Zealanders, Canadians and South Africans gathered on the Western Front. Nothing like this muster had ever been seen in British history.*

*For the first time Britain was preparing to take the leading rôle in a major continental war. Hundreds of heavy guns, newly manufactured, thousands of field guns, vast quantities of ammunition from Britain's galvanised war industry, hundreds of thousands of men—the Kitchener Armies, the last of the volunteers—assembled for the coming trial of strength.*

*As though to emphasise this historic tide-mark, now, at last, came the long-awaited contest of the two great fleets. After a year of idleness the German Navy passed to the offensive, seeking to do at least a permanent injury to the British Fleet. The clash came on May the 31st 1916; the Battle of Jutland.*

*On that misty day 259 British and German warships met and grappled in the North Sea. This was the moment for which the German Fleet had been constructed; this was the moment the Royal Navy had been waiting for ever since Fisher had begun his reforms far back in 1904. From Rosyth, Beatty's Battle-cruiser Fleet (which now included four fast battleships of the* Queen Elizabeth *class), and from Scapa Flow, Jellicoe's Grand Fleet, with twenty-four more battleships, steamed out to meet the challenge.*

*The issue of the day was curiously enigmatic. The British, in a series of unco-ordinated encounters, lost fourteen ships, the Germans eleven. The British lost twice as many men as the Germans. And they failed to destroy the German Fleet, which was their intention and Britain's expectation.*

*But the Germans also failed in their intention—to cripple the British Fleet. And the perils and losses they encountered at Jutland so discouraged them that they never sought battle again. As a New York newspaper put it: 'The German Fleet has assaulted its jailor; but it is still in jail.'*

*For Britain and the Navy the great shock of Jutland was the sudden destruction, one after the other, of three great battle-cruisers—*Indefatigable, Queen Mary *and* Invincible—*with awful loss of life.*

The Battle-cruiser Fleet was commanded by Vice-Admiral Sir David Beatty, whose flagship was H.M.S. *Lion.* I joined the *Lion* less than seven weeks after the Battle of Jutland. She was still under repair in Rosyth dockyard, and she was in a pretty good mess. There was a gaping hole where the centre turret had been, and cordite fires had left their marks all over her.

But the spirit of the ship's company was sky-high.

I was terribly disappointed to have missed the battle; my brother, in the *New Zealand,* had been in the thick of it, and, of course, everybody was talking about it.

I was tremendously excited to be in Beatty's flagship. I was one of his most ardent hero-worshippers—and he certainly looked every inch a hero. We all quoted his famous remark to his flag-captain at Jutland, when two of his ships had blown up, and his own flagship was on fire: 'There's something wrong with our bloody ships to-day, Chatfield. Turn two points to port' (i.e. nearer to the enemy).

We thought the *Lion* was the greatest ship in the world, with the bravest men and the finest admiral.

I had just turned sixteen when I joined as a midshipman. In some respects conditions were not very different from those of Nelson's days. The midshipmen slept in hammocks, which we slung wherever we could find a space—we had no proper quarters of our own. By the time I came along, all the best billets were taken. I had to sling my hammock under a police-light, which was never switched off; it was just a few inches above my face. I got used to sleeping with a handkerchief over my eyes.

On Sunday mornings we were called at 4 a.m. We had to scrub out the Mess, polish the bright-work and get everything ship-shape. One of my jobs was to look after the leather settees; on one occasion, when I failed to have one of the seams sewn up, I was beaten.

That was the traditional gun-room treatment of midshipmen—'snotties', as we were called. For instance, at meals, if the sub-lieutenant of the Mess stuck his fork into the beam above him all the junior snotties had to clear out; the last one out got beaten. Or if the Sub said, 'Breadcrumbs', all the junior snotties had to block their ears. If he then quietly said: 'All right, Battenberg, *you* can listen' and you took your fingers out, showing that you *had* been listening, you got beaten.

This happened the whole time; it was barbaric, I suppose, but we expected it. However, the whole thing got so bad that it had to be stopped by Admiral Beatty himself—so I was probably one of the last to go through it.

But naval life in general was tough and tiring in those days. Take coaling, for instance, a chore which vanished many years ago. The *Lion* was a coal-burning ship. This meant that whenever we came in from a sweep we had to coal ship. That was an exhausting, filthy business, because the coal had to be dug out of the holds of the colliers, bagged, transported to the *Lion*, then re-distributed in her holds. The whole ship's company took part in this; no one was excused. It would take from ten to twelve hours, and one became absolutely encrusted in coal-dust from head to foot. The junior snotties, I might add, only had small tin baths to wash it all off in afterwards; it hung about one for days.

All the battle-cruisers were proud of their coaling efficiency—they used to take in about 250–300 tons an hour. But morale in the *Lion* was so high that on more than one occasion we took in over 400 tons an hour.

It was all pretty strenuous for a youngster of sixteen. We were kept hard at it, keeping watch by day and night, running a picket boat when we were in harbour, and learning our profession. We didn't get much sleep. But hard work and discomfort didn't dim my enthusiasm for the Navy, or my love for my ship.

*In 1916 the war at sea took a sinister turn. The High Seas Fleet had failed in its purpose, but the German Navy had another weapon— U-boats. In September 226,000 tons of Allied shipping were sunk, in October 352,000 tons. The curve on the graph continued to rise to the fearsome figure of 849,000 tons in April 1917. This spelt out a clear prospect of disaster for an island power.*

*In November 1916 Admiral Jellicoe was brought from the Grand*

*Fleet to the Admiralty as First Sea Lord, to apply his mind to the anti-U-boat war. His successor as Commander-in-Chief was Admiral Beatty, now flying his flag in the battleship* Queen Elizabeth.

All of us in the Battle-cruiser Fleet were delighted that Beatty was going to be C.-in-C. My father had told me that Sir John Jellicoe was very clever, and assured me that he was brave too. But as far as I was concerned he was an insignificant little man in old-fashioned clothes, who looked rather like a tapir, and didn't impress me at all. He would be far better, I thought, at an Admiralty desk than commanding a fleet, which calls for guts and leadership.

When I grew older, and, I trust, wiser, I drastically revised this opinion. In fact, I became a great admirer of Jellicoe. But that was how I felt at the age of sixteen, and many others in the Battle-cruiser Fleet shared this opinion.

*At Scapa Flow the Grand Fleet awaited the enemy who never came; awaited also new ammunition and new equipment which Jutland had shown to be vitally needed; and began to absorb the lessons of the battle into training.*

*In France the Battle of the Somme, which had begun disastrously for the British Army on July 1st, now, after wavering fortunes, slowed to a stop amid the mud, ice and blizzards of a bad November. British casualties reached 415,000 in this battle—and when spring came the Allies planned to renew it and force it to the victorious conclusion which 1916 had failed to produce. By the end of that year Britain had become a land-power indeed, and was learning with revulsion the price of that condition.*

*The mood of the British people became increasingly embittered. The long casualty-lists brought this war home as none had ever done before. Air-raids, by Zeppelins and bombers, destroyed the last illusions of island security. Unrestricted U-boat warfare brought rationing and privation. Conscription came, against all British tradition: conscription for the Army, conscription of labour, mobilisation of women.*

*And there was no sign of peace.*

*In 1917 the British hardened their hearts; their anger rose against their enemies, and turned again against enemy aliens in their midst —or anyone at all who seemed to be in any way connected with the enemy.*

Once more people were in a state of hysteria—and the Government felt that they had to make further concessions to it. In July 1917 the Prime Minister, Mr. Lloyd George, advised King George V that the Royal Family should take British names. The King's family took the name of 'Windsor'. Queen Mary's family name had been 'Teck'; that was changed to 'Cambridge'. My father changed our name from 'Battenberg' to 'Mountbatten', and the King conferred on him the title of Marquess of Milford Haven.

It was all rather ludicrous. I'd been born in England, and I'd always felt completely English. Having an English name didn't make me any more English. But such was the mood of the times. . . .

Anyway, now I was Midshipman Lord Louis Mountbatten, and the 'Mountbatten story' may be said to begin at this point: July 1917—the fourth year of the Great War.

# 2
# The kings depart

When the King changed his name in response to a hysterical public agitation, and my father changed our family name from Battenberg to Mountbatten, these breaks with the past caused a good deal of consternation. All tradition was in the melting-pot at that time. The year 1917 marked the beginning of the fall of many royal houses, and we were not immune to these events. . . .

*Imperial Russia had had a terrible war.*

*Loyally supporting her Western Allies in August 1914, her unready armies at once invaded East Prussia. Before the month was out they met shattering defeat at Tannenberg.*

*The equally shattering Russian victory over the Austrians at Lemberg, the repulse of the Turks later in the year, and a stubborn winter defensive, could not make good the damage.*

*In 1915 Germany and Austria set out to crush the Russian Empire in a long-drawn-out campaign beginning with the Battle of Gorlice-Tarnow. The attempt failed; but Russian losses during that year—killed, wounded, prisoners and deserters—amounted to about two million. The giant was almost on his knees.*

*Yet in 1916 Russia revived, and a brilliant offensive under General Brusilov inflicted irreparable damage on the Empire of Austria-Hungary. But the cost was crippling. The hard winter of 1916–17 brought the Russian people to breaking-point.*

*The setbacks of the Russian Army were defeats of the Imperial régime. In 1915, in the midst of disaster, the Tsar Nicholas II made himself Commander-in-Chief of the Army. This was a grave error, for now he was blamed for all its failures. And with the Tsar at Headquarters, it was the Tsarina who effectively ruled Russia.*

*The Empress was not popular. One of the 'Hessian sisters', she was believed to have German sympathies—although in fact her affinities lay more with England. But she was known to be a firm believer in absolute monarchy; and she was a mystic deeply under the influence of the corrupt monk, Rasputin.*

*By 1917 the Imperial Family had become the focus of the disappointments, frustrations, miseries and anger of the Russian people. A bread-riot in Petrograd in March turned instantly into revolution. Within a week the Tsar had abdicated; three hundred years of Romanov rule had suddenly crashed in ruin.*

The Tsar was my father's first cousin. The Tsarina was my aunt—my mother's sister. And another of her sisters, my Aunt Elizabeth (Aunt Ella, as she was called in the family), had married the Grand Duke Serge. So our Russian connections were very close.

We used to see this side of the family quite often, either in Germany, or on visits to Russia. I loved Russia, and I was very, very fond of my Russian cousins. Among my most treasured possessions are the old albums which recall that almost unbelievable world of my boyhood, before 1914—and long before the Revolution.

My cousin Alexei was four years younger than me; he was the Tsarevitch, the heir to the throne. He had very poor health—in fact, he was a haemophilic, which was always a great worry to everyone.

His four sisters, the Grand Duchesses Olga, Marie, Anastasia and Tatiana, were all very attractive. I remember that I always secretly hoped to marry Marie. These girls seemed to get more and more beautiful every time we saw them.

We were a devoted family.

The Imperial Court was astonishing. Everything was on the grand scale: the size of the palaces, the physique of the Guards, the Cossack out-riders when we went out for drives, the splendour of the ceremonial. It was the court of an autocrat; the Tsar's powers were absolute, quite unlike those of any other European monarch. The Tsar of All the Russias was answerable only to God for the manner in which he ruled his country.

Yet anyone less like an autocrat than my Uncle Nicky it would be hard to imagine. He was a very kind-hearted, simple, charming man—but at the same time rather weak and indecisive. He was never happier than in his home, in the family circle, playing with his children.

We were shocked and dismayed when we learned that my uncle had lost his throne, and that he and my aunt and all my cousins were under arrest. It meant that all the splendour, all the happy memories were things of the past; but we didn't dream of the terrible happenings that were yet to come.

*The revolution in Russia in March 1917 was a Liberal revolution. The Imperial Family remained under arrest in the palace of Tsarskoe Selo, but they were not ill-treated. In the West the revolution was welcomed as a sign that Russia would now emerge from inefficiency, corruption and distasteful despotism, and continue the war beside the Western democracies with new vigour.*

*Almost no one outside Russia understood the deep war-weariness of her people.*

*In July 1917, inspired by the War Minister Kerensky, the Russian Army made its last brave effort to attack: the result was utter failure—with fearful consequences. Army and people alike could now think only of peace.*

*In October a second revolution brought to power the Bolsheviks, headed by Lenin and Trotsky, whose slogan was: 'Down with the war!'*

*At Brest-Litovsk, in March 1918, the Germans and Austrians forced the Bolshevik Government to accept humiliating terms of peace: Russia lost immense territories, one-third of her population, half her industrial plant, nine-tenths of her coal-mines. And inside Russia herself there was yet no peace—only civil war.*

*By the summer of 1918 the Bolshevik Government seemed to be on the point of collapse.*

*The Imperial Family had been moved into harsher exile, far to the East, at Tobolsk. With the westward advance of Admiral Kolchak's Whites and Czechs there arose the possibility of a rescue. The prisoners were moved to Ekaterinburg.*

*On July 16th 1918, just nine days before the anti-Bolshevik Czech Legion entered Ekaterinburg, the Tsar and all his family were murdered by order of the local Soviet.*

We had very little news of the family after the Bolsheviks took over. We all hoped that they would ultimately be sent abroad into exile, but we feared the worst. Even when it happened it was a long time before we heard the details, which were quite horrible.

They were all shot together. I believe that my cousin Alexei, the Tsarevitch, who was just fourteen years old, didn't die at once; he was shot three more times. And my cousin Anastasia was bayoneted eighteen times as she lay there screaming.

Even their doctor and their servants were murdered with them, and afterwards all the bodies were hacked into pieces.

The following day my Aunt Elizabeth, who founded the Nursing Sisters' Movement, and was revered almost as a saint, was also murdered by being flung down a mine-shaft.

These horrible deeds cast a shadow over the whole of my family for a very long time.

*With the end of 1917 came the knowledge that the fall of Russia would permit the Germans to bring nearly a million men to the Western Front: enough for a final tremendous gambler's throw, before the strength of America entered the field.*

*By March 1918 the Germans were ready, and on the 21st of that month a terrible blow fell on the British Army in the Somme sector. On April 9th a second blow fell, in Flanders. The Commander-in-Chief, Field Marshal Sir Douglas Haig, issued a famous Order of the Day:*

*'There is no other course open to us but to fight it out! Every position must be held to the last man: there must be no retirement. With our backs to the wall, and believing in the justice of our cause, each one of us must fight on to the end.'*

*The British fought on. For the second time the Germans were brought to a halt. But the British Army had lost almost a quarter of a million men in six weeks—as many as in the three months' advance to Passchendaele.*

*In May and June the Germans turned against the French. Their new advances carried them as near to Paris as they had been in September 1914, before the Battle of the Marne. And then, once more, they were held.*

*Their losses in these all-out attacks had been frightful—and Germany could not replace them. Allied losses had been heavy, too, but behind the Allies the limitless resources of America were now coming into the field.*

*In July 1918 there was a lull on the Western Front, a short breathing-space between great storms of war.*

   .   .   .   .   .

It was during this lull that I had the great good luck to be one of the few junior naval officers to visit the Western Front. I call it 'luck' because the Front was something that just had to be seen to be believed! Of course, I'd heard a great deal about it—one read about it every day in the papers—and I had seen a lot of films of the fighting. But none of that really prepared me for what I saw.

I went to G.H.Q., where I met Sir Douglas Haig, who made a deep impression on me. I would have been even more impressed if I had known that he was just about to win a series of great victories which did more than anything else to end the war that year.

I was shown bases, lines of communication, artillery positions— the whole amazing administrative background to fighting a major land-war: something Britain had never done before.

But, above all, I saw the Front Line itself. I thought it was abominable.

It is hardly possible to compare the utterly different styles of war that were waged by the Army and the Navy. On the face of it we in the Navy had a much less dangerous life. Naval casualties were far smaller than Army casualties (though one has to remember that naval *numbers* were also far smaller than the Army's).

A second-lieutenant in the Army, I discovered, had an expectation of life of only about six or seven weeks on the Western Front, which was a shocking thought. On the other hand, when disaster occurred at sea, it was usually pretty complete disaster. At Jutland, when the *Queen Mary* blew up, nine men were saved out of 1,275 officers, petty officers and ratings. It was a similar story with the *Indefatigable* and the *Invincible*.

I myself saw the battleship *Vanguard* blow up at anchor in Scapa Flow, and took a boat away to look for survivors—there were only two.

We didn't think about these things much; we had our jobs to do, and we got on with them. But my visit to the Western Front was to prove of the greatest value, for now I was able to understand about war on land—what the casualty lists really meant, and the horror of the conditions in which those enormous numbers of men were fighting and dying.

*In July 1918 the Allies began their final counter-offensive: French, British and Americans together in the Second Battle of the Marne.*

*In August the British armies joined in at Amiens, and once again*

*assumed the largest burden of the war. But now it was victorious
war. On August 11th, three days after Haig's stroke at Amiens, the
Kaiser said: 'We have nearly reached the limit of our powers of
resistance. The war must be ended.'*

*In September the British broke through the Hindenburg Line, the
most massive defensive system on the Western Front. In October
Germany put out feelers for peace. Before it could be attained the
world scene once more underwent a drastic change.*

*Revolution, which had already destroyed the Russian Empire and
the Romanov dynasty, now threatened the Empires of the Hohen-
zollerns and the Habsburgs.*

*On November 4th the German Fleet mutinied at Kiel. Three days
later 'Soviets' seized power in Kiel and the great port of Hamburg.
On November 9th there was revolution in Berlin.*

*On November 11th the Armistice was signed. The war was over,
but the reckoning was yet to come.*

Once again the collapse of an Empire directly affected my family.

The German Empire in 1918 was ruled by the Kaiser Wilhelm II,
who was also King of Prussia. Under him there were scores of other
rulers : there were Kings—of Saxony and Bavaria; there were Grand
Dukes—of Baden and Mecklenburg; Dukes—of Saxe-Coburg, and
so on.

The revolution swept them all away. On November 9th the Kaiser
went into his life-long exile in Holland, and one by one the other
German rulers also lost their thrones.

The Grand Duke Ernest Louis of Hesse was my mother's brother,
and my father's first cousin. Like the Kaiser, he was a grandson of
Queen Victoria—but there was never much love lost between the
two houses, Prussia and Hesse.

In 1914 my uncle was almost alone amongst the German princes
to speak out against the war. Now he lost his throne because of it.
But he was permitted—indeed, invited—to stay on in his home,
because he had always been a progressive ruler. His social and health
legislation were very advanced, but he will probably be remembered
above all as a patron of science and the arts, and the founder of the
once-famous 'Artists' Colony' in Darmstadt. Certainly, he never lost
the affections of his people. Nevertheless, when he, too, lost his
throne, another of our links with the past was broken.

·        ·        ·        ·        ·

*Peace returned, with different meanings for different men and nations. In the Allied capitals there was jubilation, deep relief, and the hope of building a new world in which such an event as the Great War could never happen again. In the defeated countries and in Russia there was revolution, famine, civil war and new bitterness which would also form part of the new world's inheritance.*

*Britain had entered the war in August 1914 as the world's greatest sea-power. Her particular victory received its acknowledgment on November 21st 1918, when the German Fleet made its last journey across the North Sea—to surrender to the Royal Navy.*

The surrender of the German Fleet was a remarkable and ironic moment. I was then serving in the Portsmouth Escort Flotilla, so I was unfortunately not there to witness it—and neither, of course, was my father, although as First Sea Lord in 1914, and previously as well, he played no small part in bringing about this event. I am sure he was there in spirit.

The German Fleet undoubtedly played a significant part in building up the war-fever. And then, when war came, this great organisation spent most of it in complete idleness. It only encountered its declared enemy—the British Grand Fleet—on one day : at Jutland. And it ended its existence in mutiny and abject surrender. Not only that—there was worse to come : just seven months later the whole of this great fleet of nearly seventy vessels, at anchor in Scapa Flow, was scuttled by its own crews.

What an ignominious end! What an irony! And what a waste!

*The British had won their war, at vast cost and with tribulation, and now they chiefly wanted to forget it. Millions of men in uniform waited impatiently to thow it off. 'We want civvie suits!' they proclaimed. 'We won the war. Give us our tickets!'*

*The clamour for demobilisation swelled, in Parliament, and above all in the Press. By April 1919 Britain had demobilised two million men.*

It was in that month that the Grand Fleet also ceased to exist. At the end of the war, when it was inspected by the King, it consisted of 370 British ships, with over 90,000 officers and men.

It contained 31 British battleships and 9 battle-cruisers; there were 37 light cruisers and 7 aircraft-carriers—an entirely new category;

there were no less than 178 destroyers, and 48 submarines. It was the most massive single demonstration of British sea-power that has ever been seen.

Now this whole magnificent array was to be dispersed. The ships we knew so well were laid up in reserve, to await obsolescence and the breakers' yards, and the wartime sailors went home.

For Regulars, of course, demob at the end of a war can be a disturbing affair. I suppose, if I thought about it at all, I realised that the Fleet would have to be cut down, and that a lot of Regular officers would have to go. But such was my youthful self-confidence that I don't believe it ever crossed my mind that I might be one of them—and, thank heaven, I wasn't!

I was eighteen and a half when the war ended. I was a sub-lieutenant and second-in-command of an anti-submarine vessel—the 'P.31'. She was very small—she only had a ship's company of fifty—but we were all very proud of her.

My pay at that time was five shillings a day—less than that of some of the petty officers when their new scales of pay came in. I had a small allowance from my father: £300 a year, which represented quite a lot in those days, and enabled me to run a small car.

I had been little more than a child—barely fourteen—when the war broke out, and although I had many very happy memories of those pre-war days, that was not really my world.

My world began now, in 1919. After the narrow existence of naval colleges, ships and bases in wartime, which was all I had known for the last five years, I had a wonderful feeling of release. I could make new friends; I could enjoy some sport; I could go to parties and dances; I could meet some girls; and I did all these things. In fact, such was my enthusiasm that I went to one play at the Gaiety twenty-four times, because I had fallen in love with the leading lady!

So that was what peace really meant to me: a whole new world at my feet. It was tremendously exciting.

And just when it might have turned rather dreary again I had a great piece of luck. The flotilla was ordered to the Baltic, as part of the naval force taking part in Allied intervention against the Bolsheviks. I was excited by the prospect of action, but I don't think I really missed anything very worth while. And instead I found myself where I had never expected to be: at Cambridge, a member of the university.

My generation of naval officers was known as the 'war babies'. We had gone to sea at an absurdly young age, and, as a result, there was a deplorable gap in our general education. This gap a wise and benevolent Admiralty decided to fill.

Sir Arthur Shipley, the Master of Christ's College, was Vice-Chancellor of Cambridge University at that time, and he arranged with the Admiralty to take the 'war babies' in relays for two terms at a time. He was a friend of my father, so I naturally went to Christ's. We wore uniform by day, and cap-and-gown at night. We attended lectures and tutorials exactly as undergraduates. As a voluntary subject I read ethnology, under Dr. A. C. Haddon, which interested me very much.

But studies apart, what was exciting about Cambridge was meeting new people, different people, and entering a new and very exciting world. I joined the Union, and took part in the debates—in fact, I was elected a member of the Union Committee. I spoke opposing the return to Party politics. I also opposed the reduction of expenditure on armaments. And in the inter-'Varsity debate against Oxford I was able to get Winston Churchill down, and together we opposed the motion that the time was ripe for a Labour Government.

All this constituted a most important formative experience. At Cambridge I met friends who helped to enlarge my ideas on many subjects. And no sooner had I left Cambridge than another wonderful, broadening experience came my way—one which brought me another very close friendship.

My cousin David, the Prince of Wales, was a most popular figure at that time. It was considered that nothing could be better for Empire relations—an Empire which was in the process of turning into a Commonweath—than a tour round it by the Prince of Wales.

In March 1920 he was due to visit New Zealand, Australia and the West Indies. He invited me to go with him as a personal aide (though officially flag-lieutenant) in the battle-cruiser *Renown*. This, I need hardly say, was the chance of a lifetime.

One heard a great deal about the Empire, of course—it was the whole vast area that was coloured red on schoolroom maps. We were all very proud of the part it had played in the war. And one of the duties of the Royal Navy was to protect it. But really one knew very little about it. Most of it was difficult to reach—there was no air travel in those days, and practically no films to reveal it to us.

So all I knew was what I had read or heard : but now I was about to
see for myself.

*The Prince of Wales and his party left Portsmouth on March 16th
1920. Mountbatten appointed himself the diarist of the journey. He
recorded that it lasted 210 days—eighty-two of them spent aboard
the* Renown—*and the Prince's party travelled 45,497 miles.*

*The first port of call was Barbados, but this was only a brief visit.
The full, official occasion for the West Indies would take place on
the way home. After Barbados came the Panama Canal, one of the
triumphs of modern engineering, with locks in gradation one above
the other, and powerful machines to pull ships through them.*

*Typically, Mountbatten calculated that it took 6,000,000,000 foot
pounds of work to raise the* Renown *to her highest point in transit
of the Canal.*

*On April 17th she crossed the Equator, and Mountbatten wrote
in his diary:*

'At two bells in the forenoon watch a fanfare of trumpets announced
the arrival of King Neptune. The Chief Herald came on to the quarter
deck leading the procession. Next came the Chief Bears, after these
followed the Judge, two of His Majesty's Bodyguard, and his Aquatic
Majesty King Neptune himself, accompanied by his Queen Amphi-
trite and his Secretary. The Doctor, the three Barbers and four more
of the Bodyguard were followed by the rest of the Bears, the Deep
Sea Police, the Barbers' Assistants and the Doctor's Assistants.'

Crossing the Line, you see, was a formidable ritual. There were
elaborate ceremonies. The Prince of Wales was invested with the
Order of the Equatorial Bath—and I was arrested for some alleged
act of fearful treachery. I was pounced on by the Deep Sea Police,
tied up and handcuffed.

Then the Instruction of the Novices began :

'H.R.H. sat down in the Barber's chair, and the Doctor took his
temperature, proclaiming it to be normal . . . His Majesty, however,
objected to this, pointing to H.R.H.'s shaking knees. The Doctor
took his temperature again and came to the conclusion that his
thermometer had stuck on the first occasion, so he gave H.R.H. a
No. 9 Pill (which was about the size of a golf-ball). The Chief Barber
then lathered him thoroughly and shaved him with a razor whose
blade was three feet long. Suddenly the chair tilted backwards, and

before he knew where he was, H.R.H. was in the grip of the Bears, who ducked him along the entire length of the bath. . . .

'Next the prisoners were brought forward . . . The warrant of Louis Francis Albert Victor Nicholas Mountbatten was read, which finished up "and the prisoner not being allowed to call any witnesses on his behalf or to give any evidence in his defence, I do judge the aforesaid to be ducked four times four".

'The Flag-Lieutenant was then put into the Barber's chair and given a double spoonful of No. 5, after which he was lathered in black, purple and white, and tipped into the bath, where he got his full sixteen duckings.'

The wonderful thing is that the entire film of this extraordinary occasion still exists, and there we both are, the Prince of Wales and myself, looking, as you may imagine, not a little alarmed by it all!

*On April 22nd the Renown arrived at Auckland, and the Prince and his party had their first experience of an Antipodean welcome. Six thousand children spelt out the word across a playing-field, but it needed no spelling. Everywhere the Prince went the people of New Zealand turned out in thousands to see him and shake hands— always prominent among them the returned Servicemen of the old Australian and New Zealand Army Corps, the Anzacs.*

*Australia, when her turn came, greeted the Prince in her own exuberant style. In just under three months he visited every state, every capital and many localities in the 'back blocks'.*

*Australia, in 1920, was more to the Left than any other part of the English-speaking world. Australian disrespect for authority was in any case a by-word. In some districts, anxiety was expressed about how the Prince might be received.*

No one need have bothered on that score. We on the Staff were often targets for the Australian sense of humour—chy-yking, it was called. Our full-dress uniforms provoked shouts of 'Oh, Percy, where did you get that hat?' and so forth. But even in districts which were supposed to be hotbeds of Bolshevism the Prince always met with tremendous affection. In fact, the problem was generally one of protecting him from his enthusiastic admirers.

He worked terribly hard; he never spared himself all through the tour. People would stream past him, literally in thousands, to shake his hand. He had a smile for each of them. But quite early on he had to start the practice of shaking hands with the left hand, because his right hand had been almost crushed with the warmth of people's greetings. He became very tired as time went by, and his programme allowed for almost no real relaxation.

On this journey I got to know my cousin very well indeed. I soon realised that under that delightful smile which charmed people everywhere, and despite all the fun that we managed to have, he was a lonely and sad person, always liable to deep depressions.

From the time when I first left home to go to school I had formed the habit of writing regularly and very fully to my mother, and, characteristically, she kept all my letters. In one of them I wrote:

'I am having a great time, but it is very difficult to keep David cheerful. At times he gets so depressed, and says he'd give anything to change places with me.'

And in another letter I wrote:

'You've no idea what a friend David is to me. He may be six years older, but in some respects he is the same age as me. How I wish he wasn't the Prince of Wales and then it would be so much easier to see lots and lots of him! He is such a marvellous person, and I suppose the best friend I have ever had. . . .'

I learnt a tremendous lot on this tour; looking back, I could even say that I came of age during this time—the result, I expect, of seeing wonderful places, meeting so many people in all walks of life, and also having to carry a certain amount of responsibility.

*The Britain to which the Prince and Mountbatten returned in October 1920 was making her first disagreeable acquaintance with post-war realities. In this month took place the 'Battle of Downing Street', between police and unemployed demonstrators.*

*The short boom was over; the first of the economic crises of the twenties had arrived. Unemployment figures rose from one and a quarter million in December 1920 to a peak of two and a half millions in 1921. Instead of the promised 'land fit for heroes to live in' of the 1918 Election campaign, the spectacle was seen of ex-soldiers begging in the streets.*

*In 1921 the coal industry was paralysed by a strike, and there were fears that the railwaymen and transport workers would join the miners. The Government proclaimed a 'State of Emergency'; troops filled the London parks, and British industrial centres took on the look of occupied cities. Steel-helmeted soldiers patrolled the streets, and sailors were drafted to the mines, to maintain the machinery and to prevent flooding or other damage.*

Others of us went to help the Army, should it be needed for the preservation of law and order. This is called 'Action in Aid of the Civil Power', and serving officers dread it.

I was put in charge of a platoon of naval ratings, and we went into camp, first at Aintree, then at Tidworth. I think that for most of those concerned the whole thing was rather a picnic—as it turned out. Being in camp alongside the Army was certainly fun.

But privately I just hoped that we would never have to be used against unfortunate people who were trying to obtain better pay and conditions. And luckily we were not used. We never even saw a striker, let alone a riot. But it was a huge relief when the Emergency ended and we could all return to our proper jobs.

I went back to my ship, which at that time was the *Repulse*, a sister-ship of the *Renown*. We were due to go up to Invergordon, and my father came aboard at Sheerness and sailed up with us.

He had just been promoted to Admiral of the Fleet—a recognition of his services to the Navy which he joined at the age of fourteen, and a partial atonement for the injustice which had forced him to retire from the post of First Sea Lord in October 1914. He thoroughly enjoyed this trip, and so did we all, listening to his wonderful fund of naval reminiscences.

When he left us at Invergordon I took a short weekend's leave, and went on to Dunrobin Castle nearby, to stay with the Duke and Duchess of Sutherland. My reason for doing so was that a very attractive young girl, whom I had recently met, called Edwina Ashley, had told me that she was going to be there.

But my weekend was absolutely shattered by a telegram, saying that my father had died suddenly of heart failure. This was the most awful shock, because I absolutely worshipped him.

*At Dunrobin Castle, when the telegram arrived, was the Prince of Wales. The knowledge of Mountbatten's grief and sense of loss strengthened the Prince's resolve to have his company again, on the Second Empire Tour, which was soon to begin.*

The 1921–2 Tour took us to India, Burma, Ceylon, Malaya and

Japan. This was my first acquaintance with countries which would one day play a very great part in my life. Every country that we went to had its fascination, but looking back, it is easy to see that the most significant was India—because there I found three loves, though on three very different planes. The first of them was India herself.

*India, when the Prince of Wales and Mountbatten arrived there in 1921, was a troubled country. It was still 'the brightest jewel' in the crown of the King-Emperor, the Prince's father. Its pomp and ceremony, its great palaces and monuments, its lavish entertainments kept alive, under the British, the ancient traditions of the Moghul Empire. And the British had added their own significant contribution: irrigation, canals, railways, industrialisation, hospitals, schools . . . and a greater political unity than ever before.*

*Against all this there remained the grinding poverty, disease, and recurring famine which afflicted the vast majority of India's enormous population. Against the background of all these factors grew the demand for Indian self-government.*

*The First World War lent new urgency to this demand. During the war 1,200,000 Indians had enlisted under the British flag. Indian troops had fought in France, at Gallipoli, in Egypt, East Africa, Palestine and Mesopotamia. Eleven Victoria Crosses paid tribute to Indian bravery on the battlefield.*

*It was understood in India and in Britain that the reward for this great effort on Britain's behalf would be a definite speeding-up of the moves towards self-government. A new Nationalist leader emerged, for whom the moves could never be too swift: Mohandas Karamchand Gandhi—Mahatma Gandhi—who preached non co-operation with the British.*

Earlier in 1921 my great-uncle Arthur, the Duke of Connaught, had also been in India, to inaugurate a most important constitutional reform. This lifted Indians out of mere consultation into real responsibility for many of the affairs of their country. It was a great step towards independence.

But for Gandhi and his followers (who at that time included Muslims as well as Hindus) this was nothing like enough. When the Prince of Wales and I arrived in Bombay in November there were riots and violence. Gandhi was demanding a boycott of the Prince's tour.

This boycott was really a failure, though it undoubtedly added to the strain on the Prince, who was still tired after the previous tour. We were never troubled by any hostile demonstrations, although sometimes the crowds in the streets were a bit thin.

Gandhi was in Bombay when we arrived. I was curious about him —he was always a remarkable figure—and I tried to contrive for him to meet the Prince, who was quite keen on the idea. But the Government of India was against it. I then asked if I might meet Gandhi myself, but the answer was 'No'. The Government really didn't want any contact at all: in fact, shortly afterwards Gandhi was put in prison. I wonder whether a meeting would have done any good? We *might* have established a useful contact.

But leaving politics aside, I did absolutely fall in love with India. We visited all the principal maharajahs and nawabs—the old ruling houses—who still lived in very great state. Many of them were immensely rich; they had their own armies, and one of them even had his own air force!

Their hospitality was on a truly princely scale. Ten of their heirs-apparent were on the Prince's staff; the result was that we became lifelong friends. These personal friendships, dating back to 1921, were to be of enormous benefit to me many years later, when they had become rulers, and I had to help them to decide their future.

And it was staying with the princes that I found my second love —polo. It was a game for which I had very little natural aptitude; in fact I wasn't even a particularly good horseman when I started. But I loved the game, and took every chance of practising it. When I was actually picked to play in a proper match it was the thrill of my life. But you can tell how good I was in those days from my diary; I wrote: 'In the last chukker, to my own intense surprise, I actually hit the ball three or four times!'

And finally, my real love, which is also noted in the diary, on February 14th 1922. I wrote:

'After dinner there was a small dance. I danced 1 and 2 with Edwina. She had 3 and 4 with David, and the fifth dance we sat out in her sitting-room, when I asked her if she would marry me, and she said she would.'

This was the Edwina Ashley I had met the previous summer. She had borrowed £100 to come out to India on a one-way ticket, to stay with the Viceroy, Lord Reading. And so we actually became engaged in Delhi.

The Prince of Wales was delighted, and most helpful. I had to have the King's permission to marry: David saw to all that. Later I discovered there had only been one really dissenting voice when we announced our engagement—the Vicereine's, Lady Reading, who wrote to Edwina's aunt and said:

'I am afraid she has definitely made up her mind about him. I hoped she would have cared for someone older, with more of a career before him.'

*Edwina Ashley was an entirely desirable match. She was twenty years old at the time of her engagement, already in the bloom of an intelligent beauty which she never lost.*

*Her grandfather, on her mother's side, was the millionaire financier Sir Ernest Cassel, who had been a friend of King Edward VII, and who, before the war, had tried to use his influence to halt the naval arms race between Britain and Germany.*

*Her father was Colonel Wilfrid Ashley, who later became a Minister, and took the title of Lord Mount Temple. Through him she was descended from the 7th Earl of Shaftesbury, the famous nineteenth-century philanthropist, and Emily Cowper, whose mother married the great Lord Palmerston.*

*Edwina Ashley thus inherited beauty, brains and wealth—and added to them all her own remarkable personality.*

Edwina and I were both keen to be married as early as possible. This rather worried my mother, who was not sure that we had really known each other long enough—and was afraid that Edwina's fortune might come between us. I tried to reassure her in my letters that everything would be all right. My mother took my word for it—and then it became just a matter of waiting until the tour was over and the *Renown* reached home.

*The Mountbatten wedding took place on July 18th 1922, at St. Margaret's, Westminster. It was the social event of the season. The King and Queen were present, and Queen Alexandra. The Prince of Wales was Mountbatten's best man.*

*Officers of H.M.S. Renown in full dress provided the guard of honour, and sailors from the ship towed away the bridal car with a gusto which called forth one or two sharp questions from the King!*

After the wedding reception I drove Edwina down to Broadlands, her father's home, part of his inheritance from Lord Palmerston. We knew that one day Edwina would inherit the house herself, and I am afraid that even before our wedding I had rather cold-bloodedly written to my mother:

'Broadlands is in a most convenient part of England for the naval world—seventy-five miles from London, thirty from Portsmouth, forty from Weymouth, and not too far from Plymouth.'

Anyway, nowhere could be nicer for a honeymoon—as I think other members of our family would agree.

I had six months on half-pay, which gave us an opportunity to do some travelling. We drove 700 miles through France and Spain to Santander, to stay with my cousin Queen Ena and King Alphonso. Then we drove across to Germany, to stay with my Uncle Ernie, the Grand Duke of Hesse, where we had a lot of fun.

And then came the big excitement: we went to America. In 1922 America was the swinging country, the place where every young person wanted to go. It was the land of apparently limitless opportunity; the land of motor-cars; the land of jazz—and movies.

We were treated as V.I.P.s (though the expression was not then in use), and met important people wherever we went. I was invited to visit the President of the United States, and I was one of the principal speakers at a Navy League dinner in Washington, packed with admirals and senior officers—very disconcerting for a young lieutenant!

But the highlight for me was Hollywood—the film capital of the world. Films fascinated me; they always have done. I already possessed my own portable 35 mm. cine-camera, but now I was taught the art by the topmost professionals, like Cecil B. de Mille.

We stayed at Pickfair, the home of our friends Mary Pickford and Douglas Fairbanks. They were away, so our host was their partner, Charlie Chaplin. He was the most delightful host imaginable. He made a film for us as a wedding present; I have a copy of it in my archives, and it can still raise a good few laughs. He called it *Nice and Friendly*. He wrote it, directed it, and appeared in it in two rôles—looking his normal self, and also as the little tramp whom he had made world-famous. Edwina and I and the rest of our party were all in it, looking very amazing. In his autobiography Charlie Chaplin reproduced a still from the film, with the caption: 'Breaking the news to Lord Mountbatten that he is no actor!' I'm afraid he was absolutely right.

Well, it was a marvellous honeymoon. It rounded off not only one of the happiest but also one of the most interesting periods of my life. The anticipation of fresh horizons and new experiences, which had excited me at the end of the war, had been more than fulfilled.

Edwina was a wonderful companion, interested in everything, and with a tremendous capacity for making friends wherever we went. It doesn't fall to many young people to enjoy experiences such as these.

But now my leave was up. It was time for me to go back to work —back to my career, in the Navy.

# 3

# The Azure Main

I picked up the threads of my naval career in January 1923. It was time to get down to hard work again, because I was determined to make a success of my profession, as my father had done.

I was pretty ambitious—why should I deny it? It simply meant that I intended to do well. But to do well in the Navy in the aftermath of a great war is not the easiest of propositions. However, I always enjoyed hard work; and now it began in a historic setting—Constantinople and the Dardanelles.

*The ugly aftermath of war was nowhere uglier than in the Middle East. When the Turkish Empire collapsed in 1918 vultures descended on the carcass: the victorious Allies, Britain, France and Italy, seized their shares; the Arabs carved out independent kingdoms; the Jews demanded a National Home; and the Greeks perceived an opportunity to revive their ancient glories.*

*In May 1919, while the Paris Peace Conference was still in session, Greek forces landed in Asia Minor. But an act intended to create a* fait accompli *succeeded only in starting a new war which dragged on for over two years.*

*Turkey—for decades 'the sick man of Europe'—had found a leader: Mustapha Kemal. Kemal was the focus of resistance to the Greeks; when the Allies formulated their peace terms, which were accepted by the Sultan's Government by the Treaty of Sèvres, Kemal rejected them; in due course he overthrew the Sultan himself; and out of abject defeat he revived the Turkish nation. As Winston Churchill wrote:*

*'Loaded with follies, stained with crimes, rotted with misgovernment, shattered by battle, worn down by long disastrous wars, his*

*Empire falling to pieces around him, the Turk was still alive.'*

*In August 1922 Mustapha Kemal's ragged army won a decisive victory over the Greeks. In September the Turks entered Smyrna. In the fire and massacre that followed it was reported that 120,000 people lost their lives. The Greek presence in Asia Minor, dating from the great days of Athens, was swept away.*

Once more an international crisis produced a family tragedy for us. Prince Andrew of Greece, the brother of King Constantine I, was my brother-in-law—he had married my elder sister Alice in 1903. Already Alice and Andrea (as the family always called him) had been in exile once with the King, when he first lost his throne in 1917. But in 1920 there was a plebiscite which brought the King back, and they returned with him to Greece.

Prince Andrew was a professional soldier. He went back to the Greek Army, and became a lieutenant-general, commanding the II Corps in Asia Minor. But he quickly conceived very serious doubts about the manner in which the war with Turkey was being conducted. He was very conscious of the Army's weakness (Greece had been almost continuously at war for ten years by 1922); he recognised the inefficiency and corruption of many of its officers, and he was extremely sceptical of the 'forward policy'—the march on Ankara which was always being talked about.

Early in 1922, when all his protests had failed, he applied for a command outside the war zone. But this did not save him when disaster hit the Greek Army later that year. Once more King Constantine was forced to abdicate. Prince Andrew was put on trial for his life in Athens. I haven't much doubt that he would have been shot—but he was saved by British intervention, at the direct instigation of King George V. The British cruiser *Calypso* arrived at Athens; Prince Andrew was released, and he and my sister went into a second exile.

On their journey they stopped at Corfu to collect their children —my four nieces, and my eighteen-month-old nephew, Prince Philip. This was just a month before I joined my next ship, the *Revenge*, at Constantinople, in the middle of a further crisis which nearly dragged Britain into war—Chanak.

*The collapse of the Greeks brought the victorious Turks face to face with the Allied Forces of Occupation. By now Allied policy was*

*seriously divided. When Mustapha Kemal's men arrived at Chanak,
on the Dardanelles Strait, France and Italy withdrew their troops,
leaving the British to handle the situation alone.*

*At Chanak there was only one infantry battalion and a squadron
of cavalry—backed, of course, by the Royal Navy. The Turks
crowded up to the British outposts, and it was touch and go whether
war might not explode at any moment out of some incident on the
picket lines. Fortunately the British troops and sailors displayed
their best phlegmatic qualities; their commanders kept their heads,
and the Commander-in-Chief, General Sir Charles Harington, displayed great ability at diplomacy. In July 1923 the Treaty of
Lausanne brought peace at last with the new Turkish Republic.*

*In October the Occupation Forces left Turkey, and the Mediter-
ranean Fleet returned to its peace stations.*

Chanak was not the only crisis the Navy had to face in the early
twenties. At home there was the inevitable outcry against large
Naval Estimates in peacetime, which led to a pretty drastic cutting-
down of ships and men. But worse still, in conjunction with the
'Ten-Year Rule' (which pronounced, year after year, that we need
not expect another major war for ten years), this meant that there
was very little new building, and many of our ships were becoming
seriously obsolete.

Also, the days of our complete naval supremacy had passed. In
1921, by the Washington Naval Treaty, we accepted parity with
the United States—indeed, we were glad to be left with that. But
the price of this concession was the ending of the Anglo-Japanese
Alliance, which meant that Japan now became a possible enemy.
And Japan was already a leading naval power in her own right.

I had seen something of the Japanese Navy myself during my
tour with the Prince of Wales in 1922. I had been lucky enough to
go aboard their latest ship, the *Mutsu*, the most powerful battleship
in the world. I was the only British officer to be allowed to make a
real inspection of her—perhaps they thought that I was too young
and silly to matter. But, in fact, I compiled a most-secret report for
the Admiralty on her armour and underwater armament. I knew
that the Japanese were rapidly becoming a force to reckon with.

So this was a difficult period of adjustment for the Royal Navy—
adjustment to economic realities, and to political realities.

·     ·     ·     ·     ·

*It was a period of adjustment for Mountbatten too. In the Revenge he became a popular officer, whose efficiency was recognised by his captain and other senior officers. Yet that captain admits that at first he had the gravest doubts about Mountbatten's presence in his ship, and even went so far as to ask the Admiralty to remove him. Aboard ship, the captain is absolute master, whose word is law; no captain desires, and no sensible captain will permit, if he can help it, having someone aboard who may not give a 'twopenny cuss' for his views or orders; and such a man, he feared, Mountbatten might prove to be. The Admiralty, however, ignored Captain Stephenson's request; his fears proved groundless. Not for the last time, a commanding officer's doubts about Mountbatten turned to gratification and pleasure.*

*During the inter-war period the character of the Royal Navy changed markedly. The Navy was under pressure. The First Sea Lord, Admiral of the Fleet Lord Beatty, fought a constant battle to defend it against the economists, on the one hand, and the claims of the other two Services, on the other. The battle against the young and demanding Royal Air Force, under Lord Trenchard, was particularly stern.*

*In the fleets themselves the lessons of the Great War were being digested. In a highly competitive, and increasingly scientific era, professionalism acquired new meanings. In the Fleets, new answers were sought to the problems of submarines, of mines, of aircraft, and of communications. This was a 'post-Jutland Navy', and it had a lot to think about.*

Very soon I had to take an important decision: what should I specialise in? My first thought was submarines, because I had had some experience in them during the war. But I decided against it: I thought that in peacetime they would be much less exciting—and they were terribly uncomfortable.

I thought of aviation. In 1918 I had learned to fly with the R.A.F., and I loved it. But the Navy had now lost control of the Fleet Air Arm, and so, in order to fly in my own Service, I should have had to obtain a commission in another Service—and that did not appeal to me.

After a lot of thought I decided on Signals. In any case, I had always been deeply interested in communications, and in what we now call electronics.

·      ·      ·      ·      ·

*Mountbatten now became what the Navy calls a 'communicator'.
At the end of 1924 he went to the Signal School at Portsmouth
to learn his new trade, and in 1925 he attended the Higher Wireless
Course at Greenwich.*

*But Mountbatten had found more than a trade; he had found a
vocation. To him, communications always meant much more than
Signals. He had already given indications of this bent. As a very
junior officer in the* Revenge *in 1923, he had produced a 'ship's news-
reel' for the amusement of the ship's company, and had explored
other means of using films to the Navy's advantage.*

I had always been extremely interested in films—indeed I still am.
This is an interest which I shared with my brother. As far back as
1916, in H.M.S. *Lion*, he brought his own cinema projector, and
trained me as assistant operator. We showed all sorts of films—
Charlie Chaplin comedies, epics like *Birth of a Nation*, whatever we
could get hold of.

It was easy to see how important this was for the morale of the
Fleet in war, but it soon proved to be just as important in peace,
especially on stations where sailors were more or less cut off from
civilisation for months on end.

My files show that as early as 1923, in the *Revenge*, I was trying
to get a proper organisation set up for showing films to the Fleet—
the birth of the idea of the Royal Naval Film Corporation. Like all
progressive innovations, it was hard going. I had a projection room
constructed next to the reading room in the *Revenge*; but when I
submitted a suggestion that other ships should copy my idea I got a
rocket from the Admiralty for 'interfering with the construction of
one of H.M. ships without obtaining Their Lordships' prior
approval'!

Even earlier than this I had realised that films could also be a
wonderful medium for instruction. So when I was flag-lieutenant in
the *Renown* in 1920, I made an instructional film to illustrate Fleet
manœuvres. I directed it myself, and did my own animation. The
idea was to show every stage from the issuing of the admiral's order
to the execution by the Fleet. I thought this would be helpful; but
Their Lordships of the Admiralty were not impressed. They said
they could see 'no possible use for instructional films in the Royal
Navy'

·        ·        ·        ·        ·

*Mountbatten's interest in films never flagged. But with the thirties, the rapid development of the film medium itself threatened to nullify his efforts. Talkies arrived—and the Navy's film projectors were for silent films only. The supply of these rapidly began to dry up. So urgent measures were obviously needed. But the lowest tender that could be obtained for converting the silent projectors to sound worked out at £800 per ship—an unthinkable sum.*

*Mountbatten decided that he could do better—using the Navy's own resources. Helped by a brilliant officer who had been his pupil at the Portsmouth Signal School (now Captain Mansfield Robinson), using the Fleet Repair Ship, and anything else he could lay his hands on, he worked out a system of conversion whose average cost was only £60 per ship. And so the Fleet continued to receive up-to-date films.*

*With the mid-Twenties came the feeling that at last the aftermath of the Great War might be dispersing. In January 1923 the French Army had marched into the Ruhr to exact from Germany the Reparations which bedevilled every economic negotiation. This war-like move cost France the sympathy of Britain and America—and awakened dangerous forces of German Nationalism.*

*Imitating the march of Mussolini's Blackshirts on Rome in the previous year, the new National Socialist Workers' Party, headed by Adolf Hitler, attempted a 'putsch' in Munich in November 1923. It failed miserably, and with its failure the more moderate elements in France and Germany gained strength. By 1925 it seemed that a true peace might be at hand. A new series of conferences produced the Treaty of Locarno, signed by Britain, France, Germany and Italy. Winston Churchill wrote:*

*'By the waters of a calm lake, the four great Western democracies plighted their solemn troth to keep the peace among themselves in all circumstances, and to stand united against any one of their number who broke the compact and marched in aggression against a brother land.'*

*Locarno seemed to spell 'peace'—but a war-damaged world had yet to glimpse prosperity. Inflation in Germany, unemployment in Germany, Britain and America, produced a new poverty, a new breeding-ground of hate. Britain's first Labour Government had come and gone in 1924, leaving the problem of unemployment*

*untouched. In 1926 came the General Strike, the event long-heralded
by the Left as the instrument of power of the working class, long
dreaded by moderate men. Once more, as troops moved in to keep
order and maintain services, British industrial towns took on a look
of war. The strike failed, but left its own aftermath of anger and
frustration.*

*And yet, with all this, the twenties won the title 'gay'. Amid all
their troubles, people obeyed the unconquerable urge to enjoy themselves. This was the age of mass-participation in sport. It was a jazz
age, brought to millions by the gramophone and radio. Film stars
were the new popular idols. The 'Bright Young People' shocked the
conventional, and gave the newspapers a new source of spice. High
society—the 'smart set'—was always in the news: and, not the least
of them, Edwina Mountbatten.*

Edwina was a year and a half younger than me. She was a Society
beauty, one of the best-dressed women in the world, a great heiress,
and so definitely one of the leaders of the 'smart set'.

I say 'smart set'—in fact, there were several. There was the Prince
of Wales's set, with which we were obviously connected, because
he and I were such close friends. But there was also a set which the
papers called 'the Mountbatten set', to which the Duke of Kent
belonged, because he was also a close friend. And so our social life
was often in the news, and many people formed the impression,
from what they read in newspapers and society magazines, that I
was just a playboy.

But I wasn't really all that good at the 'smart' life. I hope I wasn't
actually a bore, but I was quite often accused of spending most of
my time, at a dinner party or an evening out, talking to a man about
something which interested me—most likely something to do with
the Navy—instead of paying proper attention to the pretty girls.
Some of them used to be rather irritated by this—but I couldn't help
it.

The newspapers—and many of our friends—never saw that other
side of me. They didn't see all the hard work, and anyhow, hard
work is not news. But that was what my life mostly consisted of.

I am not saying that I didn't have fun. This was, as well as other
things, the Age of Speed—we were all rather speed-crazy. In fact,
it was during this period that Britain proudly achieved *all* the speed
records—on land, on water, and in the air.

I possessed a forty-knot motor-boat, which got me into bad odour with the Royal Yacht Squadron at Cowes—as a matter of fact I was blackballed in 1925 and again in 1926 when my name was proposed for membership!

I was friends with Sir Henry Segrave, who held both land and water records. I knew R. J. Mitchell, the aircraft designer, who at that time was building seaplanes to win the Schneider Trophy. I remember taking him out in my boat to watch his machine competing in one of the races. Later, of course, he developed these seaplanes into the famous Spitfire fighters of World War II.

I enjoyed fast boats—and fast cars. I remember once in 1924 driving down from our London home, Brook House in Park Lane, to the gates of Portsmouth Barracks in one hour and thirty-two minutes—and that was long before motorways, and when four-wheel brakes were scarcely known!

But work was always the main thing. In 1925 I took the Higher Wireless Course at Greenwich, and in 1927 I was appointed Assistant Fleet Wireless Officer to the Mediterranean Fleet.

*So Mountbatten found himself back in Malta, in H.M.S.* Queen Elizabeth, *in which he had served under Admiral Beatty in the Grand Fleet in 1917. Now she was the flagship of Admiral Sir Roger Keyes, another naval hero, and Commander-in-Chief, Mediterranean. Mountbatten was on the Admiral's staff.*

This was the most sought-after appointment for a newly fledged Signal Officer—but I had earned it, by coming out top in the Signal Course.

It was some time later that Admiral Keyes confessed to me that when he had seen my name on the list of officers who were to join him, he had struck it out.

'But why?' I asked. 'You didn't even know me.'

'That is why I struck it out,' he said. 'I didn't want a cousin of the King out here on my staff.'

'Then why am I here?' I asked him.

'I'll tell you,' he replied. 'I had already written to the Admiralty, saying I didn't want you; but I was thinking about it, and I turned up an old file of letters from your father. I realised that he had given me such support as a young man, and shown such confidence in me, that I couldn't do this to his son. So I sent a telegram to the

Admiralty, cancelling my letter. That's why you're here.'

And then he added: 'I felt it only fair to you to admit this.'

This sort of thing made me more than ever determined to justify myself to myself by being really proficient in every aspect of my work.

*In all spheres of his life, Mountbatten cultivated proficiency. During this period he extended his persuit of it beyond work, into sport: the sport of Polo, in which he would in due course reach an eminence which was most unusual for a serving officer.*

Polo is a marvellous game, because it combines so many skills: riding, of course, but you have to be particularly good, because of positioning the pony; then there is the thrill of hitting the ball at full speed—and you can hit a very long ball at polo. But the greatest satisfaction is to play in a really close-knit team.

Next to ice-hockey, polo is probably the fastest game in the world —and it always has a spice of danger. I can hardly think of a season when I didn't have some collision, resulting in a broken collar-bone, a dislocated shoulder, or a sprained ankle, or something like that. But that made it all the more exciting.

I was never *naturally* good at it. I was not a specially good horse-man when I began, and I didn't have a good eye for ball games. I had to plug away at it to be respectably good. But I made a point of studying the game.

I had slow-motion films made of English and American interna-tionals, to analyse the shots. I also analysed the polo stick itself, and devised a very popular one which gave increased loft and length to the shot. I used to practice hitting for hours on end, to obtain length and accuracy. And I worked out tactics with my team on the billiard table.

I had to do all these things for myself, because polo is an ama-teur game, and there are no professionals to teach you. When I once asked a famous international for advice on hitting, all he could say was:

'My dear Dickie, strike quickly! Strike like a snake!'

A fat lot of good that was!

So for the benefit of people like myself, I wrote down all the lessons I had learned in very simple language. I put them into a book, and called it *Introduction to Polo*—and I signed it 'Marco'. To my astonishment, it became a best-seller; it is now in its seventh or eighth edition, and it has been translated into several languages.

Polo was a big thing in my life in Malta—particularly captaining the Navy team, the Bluejackets, right up to the finals of the Army's Inter-Regimental Tournament at Hurlingham, against all their crack teams. I have very fond memories of the Marsa ground.

But most of Malta is a fond memory, for one reason or another. We used to live in a charming house called Casa Medina (my brother's title : we shared the house with him) at the top of a narrow, winding lane, just wide enough for one car at a time.

Edwina had got used to following the Fleet around—and the Mediterranean is not a bad place to follow it in. It was not yet the continuous playground that it is nowadays, but there was plenty of excitement to be had, as the Fleet did its rounds of cruises to 'show the flag'.

We had a family by now. My elder daughter, Patricia, was born in 1924. My second daughter, Pamela, was born in 1929, in rather extraordinary circumstances.

Edwina was one of those remarkable women who never show that they are about to have a baby, and so Pammie's arrival took us all by surprise. My ship was in Barcelona, and Edwina drove herself to meet me there over very bumpy roads—which were probably the cause of our troubles. At any rate, Pammie began to arrive very suddenly.

The only doctor in the hotel where we were staying was a retired throat specialist, which I didn't think was quite good enough. So I put a call through to Madrid, to ask my cousin, Queen Ena of Spain, for her advice. But she was away, and I was put through to King Alfonso—who jumped to all the wrong conclusions.

'You're having a baby!' he said. 'How exciting! I'll tell nobody.'

I said that wasn't the point at all : Edwina wanted help. So then he said :

'Oh, very well. I'll tell the Military Governor.'

And in due course the Military Governor of Barcelona arrived in full-dress uniform, and announced that by the King's orders he was putting sentries round the hotel. All they succeeded in doing was to try to stop the real doctor from getting in when he did arrive. It was all most extraordinary—but Edwina and Pammie seemed to be none the worse for all this confusion.

*The year of Pamela Mountbatten's birth was a year of evil memory. In January 1929 there were 1,467,000 unemployed in Britain. It was the month of the great Hunger March, when unemployed from all over the country converged in ragged columns on London. A Scottish leader, Wal Hannington, wrote:*

*'We set out to blaze the trail for over five hundred miles on the roads of Britain, calling upon the workers of the land to stir their slumbering souls and to rise against the callous governing class responsible for the terrible plight of the unemployed.'*

*But unemployment was not just a British phenomenon: in Germany there were almost two million out of work—a fertile recruiting-ground for extremism. In America there were over a million and a half—and worse was to come.*

*October 1929 was the month of the Wall Street Crash, the most seismic shock ever sustained by the capitalist system. Its effects spread rapidly through the Western world; unemployment in Germany climbed towards six million. In Britain the figure reached three and a quarter million by 1931, which meant that between six and seven million people were living on the 'Dole'—a vast and sickening human tragedy.*

I was not completely insulated from such events: Edwina and our 'progressive' friends saw to that. In any case, as the symptoms of the Slump developed—mass unemployment was, of course, the worst of them—one would have needed to be pretty thick-headed not to have realised that this was a terrible business.

On the other hand, people in the Services in those days *were*, to a large extent, insulated from civilian life. And as it happens, these years, 1929–31, were years of very intense professional activity for me. For most of this period I was the Senior Instructor in Wireless Telegraphy at the Signal School at Portsmouth, and this kept my time very well occupied.

I really enjoyed being an instructor: teaching and lecturing presented a new challenge, and I became tremendously absorbed in this work. Also, I discovered that a wide area of wireless instruction was due for overhaul; as Senior Instructor, I was in a good position to tackle this job. I devised a new and simplified way of laying out electrical diagrams, to make them more easily understandable, and I wrote the first comprehensive textbook on all the wireless sets in use in the Navy.

*In all these activities Mountbatten displayed again his immense
capacity for hard work and taking pains. Yet neither of these qualities would have been enough without the very high level of technical knowledge and the grasp of technical detail which he brought
to his work, both in the classroom and outside it.*

*It was now, while the Depression lay like a pall over most of the
nation's business, that Mountbatten was making his mark in the
Navy. In 1931 a confidential report described him as 'a natural leader,
who exerts a strong influence and constantly inspires keenness'
The report added: 'Quite unspoilt by success.' When he left the
Signal School it was noted that 'his keenness at times overbalances
his judgment . . .'; nevertheless he was 'thoroughly recommended
for promotion as likely to do well in the higher ranks of the
Service'.*

*And now the Depression touched the Navy itself. Neither a second
Labour Government in 1929, nor Ramsay Macdonald's National
Government in 1931, had been able to find more than slight pallia-
tives of the world-wide economic illness. In 1931 the announcement, badly handled, of a 10 per cent cut in Service pay produced a
mutiny in the Atlantic Fleet at Invergordon.*

*The news of this event appalled the nation and created a panic
among foreign holders of sterling. One French banker even tele-
phoned London to know if it was true that the British Fleet was
bombarding the South Coast resorts.*

I had just returned to the Mediterranean, this time as Fleet Wireless
Officer. The Invergordon mutiny shook us all; in fact it was one of
the main factors that toppled Britain off the Gold Standard.

My own conviction is that it had a lot to do with hire purchase,
which was then just getting into its stride. The amount of the cuts
in naval pay were just about equal to the amounts that a lot of men
were paying out each week for their furniture, and so forth. They
were naturally seriously alarmed in case their goods were seized
and their homes broken up.

But I am sure the mutiny was also largely due to the accidental
fact of the concentration of the whole of the Atlantic Fleet at
Invergordon, just when the news of the cuts came through. This
meant that the men could meet each other, and work up each others'
feelings.

The men of the Mediterranean Fleet were, of course, every bit as worried as the men of the Atlantic Fleet. But, as it happened, the Mediterranean Fleet was completely dispersed, and so the men could not communicate with each other, except by wireless. My Assistant Fleet Wireless Officer, my Staff Chief Petty Officer Telegraphist and I kept a continuous watch on all Fleet wavelengths, to make sure that no illicit messages were passed from ship to ship. None *were* passed, and there were no disturbances in the Mediterranean Fleet.

Being Fleet Wireless Officer was most exciting. He is responsible for radio communications throughout the entire Fleet.

But my first concern, in 1931, was not so much the Fleet as the wireless telegraphists of the Fleet. These were the men who were working with me, whatever ship they happened to belong to. They were scattered throughout the Fleet—and it was a big Fleet in those days, some seventy ships.

As specialists, practising what many people still thought of as a 'black art', their position could be rather lonely. They were often only noticed when they made a mistake. They were definitely short of what we now call 'esteem'. I felt that what was necessary was to tighten up the organisation—to give them a sense of belonging to something, instead of being all alone in their own ships. What I had to do was to impose my personality—not an easy thing to do in a Fleet of that size, when often the only instrument to do it with was a Morse key!

My second task was to educate the senior officers of the Fleet in the potentialities of wireless—radio, as we now call it—and the importance of the work their telegraphists were doing. It is surprising how long it takes for important ideas and techniques to filter right through large organisations. I concluded that the best propaganda for my ideas would be some rather dramatic demonstrations. We really went to town on these: I have always been a bit of a showman, and I thoroughly enjoy stunts of this sort.

We demonstrated the speed of communication with the Admiralty. We showed the importance of wireless discipline, and how, if a ship breaks silence, she can be identified by the pitch of her Morse, even if she only makes one dot! We simulated battle, by getting the ships themselves to transmit action signals; we had aircraft up and submarines submerged, and we fed in all their signals through loudspeakers as they came in. This is all old hat now; but it was very new then, and I think our lords and masters were duly impressed.

The Battle of Solferino, 24 June, 1859. Lord Mountbatten's grandfather, Major-General Prince Alexander of Hesse and the Rhine, rallies his Division.

Admiral Prince Louis of Battenberg, First Sea Lord, 1914, later became Marquess of Milford Haven, father of Lord Mountbatten. [*Portrait by P. A. de Laszlo, 1914.*]

The Queen's Ships: The Jubilee Review, Spithead, 1897. [*Radio Times Hulton Picture Library*]

The four Hessian sisters. Left to right : Irene, Princess Henry of Prussia;
Alix, Empress of Russia; Elizabeth, Grand Duchess Serge of Russia;
and Victoria, Princess Louis of Battenberg mother of Lord Mountbatten.

Fancy dress party, Malta, 1908. Prince Louis and Dickie in centre wearing costumes given them by the Tsar of Russia. Prince Louis is dressed as an Imperial Falconer, Dickie as a Cossack.

*... very little doubt about what I was going to be when I grew up ... Far left:* Dickie and Georgie. *Left:* Dickie in sailor suit.

*Right:* Family Naval tradition. Prince Louis of Battenberg with his two sons Georgie and Dickie, 1906. Georgie is in the uniform of a naval cadet.

*Below:* Prince and Princess Louis of Battenberg and family, 1909. Dickie on father's knee, his brother Georgie (now a midshipman) and his sister Louise.

*Above:* H.M.S. *Implacable*, Malta, 1902. Left to right, Princess Alice, Prince Louis (Captain), Princess Louis with Dickie on her knee, Princess Louise. Georgie sits at his father's feet.

*Below:* Malta, 1907. The Naval Bridge landed from the Fleet under the command of Prince Louis, mounted on extreme right.

*Above:* Coaling ship on board Prince Louis's flagship, H.M.S. *Venerable* in Grand Harbour, Malta, 1907.

*Below:* H.M.S. *Lion*, flagship of the Battlecruiser fleet, young Battenberg's first ship, which he joined in July, 1916. H.M.S. *Lion* was launched in 1910: displacement, 26,350 tons; speed, 27 knots; armament, eight 13.5-in., sixteen 4-in. guns.

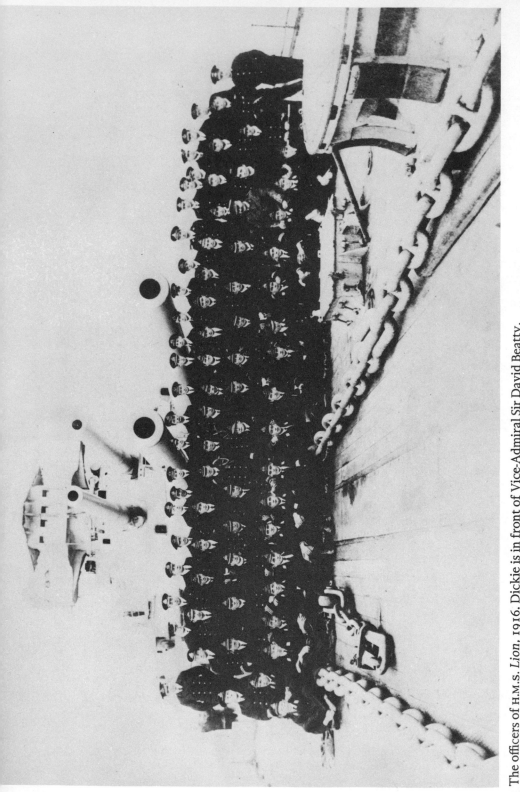

The officers of H.M.S. *Lion*, 1916. Dickie is in front of Vice-Admiral Sir David Beatty, both seated immediately below muzzle of left lower 13.5-inch gun.

A page from the personal albums of the Mountbatten family showing portraits of the Tsar, Tsarina, and their children with their signatures.

*Left:* Dickie with his two nieces, the Princesses of Greece and Denmark, in Malta, 1908.

*Below:* Friedberg Castle in Hesse, 1910. Left, the four Grand-Duchesses with Dickie. In the carriage, the Tsarevitch with Princesses Theodora and Margarita of Greece. The Tsarina is on the steps.

*Above:* Tsar Nicholas on board the Russian Imperial Yacht *Standart*, passing through the Kiel Canal, 1909. Standing next to Tsar, Grand Duke Ernest Louis of Hesse. Dickie is seated in front. The other two are the sons of Prince Henry of Prussia.

*Below:* Revolution in Russia. Students and soldiers firing at police, Petrograd, 1917.

*Above:* Tiger shooting in Nepal, 1921. Dickie standing just behind the
Prince of Wales, in centre.

*Below:* The Prince of Wales being wheeled by Lord Louis in the King's
Messenger Race, Malta, 1921.

*Above:* Burmese boat procession on the moat of Fort Dufferin, Mandalay, during Second Royal Tour, 1921–2 (Far East).

*Left:* The Prince of Wales and Dickie in the canvas bath on board H.M.S. *Renown*. First Royal Tour, 1920 (New Zealand, Australia, West Indies.)

*Right:* The Prince of Wales and Dickie in Japanese Coolie costumes on leaving Japan.

The Mountbatten wedding group 18 July, 1922. The Prince of Wales
and Prince Philip's four sisters are in this group.

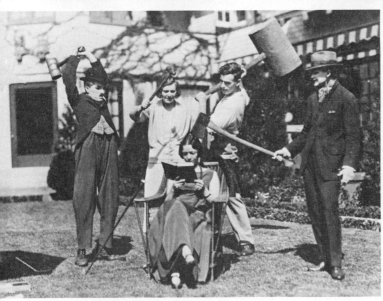

*Above:* The Mountbatten wedding at St. Margaret's, Westminster. Queen Alexandra, Queen Mary, King George V and his sister Princess Victoria.

*Below:* The honeymoon tour, Hollywood—Charlie Chaplin's wedding present, *Nice and Friendly*, a film featuring (left to right) Charlie, Edwina, Dickie, and his US Naval Aide Freddie Neilson, Mrs Neilson (sitting).

*Above:* An aerial view of Broadlands. The Victorian north wing was later removed by Lady Mountbatten, restoring the house to its classical simplicity.

*Below left:* Prince Andrew of Greece and Denmark. Portrait by de Laszlo.

*Below right:* On board the anti-submarine vessel, H.M.S. P 31, during the Peace Celebrations, 1919; Sub-Lieutenant Lord Louis Mountbatten (second-in-command) with his parents.

*It would appear that they were. Mountbatten's Confidential Report in 1933 stated that he had 'carried out the duties of Fleet Wireless Officer with marked success . . . I am confident that he will do well in any appointment he may be given.' And the Commander-in-Chief, Mediterranean, added the footnote: 'An invaluable many-sided officer.'*

*It was time for him to move on.*

By now I had reached the rank of Commander, and was due to get what every naval officer wants most—command of a ship.

But first I had to do a course at the Naval Tactical School, and while I was there something happened which not only gave me a most striking illumination of the problems of command, but also made me very glad that I had been a specialist in Signals for the last ten years.

We were still absorbing the lessons of the First World War. We were still a post-Jutland Navy, and while I was at the Tactical School the first complete presentation of the Battle of Jutland took place, based on the fullest information, German as well as British.

Admiral Jellicoe, who had commanded the Grand Fleet at Jutland, came along with his senior staff officers. Admiral Beatty, who had been my hero from the moment I joined his flagship, H.M.S. *Lion*, six weeks after the battle, was also invited, but he didn't show up.

When the presentation was over, Jellicoe opened the discussion. He told us this was the first time the whole situation had ever been made clear to him—and it all looked very plain sailing now.

But then he did a very remarkable thing. He picked up a blackboard duster, and laid it round the models representing the four nearest German battleships. Visibility, he told us, had been so bad that at no time had he ever seen more than four out of the *twenty-two* battleships of the German High Seas Fleet. And the information he received from his own ships was generally so poor that at no time had he ever had any clear idea of what the High Seas Fleet was doing. This was a revelation of the fog of war, and the stresses of command!

Winston Churchill wrote that 'Jellicoe was the only man on either side who could lose the war in an afternoon'. The crucial decision he had to make was how to deploy the Grand Fleet for battle when contact was made with the enemy. His Chief of Staff, Admiral Madden, told us that the Staff were so staggered at the manœuvre Jellicoe adopted (which had never been tried before) that they even wondered if his mind had given way under the pressure of the moment!

So the morning after the battle they analysed his decision, on the basis of all the information they then had. It took them three hours to arrive at precisely the same conclusion that he had reached in thirty seconds. My admiration for him was unbounded.

But the inescapable lesson of course, was that our failure to make essential signals had been well-nigh disastrous. I was so struck with all this that later on I gave lectures on the Battle of Jutland myself. I certainly wasn't likely to forget the vital rôle of communications when I went to my own command.

In 1934 I wrote to my mother: 'Here I am in my first command—a bit dazed but feeling very grand.' That about sums it up.

It is difficult for anyone not in the Navy to understand the feelings of a ship's company for their ship. Two sister-ships can be absolutely alike, but their personalities are quite different—a reflection, I suppose, of the composite personalities of the ship's company, the officers, and, above all, the captain. I have only once left a ship without feeling very sad at parting.

The captain's feelings, of course, are absolutely special. You have forty thousand horse-power under your hand. You can move her wherever you want. You must navigate her through all dangers. Your power is absolute—as someone once said, 'The captain can make Easter Sunday fall on Good Friday if it so pleases him.' So you are father and mother and God Almighty to every man in the ship. And you get paid—for doing the most wonderful job in the world! I can't imagine anybody who really knows about the Navy not wanting to be in the Navy.

And I had extra luck. My first command was H.M.S. *Daring*, one of our latest and newest destroyers. We were all terribly proud of her. I put up a motto—from Hakluyt, I think—'We have made every sea the highway of our daring.' But pride comes before a fall.

After only a few months we received orders to exchange ships with the China Destroyer Flotilla, old craft dating back to the First World War. This was rather depressing. I had done everything I could to identify my crew with the *Daring*.

'*Daring* by name, and daring by nature—that's us,' I told them —and all that sort of thing.

Now our new ship was called the *Wishart*, after a not-very-distinguished admiral at Portsmouth, many years ago. What on earth could I say to them about that? Well, this is what I said to them:

'We have just left behind a ship with a great name—the *Daring*: a wonderful name. We have come to the only ship in the Navy with a greater name. For our ship is called after the Almighty Himself, to whom we pray every day: "Our Father wishart in Heaven . . ." '

That was the best I could do.

*The Mountbatten treatment worked. He organised a band; he started a ship's newspaper; by every possible means he worked up the spirit of H.M.S. Wishart's company. And soon an admirable opportunity presented itself for this purpose: the Flotilla Regatta of 1935. Mountbatten coolly announced that he wanted the Wishart to carry off all the trophies.*

*Life now became a special form of hell for the officers and men of the Wishart. Mountbatten carried out a work-study analysis of rowing techniques, calculating 'economic' striking rates for each type of boat. He constructed a rowing-machine—a 'dry-puller'—on the foredeck, and sweat began to pour off everyone—including the captain, though he seemed to enjoy it.*

*The reward came on September 4th, when the Wishart swept the board at the Regatta, and became 'Cock of the Flotilla'.*

It was fine to achieve what we had set out to do in this way. We collected six out of the eleven available cups—and one of our whalers won by no less than fifteen lengths!

Better still, though, was winning both the Regatta and the Gunnery Trophy—which was almost unheard-of. We won that on hits per minute. It seemed obvious to me that the best thing for guns to do is to hit their targets. Yet, extraordinary though it may seem, I came in for a rebuke over this.

The fetish in destroyers at that time was fast shooting, and I was criticised for my slow rate of fire. When I pointed out that we would probably have sunk any one of our fast-shooting rivals before they had even hit us, I think this was regarded as being in rather bad taste! In precisely the same way, I was told that I was ruining the *style* of rowing by adopting a very fast stroke. I replied: 'I'm sorry, I hadn't realised that style was the important thing. I'd assumed that the thing that mattered was to be first past the winning-post.'

*The year 1935 closed in gloom and alarm. On October 2nd Musso-
lini's Italy invaded Abyssinia, the first of the major aggressions by
the Dictators which formed the prelude to the Second World War.*

*Britain and France reacted sharply to this Italian move, and the
Mediterranean became a flash-point. The new and outwardly imposing Italian Navy offered a clear threat to Malta and the life-lines
of the British Commonwealth. To meet this threat, the Mediterranean Fleet was strongly reinforced, and the Fleet base was transferred from Malta to Alexandria.*

We in the 'W' Class—the 1st Destroyer Flotilla—were left in
little doubt about what all this implied. When the Fleet went off to
Alexandria we were left behind. We were old ships. Our job was to
go on showing the flag in Malta, and if the worst came to the worst,
to do all we could to harass and hold up the Italians.

But when the others said their goodbyes to us, you didn't have
to be a mind-reader to see what they thought of our chances. We
were 'expendable'.

And then something else happened which opened my eyes to what
was going on. I had to take the *Wishart* to Bizerta, to discuss with
the French Admiral there the technicalities of our receiving support
from his dockyard, if Malta was bombed. I knew the Admiral spoke
perfect English, but to my amazement he now refused to talk to me
except in French—and very rude French at that. And he made his
staff do the same with my officers. In fact I found him completely
unco-operative. I realised then how fragile the Anglo-French Alliance
might prove to be, and how doubly dangerous the situation was.

Edwina had stayed behind when the other wives left Malta—she
was, in fact, broadcasting for the newly created Malta Radio. I
told her how serious I thought things had become, and found that
she had already reached the same conclusion.

This was a turning-point in our lives. Both of us—Edwina and I
—now became crusaders, and, like all prophets of doom, rather
unpopular ones. But we were sure that the dictators meant war, and
we made it our business to say so loud and clear.

*The Abyssinian crisis revealed the pitiful weakness of the League of
Nations, and the democracies which were its firmest backers. Mussolini continued his conquering march towards Addis Ababa, unde-
terred by sanctions or demonstrations of force which were palpably*

*not going to become realities. Other dictators and would-be dic-
tators took note.*

On March 7th 1936 German troops marched into the demilitarised zone of the Rhineland, in flat defiance of the Treaty of Versailles. Later that month, a 99 per cent vote in favour of official
Nazi candidates in the German elections showed the new temper of
the German people.

*In Britain, the Defence budget increased by what at that time
seemed a very large figure—£36,000,000. Part of this sum was ear-
marked for the long-overdue increase and modernisation of the Fleet
Air Arm. Mountbatten, still flushed with the Wishart's successes,
was summoned home to a new and significant appointment, in the
Naval Air Division, which bore responsibility for the Fleet Air Arm.*

By now, things were obviously hotting up. One didn't feel that one
was in a 'peacetime' Navy any more, but rather an 'eve-of-war'
Navy.

And there was a lot to be done to prepare ourselves for war.
My years in the Mediterranean had taught me a great deal. Now I
was given a chance of putting it all to further use, in a wider and
very exciting field—if time permitted.

# 4

# The stormy winds

When I came back to England in 1936 I already knew that the danger of a Second World War was very great. In the Far East, in the Mediterranean, but above all in Germany, aggressive forces were on the march. The prospect of another war was horrible—indeed, almost unbelievable—but, as crisis after crisis developed, that prospect became more certain.

The year 1936 marked the end of an epoch: the end of the old post-war world and the beginning of a new pre-war world. For members of the Royal Family the year was sad and disturbing in a special way: it began with the death of a king, and ended with the departure of another.

*King George V was not a flamboyant monarch. It was homely virtues that won him the affection of his people. This affection was spontaneously but umistakably demonstrated at the Silver Jubilee in May 1935; the loyalty to the throne then revealed astonished those who believed or proclaimed that the monarchy was a dying institution.*

*The King himself was amazed at the enthusiasm of his subjects, and their obvious pleasure that he had reigned over them for twenty-five years. 'I'd no idea they felt like that about me,' he remarked. 'I'm beginning to think they must really like me for myself.'*

*But the joy was short-lived. That autumn the King's health began to deteriorate, and on January 20th 1936 he died. During his reign Britain had undergone social revolution, faced imminent civil war, waged world war and endured damaging economic crises. Through them all the King was a symbol of stability; many feared that stability had departed with him.*

I had always had great respect for King George V, but we were never close to each other. He was a rather intimidating figure, and the younger members of his family were distinctly afraid of him. I was never actually afraid, but I can't pretend that I didn't stand in awe of him. He was really the last of the Victorians—much more of a Victorian than his own father, King Edward VII.

My cousin David, the Prince of Wales, who now became Edward VIII, was a totally different person. I had come to know him intimately—in fact, he became my best friend.

Some of the older generation rather disapproved of him, because he obviously liked to enjoy life, and disliked protocol. But he was the idol of the younger generation. His sympathy with ordinary people was so evidently genuine—whether they were soldiers, during the war, or unemployed, during the Depression.

There was a strong feeling that the new King would do something —no one could quite say what—about the social injustices which were still so plentiful at that time. His reign began with high hopes, and amid great popularity.

*It was in the fourth month of the reign of King Edward VIII that Mountbatten returned to London to take up his new post in the Naval Air Division of the Admiralty. This appointment placed him in the front line of a conflict which had been going on for nearly twenty years.*

*Ever since April 1st 1918, when the Royal Air Force came into existence, replacing the Royal Flying Corps and the Royal Naval Air Service, the Navy had been in the difficult position of not having full control of its own 'air umbrella'. The apostles of Air Power proclaimed: 'The Air is indivisible'—meaning that a true Air strategy required all Air Forces to be unified, and handled as one, whether they fought over land or water. With the Navy's air force this 'unification' ironically meant disunity: control of the Fleet Air Arm was divided between the Admiralty and the Air Ministry.*

The Naval Air Division was a tiny section in what appeared to be a backwater. But I didn't mind that, in fact, I was delighted, for two reasons: I had always been interested in flying, and I was convinced that Air Power was going to play a vital rôle in war at sea.

I was barely six years old when I made my first flight—in an airship. I made my first flight in an aeroplane in 1911, when my father had under him the embryo Royal Naval Air Service at Sheerness. I went up in a Short biplane; the pilot was Lieutenant Longmore— later to become Air Chief Marshal Sir Arthur Longmore. In 1918 I spent my leave learning to fly with the R.A.F., and I had kept it up ever since. So that was one thing.

My second reason for being delighted was the work itself. I found myself at the centre of the dispute between the Admiralty and the Air Ministry. I still have some of the papers which came on to my desk at that time. Here is one passage which shows how vital it was to change the Government's mind about this issue:

'Can anyone doubt that if we went to war tomorrow, complete chaos would reign in the Navy's Air Services? Where are the machines? Where is the trained personnel? Where is the up-to-date material? They simply don't exist. There is not a squadron of air- craft afloat today with aircraft of a type which was not in service three years ago. There is not a squadron with a type whose design is less than ten years old.'

This was a frightening situation, with international affairs shaping the way they were. And it was my job now to propose ways of bringing the Fleet Air Arm back into the Navy, and to try to per- suade the Government to do this.

*Mountbatten now displayed a capacity which remained with him, and won for him, down the years, a special reputation. Unhesitat- ingly, he used his social connections to promote the cause for which he was working. Some might call it intrigue; others might call it 'skulduggery'; others might gratefully accept the fruits of it by any name. Certainly, in 1936, any approach, by any means, which might persuade the British Government to overhaul the nation's defences, was to be welcomed.*

*In March of that year German troops entered the demilitarised Rhineland. Adolf Hitler gambled that Britain and France would not resist this open proclamation of the revival of German armed force. In 1936, as we now know, that force was not great; the wartime Allies had ample strength to overcome it. But Hitler was right: the will to fight was absent in both countries.*

*Hitler had been permitted to succeed; his prestige soared, and from now onwards he swiftly, openly, unhesitatingly rebuilt the German Army and Air Force. The balance of power in Europe had*

*been tilted irrevocably. Now dictatorship was in the ascendant
everywhere.*

*In May the Italians entered Addis Ababa, and Mussolini annexed
Abyssinia—another blow to British and French prestige. In July a
military rising in Spain against the Popular Front Government
marked the opening of the Civil War. This produced a new array
of international complications and dangers, to the advantage of the
dictators. In the democracies there were only confusion and divided
counsels.*

My great awakening had occurred the year before, during the Abyssinian crisis. But even before that I had formed a dislike of Mussolini and his Fascist movement. My Italian relations disapproved of
him, and his brutal methods of suppressing political opposition
disgusted me.

When Hitler began to come forward, some of my German relations, to my astonishment, thought he would be a good thing for
Germany. But most of them warned me about what he really stood
for, and did their best to oppose him.

From 1936 onwards both Edwina and I were increasingly worried
and depressed by world affairs, but we reacted in different ways.
Edwina became rather a tub-thumper, and horrified the died-in-the-
wool Conservatives whom we met. This gave her the reputation of
being rather red, while I was only thought to be slightly pink. In
fact, we both thought alike, but I considered it a waste of time
trying to convert reactionaries, and talked mostly to people who
shared our views and might be able to get something done.

Over and above that, of course, being in the Navy, I had to be
rather more circumspect. But there was one occasion when I
couldn't resist making my point. The King—Edward VIII—had
asked me to a dinner party one evening, and arranged matters so
that I found myself next to the Prime Minister. I told Mr. Baldwin
about the great number of airfields which were being constructed
in north-west Germany. He hadn't heard of them. He asked me how
I knew. I told him I was in the Naval Air Division, and it was my
business to know.

I asked Mr. Baldwin if he didn't think it significant that these
airfields were being built in the north-west: didn't that point to an
attack on England? He said he thought not. I then asked him if he
could account for such a build-up in that particular area. But he

just brushed that aside. I asked him whether he believed that Hitler could maintain himself in power without military aggression. He didn't see why not.

'Hitler is like a man on a bicycle,' I remember saying. 'He's got to go on pedalling or he'll fall over; he can't maintain himself stationary.'

But nothing I could say could shake Mr. Stanley Baldwin.

*In the autumn of 1936, Mr. Baldwin found his mind occupied with a crisis nearer home. In 1930[1] the King (then Prince of Wales) had begun a friendship with Mrs. Wallis Simpson, an American lady who had been previously married to Lieutenant Winfield Spencer of the United States Navy. By the time the Prince had become King this friendship had turned into love.*

*'Secrecy and concealment', wrote the King later, 'were not in my nature. We saw each other when we could.'*

*In the summer of 1936 the King and Mrs. Simpson were guests of the Mountbattens. Then Mrs. Simpson was seen as the King's guest during a cruise in the Mediterranean. In America and in Europe the Press speculated freely about future developments; but the British Press at that time had a clear sense of duty and was silent.*

*On October 27th, however, Mrs. Simpson was granted a decree nisi at Ipswich, and those who knew the state of the King's feelings realised that silence could not be preserved much longer. If the King married Mrs. Simpson she would become Queen; as Queen she would be crowned with him, with the ceremony of a religion which then held firmly that marriages should not be unmade.*

*On November 16th the King informed Mr. Baldwin that he did indeed intend to marry Mrs. Simpson, and that if the constitutional objections were too great he would abdicate. For the Prime Minister, for the country, and for the King's family, this was a thunderclap.*

I was devoted to my cousin David. He had always been a wonderful friend to me, and I had felt sure that he was going to make a wonderful king. I had known, since they had both stayed with us in the summer, that the King was seriously attached to Mrs. Simpson. But it was not until November, when I was with him during

[1] See *King George VI* by John Wheeler-Bennett: Macmillan, 1958, p. 275 et seq.

his visit to the Fleet, that I realised how utterly determined he was to marry her. The news broke shortly after this in the Press, and the crisis developed.

By then, I understood how much it meant to him to marry the woman of his choice—how lonely his position would be without her. But I couldn't possibly agree with his decision to abdicate, because I was one of those who felt that his duty to his country should have come first.

The decision placed an intolerable burden on his brother, the Duke of York. I remember, on the day of the abdication, walking up and down on the lawn with him at Fort Belvedere at Windsor, and he told me how desperately he did not want to be King, and how totally unprepared he felt. And I tried to comfort him, by telling him exactly what my father had once told his father, in equally trying circumstances: that I was sure that a naval training was the best possible preparation for being a king.

*King Edward VIII abdicated on December 10th 1936, and the following day the Duke of York (Prince Albert) mounted the throne as George VI. He was crowned in Westminster Abbey on May 12th 1937.*

*So Britain's constitutional crisis ended, but abroad there was no slackening in the succession of political crises which brought world war nearer every month.*

*The Civil War in Spain already presented a microcosm of what was to come. Openly, the two dictators, Hitler and Mussolini, backed the rebel cause. They sent troops (so-called 'volunteers') and equipment to the aid of General Franco. The Soviet Union supported the Spanish left-wing Government. Other volunteers, the International Brigades, demonstrated the solidarity of the Left by also going to fight for the Government. Meanwhile the Governments of Britain and France picked an uneasy, unrewarding course of neutrality.*

*In the Far East there was open war between Japan and China. The Japanese entered Peking and Tientsin in July. In November they took Shanghai. The League of Nations, the great hope of the post-war world, proved as ineffective in preventing war in the East as it had been over Abyssinia or Spain.*

*Britain had supported the League; but now there came about a change. On May 28th Mr. Baldwin retired, and Neville Chamberlain became Prime Minister. In November Lord Halifax paid a visit to*

*Adolf Hitler to discuss with him the future of Czechoslovakia. The policy of Appeasement had begun.*

I hated the Appeasement policey; I felt sure that it would prove disastrous. It certainly delayed the rearmament of all our Services, which was now urgently needed. There were a number of people who felt as I did, and some were in a better position to make their views known.

Churchill was the acknowledged leader of this group, but Churchill was out of office and looked like remaining so. Opposition to Appeasement was definitely a minority line, and one which could make you very unpopular. In the Government it was chiefly represented by two men, both friends of mine, and both of them ultimately had to resign. They were Duff Cooper, First Lord of the Admiralty, and Anthony Eden, the Foreign Secretary.

*Anthony Eden's resignation came in February 1938, against the background of further advances by the dictators. It was with German and Italian backing that General Franco now recaptured Teruel, after a bitter two-month winter battle. But the centre of the storm was shifting outside Spain.*

*In March 1938 German troops entered Austria, and the union of Germany and Austria which had been specifically prohibited by the Treaty of Versailles became a fact. But the Treaty of Versailles was a dead letter now; the Treaty of Locarno was a dead letter; the League of Nations was a dead letter. The democracies seemed to be utterly powerless.*

1938 was not only a bad year politically; it was especially sad for our family, because in April my brother, the second Marquess of Milford Haven, died at the age of forty-six.

Georgie was seven years older than me—just enough to be a real hero to me. To see him taken away in the prime of life by cancer was an agonising experience. I adored him. He must have been one of the cleverest men I have ever known—I think his brain was twice the size of mine. But, then, he was quite different from me. Everybody loved him; I don't think he had an enemy in the world.

He was the sort of person who, instead of reading detective stories, would sit down and read problems of higher calculus and solve them in his head. When he was a squadron gunnery officer, he could take a chart and compose complicated orders for a squadron concentration shoot in his head, and then he could dash them off on a typewriter on a wax master and have them duplicated without any revision. He was a brilliant man.

*It was in the month of this personal loss to the Mountbatten family that the final series of international crises began which remorselessly led to war.*

*In April the Sudeten Germans demanded separation from Czechoslovakia. By May, Britain and France were faced with their first decision whether to stand by Czechoslovakia according to treaty or permit Germany to destroy her.*

*In August Germany mobilised. On September 7th France called up her reservists. Then came the drama of Mr. Chamberlain's flights to Germany to meet Adolf Hitler in the hope of reaching some agreement. On September 15th he went to Berchtesgaden; on the 27th to Godesberg.*

*Chamberlain believed that he could persuade Hitler; but Hitler had gauged the temper of the democracies. He insisted on the annexation of the Sudetenland.*

*In Britain men's hearts were torn by a fear of impending shame and a horror of impending war. On September 27th the Royal Navy was mobilised at the urgent instigation of Duff Cooper. For a brief moment it appeared that Britain might steel herself to resist Hitler's demands.*

And then came Munich, and Chamberlain flew back in triumph to announce that he had obtained 'peace in our time'. Czechoslovakia, of course, was abandoned to Hitler's mercy—and Hitler had been given one more proof that he could do as he liked. Churchill described the whole transaction as 'a defeat, an unmitigated defeat'.

Duff Cooper resigned from the Admiralty, and he quotes in his autobiography, *Old Men Forget*, a letter I wrote to him at the time:

'I expect it is highly irregular of me, a serving naval officer, writing to you on relinquishing your position as First Lord, but I cannot stand by and see someone whom I admire behave in exactly the way I hope I should have the courage to behave if I had been in his shoes, without saying "Well done".'

Even now people who thought as Duff Cooper and I did were few and far between. However, there was a certain awakening. Such rearmament as we managed to achieve really began now, after Munich—but there was not much time left.

It was in this year that the Navy at last won its battle to get back the Fleet Air Arm from partial control by the Royal Air Force, which gratified me. It was too late in the day to get the new aircraft and all the things we needed before the war came—but better late than never!

Working in the Naval Air Division, the serious shortcomings in the short-range anti-aircraft protection of the Fleet were brought home to me. Our high-angled guns could not compete with low-flying attacks. For that purpose, all we had were machine guns firing solid bullets, but these really were not good enough.

I discovered that there was a new Swiss gun—the Oerlikon—a simple, robust gun with a very high rate of fire, and just the right explosive shell to stop a plane. It was not really my business, but I went to the Gunnery Division to try and interest them. I had no luck.

I even went so far as to have an Oerlikon mounted in a new motor-torpedo-boat which was being built as a private venture, in the hopes of forcing the Admiralty to take the Oerlikon with it. It seems hardly believable, but they bought the boat, on condition that the Oerlikon gun was taken out! Finally, in despair, I did a very irregular thing: I took my courage in both hands and I went and saw the new First Sea Lord, Admiral Backhouse, personally. He saw the point at once, and gave the necessary orders, although this was the eleventh hour. And so we eventually got the Oerlikon, which gradually became standard equipment throughout the Fleets.

*The consequences of Munich were not long delayed. On October 1st 1938, German troops entered the Sudetenland. Slovakia broke away from the Czechs. Hungary annexed part of southern Slovakia. It was only a matter of time (March 1939) before Germany swallowed the rest.*

*Japan withdrew from the League of Nations, and pressed her war in China forward, ignoring democratic opinion. General Franco won his final victories in Spain, and was recognised by Britain and France in February 1939. Italy, emboldened by past success, began to voice claims to Corsica, Savoy and Nice. And still the British Government clung to the policy of Appeasement. Mr. Chamberlain*

*and his Foreign Secretary, Lord Halifax, went to Rome to attempt
with the Italian dictator what they had disastrously failed to accom-
plish with Hitler.*

*In this atmosphere, Britain's rearmament was slow and difficult;
a dead hand seemed to lie on all the British Services.*

These were frustrating times. Our authorities didn't seem to want
to look ahead—and yet science was making such strides that delay
was more dangerous than ever. For instance, as far back as 1936,
I had made friends with the eminent French rocket scientist
Robert Esnault Pelterie. He foretold to me the possibility of reaching the moon with rockets within thirty years.

What was more to the point, he foretold rocket missiles within
ten years. He gave me all his work on this—in French, of course—
and I handed it to the appropriate department at the Admiralty,
because I felt sure the Navy ought to be in the forefront of this
development. But nothing happened about rocketry for several
years. I lost track of the business, and we made no use whatever
of this important work as far as I know.

*Yet Mountbatten was able to exert some significant influence.
Learning from the R.A.F., he succeeded in interesting the Admiralty
in the Typex machines which were to transform (belatedly) the
Navy's entire code and cypher system. They came too late to prevent some lamentable disasters and loss of life; but at least they
came.[1]*

*And now the curtain rose on the last acts of uneasy peace. At
the end of March 1939 Hitler denounced Germany's Non-Aggression
Pact with Poland. Another crisis was evidently impending, but this
time, unprepared as they still were, the democracies did not give
way.*

*In April Britain went so far as to introduce Conscription in
peacetime for the first time in the nation's history. But by now it
was too late to halt the march of the dictators towards war. In May
Hitler and Mussolini signed their 'Pact of Steel'. After that, week by
week, day by day, the Polish crisis intensified.*

*In August an Anglo-French Military Mission went to Moscow in a
belated attempt to recruit the Soviet Union to the anti-Axis cause.*

[1] See *Room 39: Naval Intelligence in Action 1939–45* by Donald McLachlan
(Weidenfeld & Nicolson, 1968), Ch. IV, esp. p. 78.

*But the talks failed amid the cross-purposes of complete distrust. Immediately the Soviet Government signed a Non-Aggression Pact with Germany—thus removing Hitler's last fear: a major war on two fronts. With this act, war became certain: it was now a matter of days and hours.*

It was a comfort to me to know exactly what my job was going to be when the balloon went up. In June 1939 I was appointed captain commanding the 5th Destroyer Flotilla—Captain D5. This was a wonderful command, because they were all brand-new ships of the 'J' and 'K' class, still building. My own ship, the flotilla leader, was to be H.M.S. *Kelly*. She was handed over to me by the builders, Hawthorne Leslie, on August 23rd, ten days before war broke out.

*For the first twenty-one months of the Second World War Mountbatten remained in command of his destroyer flotilla. Great events succeeded each other: the fall of Poland; Hitler's invasion of Norway; the invasion of the Low Countries; Dunkirk; the fall of France; the Battle of Britain; the Blitz; the first desert victories; defeat in Greece; the loss of Crete. Through them all the 5th Flotilla performed the arduous duties of destroyers in war, sometimes taking a direct part in the great occasions of history, more often engaged in dull but dangerous routines.*

*The story of H.M.S. Kelly during these twenty-one months of war has been told by Mountbatten's friend, Noël Coward, in his film In Which We Serve. Coward played the Captain—under a different name; he changed the name of the ship; sometimes he placed her in situations to which the Kelly did not belong (like Dunkirk). But it was Mountbatten's cap that Coward wore, in Mountbatten's manner; it was Mountbatten's words that he used in the peak moments of the story; and when Mountbatten visited the studios, and saw the life-size ship-model which Coward had had constructed, he thought for a moment that the Kelly had returned to life.*

*Coward called his film 'the story of a ship'. This is Mountbatten's story of the ship.*

The *Kelly* was launched on October 25th 1938 by the daughter of the man she was called after, Admiral Sir John Kelly. She was built by Hawthorne Leslie at Hebburn-on-Tyne; the relationship between the ship's company and the builders was, in my experience, unique. We became great friends all the way down the line: I chummed up with my opposite number, the Managing Director, Sir Robin Rowell; the First Lieutenant chummed up with the Shipyard Manager, my secretary with the secretary of the Company, our Engineer Officer with the Engineer Manager of the Yard, the Chief Bo'sun's Mate with the Foreman of Shipwrights, and so on. We became friends, and we remained friends.

On August 23rd 1939 we did our acceptance trials, and I signed for the ship. On the 25th we commissioned at Chatham. There were men in the ship's company who had served with me before, and I asked them what sort of a ship they thought I wanted. They answered:

'A happy ship.'

'What else?'

'An efficient ship.'

And that is exactly what we got: a happy and efficient ship. The day we commissioned was the day that Hitler and Stalin signed their pact; I was certain that this meant war within a few days. So I told the ship's company that instead of the normal commissioning time of three weeks I was going to give them three days. No one would take their clothes off or turn in until the job was done. Nobody did, and we finished in three days flat.

With our tails right up, we sailed for Portland to work up. We were in the middle of repainting the ship—I was over the side with a paint-brush in my hand—when the Chief Yeoman of Signals came along with the message that we were at war. And about ten minutes later he returned with another telegram from the Admiralty which just said: 'Winston is back.' It was a tremendous thrill to know that Winston Churchill was once again First Lord of the Admiralty, as he had been in 1914, when my father was First Sea Lord.

In December we returned to the Tyne—and there we met trouble. Four ships were blown up at the mouth of the river and the Tyne was closed. It was thought that they had been torpedoed, and I was ordered to go out, with the destroyer *Mohawk* under orders, to search for the submarine. I gave the necessary orders, but then I got on the telephone to the Admiral and said:

'Look, sir, I don't think these ships have been torpedoed; I think they've been mined. Even if they have been torpedoed, we shall be much too late when we get down there, and the scent will be stale.

If it's a minefield it will be very dangerous to go there until it has been cleared. Can you get the order cancelled?'

He told me that the order had come from the Commander-in-Chief, Scotland, and a bit later he rang me and said:

'The Commander-in-Chief says, "Don't bellyache; get on with your orders."'

Well, after that there was nothing I could do, so off we went. I put the *Mohawk* half a mile astern, so that not more than one of us would be blown up, and we entered the minefield—it *was* a minefield all right. It was a very funny feeling, creeping along, waiting for something to happen. And then we heard a mine grating along the bottom, just under the bridge; that was very unpleasant. It grated along midships, then under the wardroom, and finally went off between the propellers. The whole ship was shaken, we were knocked off our feet—and there we were, stopped, in the middle of a minefield. Fortunately the ship was not too badly damaged, and soon a tug came along and hauled us home to Hawthorne Leslie's, stern first.

Now on that occasion one young seaman gave way to panic. He was brought up before me, charged with deserting his post in time of war. I asked him if he knew what the punishment was. He said:

'Yes, sir.'

'What is it?'

'Death.'

'It is. Case remanded. Clear Lower Deck.'

We cleared Lower Deck, and I addressed the ship's company.

'You've just been through a harrowing experience—being mined. Out of 260 men, 259 behaved as I expected they would. One did not. One left his post. This is a most serious offence in time of war, and you may be surprised that I propose letting him off with a caution—or rather two cautions: one to him, and one to me, for having failed to impress myself sufficiently in three months on all of you, for you to know that I would never tolerate such behaviour. Nobody will ever again leave their post. I will never give the order, "Abandon Ship". The only way in which we will ever leave the ship will be if she sinks under our feet.'

Our next adventure was during the Norwegian Campaign. We took part in the evacuation of Namsos. It was a dark night, with dark blue sky overhead and black, towering cliffs on each side, as we entered the deep, magnificent fjord. At its head stood the town of

Namsos, built entirely of wood, and blazing like a Hollywood film set. We ran alongside the pier, collected our soldiers and brought them out.

It was about a week later that we were ordered to proceed at high speed to the island of Silt, to intercept and destroy some German minelayers. We hared across the North Sea at high speed all day, and then, about half-past ten that night, when visibility was pretty shocking, the port lookout called out:

'Torpedo track port!'

I looked, and saw a torpedo track which passed under my feet, and I said:

'Thank God! It's run too low'—because obviously it had not gone off; and looking out again I saw a motor-torpedo-boat disappearing into the mist.

At that moment the second torpedo hit us, exploded, and made a great hole in Number 1 Boiler Room. The Officer of the Watch in the *Kandahar*—our next astern—was my nephew, Lord Milford Haven. He said to his captain:

'Can't we stop and try to pick up survivors from the *Kelly*?' And his captain replied:

'What's the good? You saw the explosion; nobody can survive an explosion like that.'

Fortunately a destroyer from another flotilla, the *Bulldog*, came up shortly afterwards, saw that we were still afloat, and asked what she could do. I said:

'Take us in tow.'

And that was the beginning of a very long haul. First we jettisoned every bit of topweight that we could move. We shot off ten torpedoes and all our depth-charges; we cut our boats adrift; we threw ammunition overboard; we unbolted the lockers, and threw them out too. And so we were able to remain afloat—rather unsteady, difficult to manage, but the *Kelly* was afloat, and that was all that mattered to me.

I remained on the bridge for the whole of our return trip. Late the first night, we suddenly heard the sound of an E-boat engine, and then she arrived, at full speed. She hit the *Bulldog* a glancing blow, bounced off her and came right inboard on the *Kelly*. Our starboard gunwale was awash, and so she was able to come right on board us with a rush, firing her 20 mm. gun. I remember ducking down behind the bridge screen, which was only canvas, and thinking to myself: 'What a damn silly thing to do!' So I straightened up and watched the rest of the action. The E-boat (MTB 40, we now know it was) shore off davits and guard rails as she passed down *Kelly*'s side, and then vanished into the night.

And then came the Luftwaffe. We were transferring our wounded to the *Kandahar* when they first appeared. The first attack was driven off, but we knew they would be back—and they were. We buried our dead at sea—as many of them as we could find—and that was an eerie and harrowing experience; I had to read the Burial Service while helm orders were passed down the ship:

'Ashes to ashes . . . starboard ten . . . dust to dust . . . midships . . .'

By now there were quite a few ships clustered round us, and the Admiral signalled me saying that with Hitler invading the Low Countries this was a waste of force; he suggested that we should open the seacocks and scuttle the *Kelly*. To this I replied:

'I absolutely refuse to scuttle. We don't want any help. We have enough ammunition to defend ourselves. Please send a tug to complete the tow.'

So in due course a tug arrived to bring us home. But the night before it appeared, we were nearly done for after all; the sea got up, and the ship started to develop a very unpleasant movement. I could feel that we were very near complete loss of stability. I racked my brains to think of more topweight that I could get rid of. And then I had a brainwave:

'The ship's company. They weigh a hell of a lot. Let's get rid of the ship's company!'

So the whole ship's company was transferred to the other destroyers, with the Luftwaffe bombing the open boats as they went across. The next morning the tug appeared, and we were on the last lap. Six officers and twelve men came back aboard—just enough to handle the ship and man the close-range weapons. I worked a .5-inch multiple machine-gun, and I must say that it's much more fun actually firing a gun than just sitting there when you are being attacked!

And so we came home, after ninety-one hours in tow: home to Hawthorne Leslie's, and I'll never forget the heart-warming cheer from all the shipyard workers as we came into the Tyne.

Well, all this meant that the *Kelly* was out of action for quite a long spell. Our crew was largely dispersed, and I led the flotilla in various ships at different times. We took part in the bombardment of

Cherbourg; we had a daylight action with German destroyers, and a night action, too. On that occasion I was in the *Javelin*. We managed to get both our bow and our stern blown off by torpedoes, but we were able to bring the middle of the ship home nevertheless. They were well-built vessels, the 'J' and 'K' class.

It was about this time, I believe, that a certain admiral coined a phrase about me: 'I know of nobody I'd sooner be with in a tight corner than Dickie Mountbatten, and I know of nobody who could get me into one quicker.'

In November 1940 the *Kelly* was re-commissioned; it was wonderful how hard her old company tried to get back to her, and I was glad to see some familiar faces around me again. This time we were soon on a new stamping-ground—the Mediterranean. Hitler's dive-bombers had practically closed the western end of the Mediterranean, and when the 5th Flotilla made the passage from Gibraltar to Malta in April 1941 we were the first to do so for a long time. The battlements of Valetta were black with cheering people, delighted to see the Navy back again.

We had an exciting time. We went out on night sweeps to try to intercept Rommel's supply ships, carrying stores and petrol to the Afrika Korps. We bombarded Benghazi. But the Mediterranean was becoming more and more dangerous. Malta was being bombed the whole time. I didn't like to think what people would say if the *Kelly* was sunk in harbour, and when they asked where Dickie Mountbatten was, were told that he had been in an air-raid shelter. So although I insisted that half the ships' companies of the flotilla must sleep in shelters every night, I stayed aboard. There were twenty-one raids during this time, and I've never been so frightened in my life. It's hair-raising when you can do nothing about it!

By now, things were going badly all round. Our forces had been driven ignominiously out of Greece, and in May the Germans were attacking Crete. The Navy was very hard put to it, in the face of German air superiority, to support the Army, but we had to do everything we could. I was ordered to take one division of the flotilla to Maleme to give fire-support to the New Zealanders who were trying to recapture the airfield there. There were only three of us in company—*Kelly*, *Kashmir* and *Kipling*. By a merciful providence, the *Kipling* developed steering trouble, and I ordered her to part company. That left just the two of us. We ran into some caiques carrying German troops, and sank at least one of them. I

still remember the sight of Germans in full marching order jumping
into the sea.

We put down our barrage with our 4·7-inch guns to support the
New Zealanders. Then it began to get light, and it was time for us
to go. We had the good luck to run into a German ammunition
ship, and when we had finished with her she was going off like a
firework display on the 5th of November. But that was the last of
our luck. Well, very nearly the last.

The German high-level medium bombers soon found us, and
began their attacks. I wasn't too worried, because we could see
them coming, and we could manœuvre the ships to dodge the bombs.
But at about eight o'clock that morning—May 23rd—our doom
appeared on the horizon, in the form of twenty-four Junkers 87
dive-bombers. These were the dreaded Stukas, who made vertical
dives on their targets, and whose proud boast was that they never
missed, even if they had to kill themselves in the process.

I made a signal to the *Kashmir* to act independently, and put
the telegraph down to 'Full Ahead'. We must have been doing
thirty-three or thirty-four knots. The Stukas came down in waves of
three. The first wave went down on to the *Kashmir*, the second made
for the *Kelly*. Both of us were doing our best to steer in such a
fashion as to make the bombing dive steeper and steeper, to make
them miss the ships and dive into the sea. But the third wave of
bombs hit the *Kashmir*, and I saw that she was finished. I remember
saying:

'Oh God, now we're stuck here! We shall never get away. We've
got to pick up the *Kashmirs*.'

The next wave was coming in on us, and I ordered:

'Hard a-starboard.'

With the wheel hard a-starboard, doing some thirty-three knots,
the ship was listing heavily over to port. And then one Stuka came
in lower than any others—so low that he was one of the three or
four we shot into the sea; but the bomb was released so close to
the ship that it couldn't miss. It hit square on 'X' gun-deck and
killed the crew of the twin 4·7-inch gun mounting.

I immediately gave the order: 'Midships.'

And then: 'Hard a-port.'

But we only listed over more heavily. I gave the order:

'Stop engines.'

I heard the coxswain shout up the voice-pipe:

'Ship won't answer the helm, sir. No reply to the engine-room telegraphs!'

And then I knew we were for it.

I shouted out: 'Keep all guns firing!' because I could see another wave coming in. It was an unnecessary order, because all the guns *were* firing. Nobody stopped. As she went over I could see some of the gun-crews being washed away from their guns while still trying to keep them in action.

I realised that the ship was rolling right over, and water was coming up in a raging torrent, because we were still doing about thirty knots. I thought: 'Whatever happens I must stay with the ship as long as I can. I must be the last to leave her.'

When she was right over I climbed up on to the distance-correction indicator of the station-keeping device which I had invented, and which was fitted throughout the flotilla. I clung round the gyro-compass pedestal, with the sea still swirling all over the bridge because of our speed through the water. I held on as long as I could, and took a deep breath as the sea closed over my head.

Somehow I managed to pull myself under the bridge-screens in the darkness. I was already beginning to need air, so I held one hand over my mouth, and one over my nose, hoping I would have the strength to keep them there. I thought my lungs were going to burst, but at last I came to the surface, without having taken in any sea-water. I looked round, and there was the stern of the ship passing not more than a dozen yards away, with the propellers still going round. I saw the Navigator, Lieutenant Butler-Bowden, close to me, and thinking that the propellers were going to hit us, I shouted to him:

'Swim like hell!'

So we swam like hell, and the ship missed us by about six or seven yards, and then up popped one of the stoker petty officers, covered with oil fuel, as I was, and he took one look at me and said:

'Funny how the scum always comes to the top, isn't it, sir?'

There was one Carley raft afloat—there had only been time to release one, before the ship went down—so I yelled out:

'Everybody swim to the raft!'

I found I still had my tin hat on, and thinking that it was rather silly to swim in a tin hat I took it off and threw it away. Never have I regretted an action so quickly, because only a few minutes later I saw a row of splashes between us and the raft. The Ju 87s were back, machine-gunning us in the water. I felt very naked without my tin hat.

I reached the raft, and clung on to the side. We put the wounded inside it, and the rest of us clung to the outside or to each other. The Stukas came back again, firing at us, and a number of men were killed. When this happened, or when someone died of his injuries, we gently took them out of the raft, and more recently wounded men took their places. It was a gruesome and unpleasant business, and yet the sea was calm, the sun was shining, and this was the same Mediterranean in which I had had so many bathes in the days before the war. We sang to keep up our courage in the water, 'Roll Out the Barrel', and songs like that, and it seemed to help.

And then the miracle happened: there was the *Kipling*. I don't think I've ever been so pleased to see any ship in my life. Commander St. Clair Ford had seen the dive-bombing, decided that they would probably sink us, and had very gallantly come along to help, knowing that he would draw the attacks on to his own ship. Just as he arrived, the *Kelly*, whose bottom was still just visible, started to go down altogether. I called out:

'Three cheers for the old ship!'

For me it was the saddest moment of the day.

*Kipling* actually nudged the *Kelly* in the water as she went down, and sustained some damage, but it was not important. Then she lowered scrambling nets, and we all swam to her. I towed a badly wounded man, but by the time I got to the *Kipling* he was dead and I let go of him. When I got aboard I went up on the bridge, but beyond asking him to go over and collect the survivors of the *Kashmir*, I naturally didn't interfere with Commander St. Clair Ford in the handling of his ship.

Picking up the *Kashmirs* was the devil of a job. She had gone down more slowly than the *Kelly*, and in an upright position, so there were five Carley rafts floating, and five groups of men to be picked up. This would have presented no problem but for our next lot of visitors—a squadron of Ju 88s. It was lucky for us that they were 88s and not 87s, because their bombing was much less accurate; even so, every time the *Kipling* came alongside a raft, Commander St. Clair Ford had to go ahead with the wheel hard over to avoid being hit. The whole business seemed to be quite hopeless.

Now everything resolved into a battle of wits between St. Clair

Ford and the bombers. With great skill and courage he nosed the
*Kipling* from raft to raft, but it was a long and painful procedure,
and the Ju 88s never let up. After about two hours some of my
staff officers came to me and pointed out that the *Kipling* now had
aboard all the *Kelly* survivors, and about half the *Kashmir* survivors, as well as her own company. It seemed to be just a matter
of time before one of the bombers scored a hit, in which case we
might lose another five or six hundred lives. Why not call it a day?
I decided that we should stay and carry on picking up the *Kashmirs*.

After about another hour there was only one raft left to be
rescued, and the staff came back again, urging that the right decision was to make sure of saving the men already on board. But I
felt it would be better for us all to be sunk together than to leave any
of our flotilla mates struggling in the water without any hope of
being saved.

In the end we cleared all the rafts. And then at last we could turn
for home—Alexandria—a long way away. And because of her
damage the *Kipling* could only do about seventeen knots. All her
decks were crowded with survivors, many of them severely
wounded, some of them dying. I went round with a notebook and
pencil, and collected messages to be sent to their families at home.
And then I went back to the bridge. The bombers were still after
us; I counted over eighty near-misses as the *Kipling* limped home.
But thanks to her captain and his ship's company we were not hit.

At last the bombers went away, but our troubles were not yet
over. We ran out of fuel. We were very glad to see the *Protector*
come out to meet us, and fill up our tanks a bit! And so at last
we arrived at Alexandria, and the ships' companies of the Mediterranean Fleet cleared lower deck and cheered us in.

I went ashore in the first boat, and when I reached the landing
stage almost the first person I saw was a cheery young midshipman, grinning all over his face. It was my nephew Philip.

'What are you grinning at?' I asked him.

'You've no idea how funny you look,' he replied. 'Your face is
absolutely brown and your eyes are bright red.'

'What's so funny about that? You chaps who fight your battles
in big ships never get dirty.'

But I was very glad to see him.

And then we came to the moment which I was dreading: saying
'Goodbye' to my *Kelly* shipmates. I feared that this really was the

end of the *Kelly*. As long as we were together the spirit of the ship still seemed to be alive, but when we all went our different ways I was sure it would evaporate. So when it came to shaking hands with the survivors—there weren't very many of them, only about forty or fifty unwounded men all told—it was almost more than I could bear.

But I was wrong. I was quite wrong. The spirit of the ship did not die. I had underestimated what the Lower Deck could do. It was the Lower Deck—not me, not the officers, not even the petty officers—who dreamed up the idea of the *Kelly* Reunion Association. It meets every year, and I make a point of attending whenever I possibly can. And so the spirit of the *Kelly* lives on.

# 5
# United we conquer

In June 1941 I was back in London, waiting for another job. But first I had a special mission to perform. I had been instructed by the Commanders-in-Chief, Middle East (Field Marshal Wavell, Admiral Cunningham and Air Marshal Tedder) to report their views on the situation personally to the Prime Minister. So my first port of call was Whitehall.

The Prime Minister asked me to lunch at No. 10 Downing Street on Saturday, June 21st. Lunch was laid in what was then the downstairs dining-room. The only other person present was Lord Beaverbrook.

Winston Churchill arrived about twenty minutes late, and at once told us that he had definite information that the Germans were going to attack Russia on the 22nd—the very next day.

*Operation Barbarossa, Hitler's invasion of the Soviet Union, began at four o'clock in the morning on June 22nd. The Soviet forces were taken utterly by surprise, and immediately sustained severe and costly defeats.*

*On the very day of the attack Churchill had broadcast:*

*'Any man or State who fights on against Nazidom will have our aid. Any man or State who marches with Hitler is our foe . . . That is our policy and that is our declaration. It follows, therefore, that we shall give whatever help we can to Russia and the Russian people . . .'*

*The Russians were now Britain's allies, and Hitler's treacherous attack had produced a result which he had certainly not intended:*

the first step towards the forging of what Churchill called 'The Grand Alliance'.

Another step followed shortly afterwards. In August, only a few weeks after the attack on Russia, Churchill and President Roosevelt met at Placentia Bay, Newfoundland. From this meeting emerged the Atlantic Charter. America was not yet at war, but by this meeting and this declaration the already strong links between American and British policy were made stronger.

It was in that same month—August—that Mountbatten took up his new command. The aircraft-carrier Illustrious, severely damaged in Malta, was being repaired in the U.S. Navy Yard at Norfolk, Virginia. Mountbatten was appointed captain of this splendid ship, and although it would clearly be some time before she was ready to go to war again, he entered upon his new command with great elation.

There was not a lot for me to do on board while the Illustrious was refitting, so I was delighted to be invited to visit the U.S. Pacific Fleet, and lecture to the officers about what the war at sea was like.

The Fleet Base was Pearl Harbour, over two thousand miles out in the Pacific Ocean from San Francisco. After two years of war I was appalled to see how unprepared the Americans were, and how vulnerable Pearl Harbour was to a surprise attack. I told them so, and although some of their senior officers seemed to think I was being unduly alarmist, the C.-in-C., Admiral Kimmel, agreed with me.

I was received with wonderful kindness during this period in America. President Roosevelt invited me to dinner at the White House, where I met Harry Hopkins, General Arnold, the Chief of the Army Air staff, and other important officers. When I came back from Pearl Harbour, I had the great honour of being invited to stay at the White House, but my time was cut short by a signal from Winston Churchill:

October 10th, 1941.

Prime Minister to Lord Louis Mountbatten:
We want you home here at once for something which you will find of the highest interest.

When I got back to England I went straight to Chequers, and

Winston told me that I was to be Adviser on Combined Operations.
I can't have looked very pleased, because he said to me, rather
truculently:

'Well, what have you got to say to that?'

I said I'd rather be back at sea in the *Illustrious*. That really made
him snort!

'Have you no sense of glory? Here I give you a chance to take a
part in the higher leadership of the war, and all you want to do is to
go back to sea! What can you hope to achieve, except to be sunk
in a bigger and more expensive ship?'

So that was that; no further argument! On October 27th 1941 I
took over from Admiral of the Fleet Lord Keyes, and became
Adviser on Combined Operations.

*Combined Operations Command was born in adversity. On June
4th 1940 the last evacuations of British troops from the beaches of
Dunkirk were carried out. The German armies stood along the
English Channel. France was visibly crumbling under their attack.
England prepared herself for invasion.*

*Everyone was thinking of defence. Churchill proclaimed Britain's
defiance of the triumphant enemy in the House of Commons with
fighting words, but the hard core of their meaning was nevertheless
defensive:*

*'We shall defend our island, whatever the cost may be. We
shall fight on the beaches, we shall fight on the landing-grounds, we
shall fight in the fields and in the streets, we shall fight in the hills;
we shall never surrender . . .'*

*But Churchill's mind could never be satisfied with such a pro-
gramme. On that same day he minuted to General Ismay:*

*'How wonderful it would be if the Germans could be made to
wonder where they were going to be struck next, instead of forcing
us to try to wall in the island and roof it over!'*

*Two days later:*

*'We have got to get out of our minds the idea that the Channel
ports and all the country between them are enemy territory . . .
Enterprises must be prepared with specially trained troops of the
hunter class, who can develop a reign of terror down these coasts
. . . I look to the Joint Chiefs of Staff to propose me measures for a
vigorous enterprising and ceaseless offensive against the whole
German-occupied coastline.'*

*Out of this impulse Combined Operations Command was created
—without loss of time. There were no landing-craft; none at all.
There were only forty Thompson sub-machine-guns (Tommy-guns)
in the whole country. Yet the first raid on the German-held coast
took place on June 23rd—only nineteen days after Dunkirk. It was
a small affair, a small beginning. Out of it great things grew.*

*In July Churchill appointed his old friend and ardent supporter
since the frustrating days of Gallipoli, Admiral of the Fleet Lord
Keyes, to be Director of Combined Operations. Twenty-two years
earlier, on St. George's Day, April 23rd 1918, Keyes had carried out
the famous Zeebrugge Raid. He looked forward to bigger and better
Zeebrugges in 1940.*

*Under Keyes the new Command began to put on muscle. Com-
mandos were raised and trained in their own ferocious style of
warfare; landing-craft were built, and crews, entirely drawn from
the Royal Naval Volunteer Reserve—were trained; ships were ear-
marked for amphibious warfare; special equipment was designed.
But every Service had equally imperious demands: British production could not keep pace. The whole national effort was at full
stretch, at sea, in the air, and on the battlefields of the Middle East.
Time after time Keyes found his bold plans thwarted, his forces
diverted to other uses.*

*His relations with the Chiefs of Staff became strained; by October
1941 they had reached breaking-point. Churchill wrote:*

*'I reached the conclusion with much regret on personal grounds
that the appointment of a new and young figure would be in the
public interest.'*

It was embarrassing for me—a mere captain—to have to take over
from this famous Admiral of the Fleet, who had served under my
father, and who had been kind to me when he was Commander-in-
Chief of the Mediterranean Fleet, and I was a two-striper on his
Staff in the 1920s.

Lord Keyes was very friendly about the turnover, but naturally
sad and upset.

'Dickie,' he said, 'the trouble is that the British have lost the will
to fight . . . The Chiefs of Staff are the greatest cowards I have ever
met.'

I believe he told them that to their faces, so no wonder he and
they fell out!

Anyway, Winston had given me my directive, and now it was up to me. My task, he told me, was twofold: I was to continue the Commando raids, in order to keep up the offensive spirit, gain essential experience, and to harass the enemy; but, above all, I was to prepare in every possible way for the great counter-invasion of Europe.

Everyone else at that time still believed that our backs were to the wall. Yet if the Russians could hold on, as they were doing, a large part of Hitler's forces would be tied down—in which case our invasion would begin to look like a real possibility. Winston summed up my job in one sentence:

'I want you to turn the south coast of England from a bastion of defence into a springboard of attack.'

So from now onwards my main preoccupation was this vast Combined Operation which was to be the climax of the war. I don't think anyone appreciated just how enormous it was, or how complex all the problems would prove to be. But bit by bit we found out, and bit by bit we overcame them.

*The eyes of the world, in October and November 1941, were on the Russian Front. If Russia fell, Britain would be alone in the war again, and all her hopeful plans would have to be shelved once more.*

*It seemed that Russia might easily fall. Leningrad was besieged; Kiev, Kharkov and Rostov were in German hands. On November 15th, with the thermometer dropping to below zero, the Germans launched a final attack on Moscow. By December 2nd they were in the suburbs of the Russian Capital. And there they stopped.*

*Without special equipment for winter fighting, without even winter clothing, Hitler's armies were trapped in the snow as Napoleon had been in 1812. And then, to the world's astonishment, on December 6th the Russians struck back. Stalin had already admitted to one and three-quarter million casualties, and huge losses of equipment. And yet the Russians struck back. Hitler, for the first time, was on the defensive.*

*On December 7th came the second turning-point of the war: Pearl Harbour.*

*Hot on the news of the Russian counter-attack came the staggering shock of Japan's aggression, and the virtual destruction of the American Pacific Fleet inside its base. A new enemy; a fresh defeat; that was the short-term view. The long-term view was different.*

'I could not foretell the course of events', wrote Churchill. 'I do not pretend to have measured accurately the martial might of Japan, but now at this very moment I knew the United States was in the war, up to the neck and in to the death. So we had won after all!'

What a typically Churchillian way of looking at an event which had all the hall-marks of disaster!

Because it was not simply the American Pacific Fleet which sustained terrible damage on December 7th. The Japanese attacked us at the same time. On the same day as Pearl Harbour they bombed Hong Kong. The next day they landed in Malaya. The day after that they landed in the Philippines. And the day after that our two great ships, the *Prince of Wales* and the *Repulse,* were sunk off Singapore. On December 17th the Japanese invaded Borneo. On the 23rd they captured Wake Island. On the 25th Hong Kong surrendered. It looked as though they might even get into Australia and New Zealand. There wasn't much to stop them.

From the immediate point of view this was the worst moment so far. We couldn't yet see the fruits of the Russian counter-offensive. Our own campaign in the Western Desert wasn't going too well. The Americans had their hands full. And now a whole new Far Eastern theatre of war had opened up, with its own insatiable demands.

Yet Winston was right: we *had* won the war. Because now we knew that the full resources of American man-power and American production would be behind us. To me, that meant everything. I had just spent five weeks taking stock of my new assignment, and realised that the root of our problems was the absolute shortage of every single thing we needed. But with America mobilised all that would change. So now Combined Operations, Headquarters could really begin to think big.

*It was a measure of Britain's capacity for Combined Operations in December 1941 that Mountbatten's first raiding venture, small as it was, should be turned into a big propaganda occasion.*

*On Boxing Day a combined force set out to attack the islands of Vaagso and Maaloy in South Norway, and the Lofoten Islands in the north. The raids were successful. Fish-oil factories, a power station, wireless stations and coastal defences were demolished; 150 Germans were killed, 98 were captured; some 15,000 tons of shipping were destroyed. British casualties were light.*

*It was only a small affair, involving a cruiser and four destroyers of the Navy, some six hundred Commandos, and a few R.A.F. squadrons. But its significance was considerable: this was the first time that all three Services had co-operated in this way, and it showed what could be done. The effect on the enemy was to make Hitler so nervous about Norway that he tied down there a garrison of over 370,000 men.*

Just two months after this—February 1942—we had another success which I was even prouder of, because it brought inter-Service co-operation a stage further.

We knew that the Germans had some rather special Radar equipment at Bruneval, about twelve miles north of Le Havre. We decided that it was essential to examine it. For this job we used paratroops, as well as the landing parties.

The whole thing went like clockwork. The paratroops demolished the German radar station, got hold of the pieces of equipment we so badly wanted to see, and were taken off by the landing-craft at the appointed time, with the loss of only one man killed and seven missing. That was a Combined Operation if you like!

But our biggest and most dramatic raid took place on March 28th, on St. Nazaire. This time the object of the exercise was to put out of action the great dry dock in St. Nazaire harbour—the only one on the Atlantic coast big enough to take the giant German battleship *Tirpitz*.

Our plan was to ram the gate of the dock with a ship crammed with high explosive, the destroyer *Campbeltown*. This was a most hazardous business, entailing a long run-in under heavy fire. But the *Campbeltown* made it. Torpedoes were fired into the harbour installations; Commandos landed and carried out more demolitions. And the next day, when it was all over, and she was crowded with German officers inspecting her, the *Campbeltown* exploded and blew them all sky-high. However, the main thing was that the *Tirpitz* was never able to come into the Atlantic.

Our casualties at St. Nazaire were heavy, as we had to expect. The military and naval force commanders both won the V.C., and

so did three others: the largest number in one operation since the
1/Lancashire Fusiliers won 'six V.C.s before breakfast' in another
famous Combined Operation at Gallipoli in 1915.

By now my own status had changed significantly. Ten days before the St. Nazaire raid my designation was altered to 'Chief of
Combined Operations'. This was not just a form of words; it carried
with it a tremendous honour and a tremendous responsibility: I
now became the fourth member of the Chiefs of Staff Committee,
the body which directed British strategy in every theatre of war.

*To support his new status, Mountbatten received a remarkable pro-
motion: from Commodore, he moved up the Navy List to Acting
Vice-Admiral, at the age of forty-one. Nelson had been made a Vice-
Admiral at forty-three, Beatty at forty-four. But this was not all:
Mountbatten also became an Honorary Lieutenant-General and an
Honorary Air Marshal. This was the first time that anyone, except
the King, had held rank in all three Services.*

*A naval historian, Commander Kenneth Edwards,[1] writing in
1943, remarked that all this was not necessarily to his advantage:
'He has, in effect, been lifted out of his generation, and unless he can
revert to the rank of Captain and be given a command at sea his
subsequent naval career may be cut unduly short.'*

He was quite right, of course, though I dare say he was as surprised as I was at the manner in which his prophecy was fulfilled!

I got a great kick out of holding rank in all three Services (though
in fact I never did dress up as a General or Air Marshal) because I
had now become a firm believer in inter-Service co-operation.
Indeed, it became a guiding principle right through the rest of my
career.

In 1942 it was still a very unfamiliar idea, and it met with a good
deal of resistance. There were soldiers, sailors and airmen who really
did seem to find it most difficult to discover any virtue in working
with other Services than their own. Of course, people like that were
no good to Combined Operations; forunately, there were plenty
of the other kind.

The real difficulty was the Service Ministries—the Admiralty,
the War Office and the Air Ministry—each of which had its own

[1] *Men of Action*; Collins, 1943.

way of doing business, and bitterly resented a new organisation cutting through its cherished red tape. It was there (and perhaps most of all in the Admiralty, because I made so many demands on them) that I met with obstruction. But my new position and my three ranks, and, above all, the backing of the Minister of Defence (who was also the Prime Minister: Winston), helped me to overcome obstacles and generally get what was wanted.

The men I was working with now were the professional heads of the three Services; we were fortunate in having men of such ability in this crisis of the war. They were all a lot senior to me: Peter Portal[1] was the nearest to me in age—seven years older—and yet had risen to be Chief of the Air Staff. He showed me great friendship from the very beginning.

'Age,' he told me, 'has nothing to do with this job; what matters is whether you know what you are doing and can hold your own.'

Admiral of the Fleet Sir Dudley Pound was the most distinguished of the Chiefs. He was twenty-three years older than me; he had entered the Navy as a cadet in 1891; he had commanded a battleship at the Battle of Jutland in 1916; and he was my captain in the *Repulse* in 1921, when I was a junior lieutenant. Now he was First Sea Lord. But despite our difference in rank and age he was very friendly and helpful.

It was Sir Dudley Pound who explained to me why the Admiralty was so sticky about Combined Operations. The Navy was fighting the Battle of the Atlantic. If we lost that battle the war would be lost. And in 1942 it seemed that this might very well happen.

In the first seven months of 1942 U-boats alone accounted for over three million tons of Allied shipping in the Atlantic, including 181 British ships. So it was not to be wondered at, after all, if the Admiralty looked askance at our demands for ships, shipbuilding facilities and men. But Dudley Pound did his best to help me get what I needed.

He was getting very tired now—he died in harness the following year—and to lighten his burden the chairmanship of the Committee was taken over by the new Chief of the Imperial General Staff, General Sir Alan Brooke. He was seventeen years older than me, and a man of great character and ability.

Brooke always said exactly what he thought, even to Winston

[1] Air Chief Marshal Sir Charles Portal.

Churchill, who took that from him, and always called him by his nickname—'Brookie'. Alanbrooke (as he later became) had a wide, inter-Service view, and a very incisive mind. He and I had several disagreements, but he was never rude in public, and always very kind and considerate in private.

They all knew that I used to see Winston by myself, and this worried them at first. Lord Alanbrooke wrote in the notes to his diary :

*'Dickie's visits to Chequers were always dangerous moments and there was no knowing what discussions he might be led into and . . . let is in for. He was most loyal and on those occasions frequently asked me what he was to say that night to the P.M. . . . On Monday morning he always gave us a full account of what had happened to him.'*[1]

The point is that I saw straight away that the whole position would be unworkable if I didn't play fair. Inevitably there was friction between a Prime Minister (also Minister of Defence) who was full of ideas for aggressive action and the Chiefs of Staff who had to carry on the war from day to day with limited resources.

In this connection I must mention one other man who played an absolutely vital part : General Sir Hastings Ismay—'Pug' Ismay—Churchill's personal representative, who always attended our meetings. He was the mediator. It was his never-failing tact which smoothed over many awkward moments and helped us to reach right conclusions without a fatal clash of wills with Winston.

I remember the first night I attended a Defence Committee meeting.

'Don't be nervous,' said Pug. 'This is the best evening show in London—it's much better than the Palladium.'

*The American reaction to Pearl Harbour was impressive. In January 1942 Churchill, conferring with the American leaders in Washington, reported to Mr. Attlee (Deputy Prime Minister) in London:*

*'A series of meetings has been held on supply issues . . . It was decided to raise United States output of merchant shipping in 1942 to 8,000,000 tons deadweight and in 1943 to 10,000,000 tons deadweight . . . War weapons programmes for 1942 were determined as follows:*

[1] Sir Arthur Bryant: *The Turn Of The Tide*; Collins, 1957.

| | |
|---|---|
| *Operational aircraft* | 45,000 |
| *Tanks* | 45,000 |
| *Anti-aircraft guns* | 20,000 |
| *Anti-tank guns* | 14,900 |
| *Ground and tank machine-guns* | 500,000.' |

*A few days later he added:*
'The United States Army is being raised . . . to a total strength of about 60 divisions and 10 armoured divisions. About 3¾ million men are at present held or about to be called up for the Army and Air Forces. Reserves of manpower are practically unlimited . . .

The naval superiority of the United States . . . ought to be regained by the summer of 1942 . . .'

*This was mobilisation for war on the grand scale—but it posed a mighty question: how should the Allies use this great array of force when it became available?*

Very shortly after I joined the Chiefs of Staff Committee a series of crucial Anglo-American discussions took place which determined the entire future shape of the war.

The Americans had decided, long before Pearl Harbour, that even if it was Japan that dragged them into the war they would make Germany their first enemy. This was a brave decision. It was braver still to stick to it in the face of the humiliating beatings which Japan was handing out to them.

When Winston went to Washington at the turn of the year this decision was reaffirmed; so now we could look forward to a massive American build-up in the European theatre. During that same Washington visit something else of cardinal importance was decided: a Combined Chiefs of Staff Committee was set up, consisting of the American and British Chiefs of Staff (or their representatives) sitting together in one body to determine policy. This was a real step forward—something that had never been done before.

But sitting together round a table didn't necessarily mean that they agreed with each other. I've described how Churchill's mind was working: how he gave me the directive to 'turn the south coast of England into a spring-board of attack'. This could only be for one purpose: the invasion of north-west Europe.

It has often been suggested that the British were cool about this idea, while the Americans were all for it. We weren't cool—far from it; everyone knew it had to be done. But after two years of indescribable difficulties and shortages we were very much concerned with ways and means. And, of course, we had certain other pressing problems, too.

For one thing, we had a major campaign on our hands in the Middle East. Two days after Pearl Harbour our Eighth Army under General Ritchie relieved Tobruk after a siege of nearly eight months. On December 24th we took Benghazi and cleared the Germans out of Cyrenaica. But then General Rommel struck back, and once more the Desert campaign was in the balance. Reinforcements to the Middle East were diverted to deal with the Japanese. And meanwhile the Battle of the Atlantic had yet to be won. All these things were using resources which we would need for the invasion of Europe.

The Americans were still in their first flush of enthusiasm; they found it hard to understand our difficulties, and they hadn't yet entirely got to grips with their own. The American Chiefs of Staff now put forward a plan for invading Europe in the spring of 1943. They called this by the code-name Roundup. They also suggested that we should prepare to make a landing in 1942, if things became desperate on the Russian Front, or, conversely, if Germany looked like collapsing. This operation was called Sledgehammer.

*The great debate now started—a two-way transatlantic traffic of ideas. On April 8th Harry Hopkins, personal adviser to President Roosevelt, and General George Marshall, Chief of Staff of the United States Army, arrived in London to discuss the American plan with the British Government and Chiefs of Staff.*

On April 14th our Chiefs of Staff accepted the American plan in principle. I'm afraid the Americans thought we had accepted it completely, and this was the beginning of a series of unfortunate misunderstandings. Anyway, two days later Force Commanders were actually appointed, and set up their offices in my Combined Operations Headquarters to study the operation. It only took them a fortnight to confirm that any large-scale Anglo-American landing in 1942 was quite out of the question.

This was unpalatable news for General Marshall, who was afraid that unless we got a move on in Europe, the U.S. Navy and public opinion would insist on diverting American strength to the Pacific.

It was during this visit that I started my friendship with Marshall. What an invaluable friendship that was! He was and remained the absolute key man in the American military effort all through the war—a terrific personality. On this occasion he paid me the great compliment of asking, off his own bat, to come and inspect Combined Operations Headquarters before accepting the invitations of the other Service Ministries. I was only too pleased, of course, and he came round that afternoon.

He was really excited at the sight of Army, Navy and Air Force officers all working together on joint projects.

'This is inspiring,' he said. 'How have you done it?'

'Well,' I replied, 'it's very simple. They all speak English, so they can all understand each other.'

And then, suddenly, the penny dropped, and on the spur of the moment I said:

'Come to think of it, General, you Americans talk English too, after a fashion. Why don't you send some American soldiers, sailors and airmen to join us in this headquarters?'

The idea appealed to Marshall immediately, and that is how the first integrated Allied Headquarters came into existence.

*The strategic debate continued, in a climate not best suited to rational thought. From the moment when Hitler attacked the Soviet Union demands for a 'Second Front Now!' were put forward vehemently by the Soviet Government, and echoed by Communists and their supporters in Britain. The very people who had denounced the war as 'capitalist and imperialist' changed their tune overnight, and shouted for operations which could only result in the vain sacrifice of many British lives.*

*'We did not,' said Churchill, 'allow these somewhat sorry and ignominious facts to disturb our thought, and fixed our gaze upon the heroic sacrifices of the Russian people under the calamities which their Government had brought upon them, and their passionate defence of their native soil. This, while the struggle lasted, made amends for all.'*

*Agreement between the two Western Allies seemed to remain a long way off. To try to bring it closer, Mountbatten was despatched to Washington as spokesman of the British point of view.*

I arrived in Washington on June 3rd—which was also the date of the Battle of Midway. We couldn't appreciate it at the time, but this proved to be the turning-point in the war against Japan. It was in this battle that the U.S. Navy regained the initiative, and never lost it again. The Japanese lost four aircraft-carriers, with 250 planes and their pilots. Japanese production could never make good this damage, while the Americans could replace their losses several times over.

What I had to do in Washington on this occasion was probably my most important task of the whole war. I had to try to persuade Roosevelt and his advisers that our entire strategy needed rethinking. I pointed out that the Germans had twenty-five divisions stationed in France. With the pitiful number of landing-craft we possessed they could easily destroy any landing without shifting a man from the Russian Front.

The Americans were rather shattered by this. In fact, the Chiefs of Staff and the Secretary for War, Mr. Stimson, were convinced that I had 'put one over' on the President. This, I'm afraid, was partly due to Roosevelt's unfortunate decision to talk to me in private, much against my wishes.

Such procedures helped to build up a certain atmosphere of distrust, which had already developed out of his close friendship with Churchill. The American Chiefs had the feeling that important decisions were taken behind their backs. They didn't like this, and I don't blame them. When I was allowed to see them I worked hard to re-establish a position of trust.

But the root of the problem didn't lie in personal preferences or differences of opinion. It lay in the inexorable realities: availability of landing-craft, and production figures. Roosevelt was the first to grasp the point, and go on to the next question: what, then, *could* the British and Americans do in 1942?

And this drew him back to something which he and Churchill had already tentatively discussed: the possibility of a landing, not in Europe, but in French North Africa. Once this was accepted, the subsequent Mediterranean strategy inevitably followed from it—the invasion of Sicily and then Italy. And once these were under way, equally inevitably, the invasion of north-west Europe had to be pushed back to 1944. I was already reaching the conclusion that this would, in any case, be the earliest date we could manage—but

I wouldn't have dared to say so bluntly, in Washington in June
1942!

What I *did* say, however, prepared the way for Churchill's next
visit, later in the month. The great debate didn't end with that, but
stage by stage the realities of the situation forced themselves on us
and on the Americans, until finally, in July, it was agreed that we
must rule out Sledgehammer in 1942, and that we *would* invade
North Africa in the autumn. So that became our target, and so the
fundamental shape of the war was decided.

*Mountbatten returned to England to plunge into the final stages of
preparation for an event which underlined all the arguments against
cross-Channel invasion in 1942. Combined Operations Headquarters had reached the conclusion that, to succeed, the invading
forces must capture a deep-water port. Could it be done? No one
knew. No one knew, either, what the problems of transporting a
large army on to enemy-held beaches would be.*

*Now, at last, an opportunity presented itself of answering both
these questions. At last, enough landing-craft existed to lift one
division. It was decided to make an attempt on a port. It would
have to be a port within range of air-cover. The choice had fallen
on Dieppe.*

*The ill-fated Dieppe Raid took place on August 19th. The bulk
of the military forces engaged were Canadians. Meeting a murderous
fire on the beaches from unsubdued defences, they lost 3,363 officers
and men out of just under 5,000 engaged. The Royal Regiment of
Canada returned with only 2 officers and 63 men out of 26 officers
and 528 men who set out. The Royal Navy, the Commandos and
the R.A.F. added another 1,000 to the total loss. Dieppe had all the
appearances of catastrophe.*

It is only in the most immediate sense that Dieppe can be called a
catastrophe. The losses, of course, were very disturbing. Yet it is
some mitigation to remember that a high proportion of our casualties were taken prisoner—so they did at least survive.

But costly as it was, Dieppe taught us lessons which had to be
learnt. Nothing like what we were planning to do had ever happened
before. This was the *only* experience we had to go on, and I see no
other way of learning the lessons than by experience. In fact, as
Bernard Fergusson said in his history of Combined Ops.: 'Dieppe

lifted the discussions about the invasion of Europe out of the academic sphere into the practical.'[1]

This operation taught us the need for heavy fire-support—which led us to rocket-ships, and L.C.G.s (landing-craft with guns). It taught the need for better pilotage of the invasion armada. It taught us about beach obstacles, and made us find means of overcoming them. It taught us about the problems of the follow-up over the beaches. It confirmed the need for headquarters ships from which the amphibious battle could be controlled.

But, above all, it helped me to evolve what I call my 'philosophy of invasion'. Dieppe, after all, was a raid; we never intended to do more than go in and come out again. The invasion itself would be a different matter: we would not only have to blast our way through every defence, but we would have to remain ashore. This meant building up our forces faster than the enemy could build up against us.

It seemed to me that the problem resolved itself into three elements. First, there was the question of where to land. Clearly, a decisive factor would be the extent of air-cover—but this left us a fair number of places to choose from. Most senior commanders argued strongly for the shortest possible route: the Dover–Calais line. The Germans were convinced that we would come this way, and we encouraged this belief with an elaborate and very successful deception plan. But I was convinced that the longer way would prove the surest way in the end. I stuck out for Normandy.

Now Dieppe had demonstrated that you cannot capture a port without so damaging its facilities as to make it useless. Yet we had to have a sheltered harbour, with piers and landing facilities, to enable us to build up our forces quickly, without interruption, because we knew that we could never count on more than four consecutive days of weather calm enough to continue landings on the Normandy beaches.

So we were inexorably forced to the conclusion that we would have to 'take our harbour with us'. And out of that conclusion, far-fetched though it seemed to be to many at the time, were born the famous 'Mulberry' artificial harbours, which ultimately played such a vital part.

Finally, and this is where my scientists (headed by Sir Solly Zuckerman) came in, there was what was called the 'Interdiction Plan'. This

[1] *The Watery Maze*: Collins, 1961.

was intended to prevent the enemy concentrating against us during the dangerous period of the build-up. Solly Zuckerman suggested that the Air Force should bomb all the road and rail junctions, bridges and tunnels along the German lines of communication, and so keep their reinforcements out of the invasion area. There was tremendous opposition from the 'bomber barons', who had their own strategy of Air Power, but General Eisenhower saw the point and forced it through.

All in all, as each month drew us nearer to the date of the invasion, we at Combined Operations Headquarters found that we had plenty to get on with!

*Into Mountbatten's headquarters now flowed a seemingly endless stream of ideas, some—like Pluto, the Pipe-Line Under The Ocean which carried petrol to the Normandy beach-head—brilliant; some of them, terrible. Gadgets and gimmicks abounded at that time. Combined Operations Headquarters was regarded by some as a cranks' paradise, 'the only lunatic asylum run by its inmates'; its Chief's predilection for strange fancies became a legend. One of his staff officers wrote:*

> *Mountbatten was a likely lad;*
> *A nimble brain Mountbatten had,*
> *And this most amiable trait:*
> *Of each new plan which came his way*
> *He'd always claim in accents pat,*
> *'Why I myself invented that!'*
> *Adding when he remembered it,*
> *For any scoffer's benefit,*
> *Roughly the point in his career*
> *When he'd conceived the bright idea—*
> *As 'August 1934',*
> *Or 'Some time during the Boer War'.*

*etc., etc.*

*Yet the serious and invaluable contribution behind all this received its acknowledgment. In June 1944, about a week after D-Day, when Mountbatten had long departed to a new and distant field, the Allied leaders visited the Normandy beach-head. They sent this telegram to Mountbatten:*

'Today we visited the British and American armies on the soil of France. We sailed through vast fleets of ships with landing-craft of many types pouring more men, vehicles and stores ashore. We saw clearly the manœuvre in process of rapid development. We have shared our secrets in common and helped each other all we could. We wish to tell you at this moment in your arduous campaign that we realise that much of this remarkable technique, and therefore the success of the venture, has its origin in developments effected by you and your Staff of Combined Operations. Signed: Arnold, Marshall, King, Brooke, Smuts, Churchill.'

This great result was still in the distant future, and before it could come about the war had taken many turns.

On October 23rd 1942 the Eighth Army, now under Lieutenant-General Sir Bernard Montgomery, began the Battle of El Alamein, the decisive victory of the Desert war. Shortly afterwards, Mountbatten's work produced a significant result. On November 7th the landing in North Africa promised the encirclement of the Axis forces. This was Operation Torch, the largest Combined Operation yet seen —a success, but with more lessons to be learned from it. By May, the Axis was beaten in Africa, and on May 12th 250,415 German and Italian troops laid down their arms.

More Combined Operations followed: on July 10th the Allies invaded Sicily. A fortnight later Mussolini fell: Fascism in Italy was beaten. The first of the dictators had gone. Allied forces prepared to land on Italian soil—the mainland of Europe at last.

Already the tide had turned on the Eastern Front: the German surrender at Stalingrad in January marked the beginning of the series of sustained Russian offensives which crippled Germany.

Only in the Far East was the news still bad. On Guadalcanal the Americans were discovering the terrible tenacity of the Japanese soldier in defence. In Burma the British were defeated again. Nothing seemed to go right in that sector of the war.

Once more the Allied leaders gathered, this time at Quebec. They had much to discuss—among other things, the creation of a new South East Asia Command, which would include Burma, and the appointment of a Supreme Allied Commander for that theatre. On August 22nd Churchill reported to Attlee:

'The President and General Marshall are very keen on Mountbatten's appointment. . . . There is no doubt of the need of a young and vigorous mind in this lethargic and stagnant Indian scene. . . .'

*Three days later the announcement was made officially from the Citadel at Quebec:*

'It has been decided to set up a separate South East Asia Command for conducting operations based on India and Ceylon against Japan. . . . The King has been pleased to approve the appointment of Acting Vice-Admiral the Lord Louis Mountbatten, G.C.V.O., D.S.O., A.D.C., to be the Supreme Allied Commander, South East Asia.'

I had been wondering what was going to become of me. During that summer I had begun to see that my work at Combined Operations was really done. A new organisation had been set up, under a Chief of Staff to the future Supreme Allied Commander, and detailed preparation for D-Day was really his responsibility now.

Once the invasion was off the mark, if the landings were successful, it was hard to see where I would fit in. In fact, the more successful the show was, the less there would be for me to do.

I now wanted to do something that perhaps only a professional sailor will understand. I wanted to go back in command of a ship. It was a shock when Winston told me what they wanted me to do instead. I asked for twenty-four hours to think it over.

'Why?' he asked. 'Don't you think you can do it?'

I replied that I had a congenital weakness for thinking I could do anything. But I wanted to know how each of the British and American Chiefs of Staff felt about it. When I found that I had their full backing—and, above all, President Roosevelt's—of course I accepted right away.

I went to my room, sat down, pulled out a blank sheet of paper, and began to write down all the things I would have to do. I was starting from scratch.

# 6

## The Imperial Enemy

---

*The Imperial forces of Japan completed their conquests with astonishing and alarming speed. One after another, British possessions in the Far East were overrun.*

*The island of Hong Kong was bombed on the same day as Pearl Harbour: December 7th 1941. Eleven days later Japanese troops landed. On Christmas Day Hong Kong surrendered.*

*On the day after Pearl Harbour, Malaya was attacked. By the end of December, the Japanese reached Singapore. On February 15th 1942 Britain's great Far Eastern base capitulated. The Japanese took 85,000 prisoners in Singapore; this was the greatest disaster ever inflicted on British arms.*

*Already the Japanese were in Burma. By March 10th Rangoon was in their hands, and from Rangoon they advanced into Upper Burma. In six months they had destroyed the British Empire in the Far East: they stood at the gates of India, and there they remained.*

*On October 7th 1943 the newly appointed Supreme Allied Commander, South East Asia, arrived in Delhi. Mountbatten was forty-three years old. His task was to dispel the despondency of defeat and stagnation; to impart a youthful impulse to willing but tired men; to grip the British war against Japan.*

So now I was a Supreme Allied Commander—a very grand title indeed. What is more, it was a very grand job: there were not many of us about!

No two Supreme Commands were quite alike. Mine, I think, was the most diverse: the bulk of my forces were Indian, British and Gurkhas; I had a considerable number of Americans in the Command, and a lot of Chinese—not to mention East and West Africans.

There were Burmese, there were Australians, and there were French and Dutch. Somehow, all these elements had to be welded into one force.

The first man to meet this problem was Lord Wavell. He was made Supreme Commander of the A.B.D.A. Command (American, British, Dutch and Australian) at the beginning of 1942. I was now inheriting a part of his area of responsibility.

Now, in the war against Japan, there were four of us: Admiral Nimitz in the Central Pacific, holding the Japanese Navy in check and guarding the life-lines; General MacArthur, in the South West Pacific, based on Australia; myself in South East Asia, based on India; and Generalissimo Chiang Kai-shek in China. We four formed the ring around Japan, and it was our job, in 1944, to tighten it into a noose.

*For the time being, only the Air Forces of South East Asia Command could strike the enemy. While the bombers harassed the extended Japanese communications, the Navy awaited reinforcements, the Army was undergoing the familiar process of regrouping and building up for a new offensive—and Mountbatten was organising his new Command from scratch.*

I set up my Command Headquarters in New Delhi, in what is now the Ministry of Education. Running the Command—SEAC, as it was called—involved a whole series of relationships with key people.

First there was Field Marshal Lord Wavell; he was now Viceroy of India—and India was my base. He was also my official political link with the Government at home. Fortunately, we got on very well together.

Then there was General Auchinleck, the Commander-in-Chief in India. Auchinleck provided and trained most of my troops. He had to revive the spirit and efficiency of the Indian Army after many defeats—and then hand most of it over to me! All of us in SEAC owed him a very great debt.

My Deputy was Lieutenant-General Joseph Stilwell of the United States Army: 'Vinegar Joe'. He contrived to wear five hats at once, because as well as being Deputy Supreme Commander, he was also Chief of Staff to Chiang Kai-shek, American Lend-Lease Administrator in China, Commander of all U.S. Forces in the China-Burma-

India theatre, and field commander of my five Chinese divisions in Burma. That was the job he liked best.

Our personal relationship worked well, though he didn't like the British; he was rude, and he was prejudiced. He didn't like staff duties, and he certainly didn't like coming to Supreme Headquarters. But when it came to training the Chinese soldiers and leading them in battle, Stillwell was terrific.

Generalissimo Chiang Kai-shek was always a problem. He spoke no English, he didn't think much of British fighting capacity, and he had no conception of our logistical problems. All he really wanted from us was that we should open up and guard the lines of communication through which the Americans could pour supplies into China. And that was largely a political problem—perhaps the worst headache I had to cope with in South East Asia Command.

*Pressure on Japan was mounting. In the Pacific General MacArthur and Admiral Nimitz concerted attacks upon the Japanese bases. The Australians pressed their offensive in New Guinea; American troops landed at Bougainville. Everywhere the Japanese resisted fanatically.*

*In November 1943 the United States Navy struck at the Gilbert Islands. The 2nd Marine Division captured Tarawa Atoll after ferocious fighting. Marine casualties were heavy; the Japanese were annihilated.*

*All eyes turned to Mountbatten's new Command. The least the British could do was to effect a diversion of Japanese strength from the Americans in the Pacific. Better still would be a successful offensive of their own, reversing the long chapter of British defeats. But first there were serious difficulties to be overcome.*

Without doubt, the most serious thing of all was that, as a result of all our defeats, a myth had grown up of Japanese invincibility: 'the invincible Jap', 'the man who couldn't be beaten in the jungle', and so on. It was absolutely essential to break this myth, and break it quickly.

*Everything was wrong in Burma. Soldiers trained for desert fighting found themselves groping in thick jungle. Men from the high Himalayas, or the hot plains of the Punjab, or Glasgow, or Birmingham, had to endure the five months' continuous downpour of the Mon-*

H.M.S. *Queen Elizabeth* at her first action, Gallipoli, 1915. Dickie joined her as a Midshipman in 1917 and served in her again as a Lieutenant in 1927 and as a Commander in 1932. In World War II she was for a time flagship of the Mediterranean Fleet, then served under Mountbatten's Supreme Command in the Far East Fleet. *Queen Elizabeth* was launched in 1913; displacement, 27,500 tons; speed, 25 knots; armament, eight 15-in., twelve 6-in. guns.

Family group in garden of Brook House, Park Lane, 1924. Left to right:
top row, the Crown Prince of Sweden (Gustaf), Lord Louis Mountbatten
(Dickie), the Marquess of Milford Haven (Georgie), Prince Andrew of
Greece (Andrea). Middle row, Lady Louis Mountbatten (Edwina), the
Marchioness of Milford Haven (Nada). Bottom row, the Crown Princess
of Sweden (Louise), the Dowager Marchioness of Milford Haven (Victoria),
Princess Andrew of Greece (Alice).

Adsdean, 1926. Prince Philip, Patricia and Lord Louis.

*Above:* Polo, 1926. Mountbatten, the Duke of Peneranda and Señor Martinez de Hoz in play during the final of the Prix du Casino at Deauville.

*Below:* On leave from the Fleet in Egypt, 1928. Left to right, Lord Milford Haven, two friends, Lady Louis, Lord Louis, Lady Milford Haven.

*Above:* H.M.S. *Wishart* on full power trial at 33.2 knots, 1935.
*Below:* The professional at work. Manœuvres in H.M.S. *Wishart*, 1935.

*Above:* Cannes, 1935. On board the *Wishart* with the Prince of Wales and Mrs. Simpson.
*Below:* Balmoral, 1936. Mrs. Simpson, Lord Louis, King Edward VIII.

Wings of the Navy before the two wars.
*Above:* The Short bi-plane in which Lord Louis made his first aeroplane flight in 1911 at Eastchurch piloted by Lieutenant Longmore, R.N. (later Air Chief Marshal Sir Arthur Longmore).

*Below:* Fairey Swordfish flying over their parent aircraft carrier H.M.S. *Ark Royal*, 1939. [*Charles Brown*]

H.M.S. *Kelly* carrying out her first full power trials off the Tyne, August, 1939.

*Above:* King George VI visits the Fleet, June, 1938.
*Below:* Outbreak of War. The Duke of Windsor returns to England on board H.M.S. *Kelly*.

*Above:* The stricken *Kelly*, torpedoed by a German E-boat in the night of 10 May, 1940.

*Left:* Mountbatten, after 90 hours on the bridge, gets her home.

*Right:* In dock, showing the gaping hole where the torpedo hit.

*Above:* The Mediterranean Fleet cheers H.M.S. *Kipling*, bringing back the survivors of the *Kelly* and *Kashmir*, sunk in the Battle of Crete on 23 May, 1914.

*Below:* Noel Coward's film *In Which We Serve* was inspired by the story of the *Kelly*. Coward, as Captain, with survivors watch their ship go down.

Farewell family group at Broadlands, before Lord Louis' departure for
S.E.A.C., September, 1943. Left to right : Pamela, Patricia (now a Wren
rating), Lady Louis.

*Above:* Lord Louis inspects his Royal Marine guard on taking over command of the aircraft carrier *Illustrious* at Norfolk Navy Yard, Virginia, September, 1941.

*Below:* The King visits Combined Operations H.Q., Richmond Terrace, Whitehall, 1942.

*Above:* Casablanca Conference, January, 1943. Standing behind President Roosevelt, the U.S. Chiefs of Staff, General Arnold (U.S.A.A.F.), Admiral King (U.S.N.), General Marshall (U.S. Army). Standing behind Mr. Churchill, the British Chiefs of Staff, Admiral of the Fleet Sir Dudley Pound, Marshal of the R.A.F. Sir Charles Portal, General Sir Alan Brooke, Field-Marshal Sir John Dill (British Liaison Officer with U.S. Chiefs of Staff), Vice-Admiral Lord Louis Mountbatten (Chief of Combined Operations).

*Left:* Mountbatten and the Prime Minister at Quebec (Quadrant Conference) August, 1943.

*Above:* The Dieppe raid. Wounded men climbing on board a destroyer while the action was taking place. [*Imperial War Museum*]

*Below:* The St. Nazaire Raid. H.M.S. *Campbeltown* in the sluice gates just before blowing up, 28 March, 1942. [*Imperial War Museum*]

*Above:* The Chief of Combined Operations addresses a group of Commandos and Wrens in Scotland, 1943.

*Below:* March, 1943. Mountbatten with Naval Commandos.

*soon, under the gloom of dripping trees, attacked by leeches and malaria-carrying mosquitoes.*

*Food supplies were uncertain. Medical supplies were short. News and mail were rare. Home leave was non-existent. Sickness, and the fear of sickness, were always present. None of this would have mattered too much if they had been winning. But it was only too obvious that they were not winning. They were not in a winning frame of mind.*

*The Supreme Commander's first offensive was upon the spirits of his men. Mountbatten toured his whole Command—all Services, all nations—to meet the men, to sweep away the old depression, to instil the idea of winning.*

I can remember gathering men round me and saying: 'I hear you call this the Forgotten Front. I hear you call yourselves the Forgotten Army. Well, let me tell you that this is *not* the Forgotten Front, and you are *not* the Forgotten Army. In fact, nobody has even heard of you.'

And then, after a stunned silence, when the message had sunk in, I would go on:

'But they *will* hear of you, because this is what we are going to do . . .'

And then I would put them in the picture, and everybody cheered up.

But there was more to it than pep-talks. We obtained special broadcasts for the Forces on All India Radio. I demanded films for them, gramophones, theatrical shows, and so on, and bit by bit we got all these things. I also arranged for SEAC news stories to be published in our Press at home.

But perhaps the best thing of all was starting our own newspaper, to keep everyone in touch with home and the outside world. It was simply called SEAC, and it was edited by Frank Owen, who had been editor of the *Evening Standard* before the war. I pulled him out as a second-lieutenant to tackle this job; I gave him a completely free hand, and he did it brilliantly.

After a while the men began to feel that people actually cared about them—and that was an immediate tonic for morale.

*A new wind blew through SEAC. In the back areas training continued—but training with a difference, training with a really*

*offensive feel about it. And this time there was a strong suggestion
that it would not all end as usual in miserable retreat. There was
also training for Combined Operations, for the Supreme Commander, after all, was the man who had perfected their techniques.*

*A new formation had come into existence, with a new name
which had yet to make itself known: the Fourteenth Army. Its commander was known in India, but his name meant little elsewhere:
Lieutenant-General W. J. Slim. Slim and Mountbatten understood
each other; they had the same ideas about how the war should be
conducted.*

When I was sent out to South East Asia I was left in no doubt about
what I was supposed to do. The Prime Minister gave me a Directive
which said : 'Your first duty is to engage the enemy as closely and
continuously as possible, so that his forces may be worn down and
consumed by attrition, and to establish our superiority to the extent
of forcing a diversion of his forces from the Pacific theatre.'

Not much doubt about the meaning of that—or who the author
was!

There was not much doubt, either, about how it was to be done.
There was to be an advance in northern Burma, certainly; but this
was really only for the purpose of opening up and safeguarding our
communications with China—the famous 'Burma Road'.

My main strategy was to be amphibious. That was why I moved
my headquarters to Kandy, in Ceylon. I was to form a Combined
Striking Force to attack the Japanese flank along the long coast of
Burma. Well, I'm afraid we were all in for a big disappointment.

*Once more, everything turned on priorities. Every Allied campaign
made its demands on man-power, guns, tanks, aircraft . . . shipping.
Shipping was the most difficult problem of all—shipping and landing-
craft. The Battle of the Atlantic, the Mediterranean war, the Russian
convoys, the Pacific war, all demanded ships, and still more ships;
and the great invasion of north-west Europe was coming closer each
day, with its own immense demands.*

*In November 1943 the Allied leaders assembled in Cairo. They
applied their minds to the war against Japan, and the rôle of
South East Asia Command. Mountbatten was ordered to work out
details for a large amphibious operation across the Bay of Bengal.
Then, on November 28th, Mr. Churchill and President Roosevelt*

met *Marshal Stalin at Teheran. At this conference the date of the invasion of Europe was settled: May 1944. So the greatest seaborne operation in history was only five months distant.*

*It was against the background of this decision that Mountbatten submitted his proposals for the attack across the Bay of Bengal. 'They made,' said Churchill, 'a very bad impression.' He wrote to Mountbatten:*

*'Everyone has been unpleasantly affected by your request to use 50,000 British and Imperial troops . . . against 5,000 Japanese. I was astounded to hear of such a requirement. . . . The Americans have been taking their islands on the basis of two and a half to one. . . . While such standards as those you have accepted prevail there is not much hope of making any form of amphibious war.'*

*The expedition was cancelled.*

I was absolutely horrified. It was so unjust! I was not asking for anything; we already had all the shipping and landing-craft we needed—I'd seen to that.

I'd been instructed to carry out amphibious operations, and our troops were training hard for them. I knew our calculations were not exaggerated: we above all could not afford a failure—we had to be absolutely certain of success.

But there it was: bitterly disappointing. And there was worse in store. I now learned that, so far from being able to build up a striking force, I must send practically all my landing-ships and landing-craft back to Europe for the invasion of France. This was a bad moment.

You didn't have to be a strategic genius to see that amphibious operations—getting in behind the Japanese—were the best way of attacking Burma, or that a fearful land advance straight down from the top end was just about the worst way. A lance-corporal could have told you that.

But this was now what we were going to have to do. It was up to the soldiers and airmen to carry the can and find a way of doing it. It was up to me to break the news to them, and help as best I could.

*Fortunately for the Allied cause, the Japanese commanders also had their problems. Japan, now, was on the defensive—but that word was hardly uttered in the Japanese military vocabulary.*

*Unbroken victory had taught the Japanese to despise the British and Indian forces. Extreme Indian nationalists had joined up with the Japanese, and preached that India was only waiting for a chance to rise en masse against British imperialism. So it was argued that the best defence of Burma would be to advance into India. And if India then did rise against the British, further glittering prospects might open up—even a march on Delhi.*

*Backed by the forceful personality of General Mutaguchi, commanding the Japanese 15th Army on the central front, these views prevailed. So now both sides were preparing to take the offensive. The question was: which would strike first? In any case, there was bound to be a head-on collision between the main body of the Japanese, and the main body of Mountbatten's South East Asia Command.*

So now what it all boiled down to was beating the Japanese Army in Burma. The Japanese were formidable fighters. They were not quite so good as some people—mistakenly, in my opinion—had cracked them up to be. I did not believe that they were invincible supermen. But there was no doubt that the Japanese were the very devil to beat.

We knew that the Japanese soldier was very hardy. He could march long distances. He could carry a heavy load. He could exist on what the British soldier would consider miserable rations. The most impressive thing about the Japanese was that they never gave up. In attack they would come at you again and again and again, regardless of casualties. In defence they really did hold on 'to the last man'. You had to kill them, absolutely wipe them out. They would hardly ever surrender.

But I was sure that the Japanese must have weaknesses. They were human, after all, not super-human. They were mostly town-dwellers, with no more natural aptitude in the jungle than our British troops. They tended to be inflexible, and found it hard to adapt themselves to changing circumstances. They could stand a great deal, but I was sure that factors like hunger, fatigue and sickness—malaria, dysentery, and all the other horrible tropical diseases—affected the Japanese as much as they affected us.

If we could overcome these things, then we could make the land and the climate of Burma, with all the hardships and difficulties they presented, fight on our side.

*It was the Japanese who struck first. On February 4th 1944 they launched a diversionary offensive in Arakan, to draw British reserves from the central front. Once more the Japanese attempted their well-tried tactics of infiltration and encirclement. Full of confidence, they attacked with only 12,000 men—less than one division—against the two British/Indian divisions of the XV Corps. The Japanese carried only seven days' supplies; the retreating British would once more provide what they needed from captured dumps.*

*But this time the British did not retreat. Part of the 7th Indian Division was soon encircled, and the Divisional Headquarters over-run. But the troops, under Brigadier Geoffrey Evans, stood fast on their administrative box. Supplied by air, the 7th Division held on for 18 days, and when the relief columns arrived it was the Japanese who were encircled—and their supplies had practically run out. At last the tables were turned: the Japanese were forced to retreat with a loss of nearly 50 per cent of their strength.*

*The Battle of the 'Admin. Box', wrote Field Marshal Lord Slim, 'was the turning-point of the Burma campaign. For the first time a British force had met, held, and decisively defeated a major Japanese attack, and followed this up by driving the enemy out of the strongest possible natural positions that they had been preparing for months and were determined to hold at all costs.'[1]*

This was a nasty shock for the Japanese—finding that their time-honoured tactics no longer worked.

I always insisted that the campaign in Burma resolved itself into three 'M's': Morale, Monsoon, Malaria. Arakan showed that the first problem—Morale—was solved, thanks to all the great work which General Auchinleck and India Command were putting in for us in their training camps, thanks to General Slim and his commanders in the field, and thanks to the thousands of regimental officers and N.C.O.s on whom it all depended. The Army's morale was sound.

*The morale of one part of the Army was not merely sound: it was effervescent. Major-General Orde Wingate's famous Chindits had already, in 1943, shown conclusively that British, Gurkha and Burmese troops could march in the jungle, live in the jungle and fight in the jungle. Now, with three times the strength of 1943, borne in*

[1] Slim: *Defeat into Victory*; Cassell, 1956.

*gliders, Wingate was preparing to return to the Japanese back areas in Burma.*

*Wingate believed passionately in his theory of long-range penetration warfare. He despised normal formations and normal methods. Ostensibly the spearhead of the main offensive by the Fourteenth Army, he saw his force as a potential war-winner in its own right. 'The Fourteenth Army,' he told Mountbatten, 'can hardly be expecting ever to operate beyond the mountain barrier with its present establishment, after the experiences of the past two years. . . .'*

I first met Orde Wingate in August 1943, when we were on our way to the Quebec Conference together. I had many talks with him, and I saw at once that he was a very remarkable man, and that there was a lot to be said for his ideas. Mr. Churchill gave him full backing, and so did the Combined Chiefs of Staff.

*Despite the difficulty of meeting Wingat's insatiable demands, and despite the evidently impending Japanese attack, the 1944 Chindit campaign was approved. The fly-in to Burma took place on March 5th. Chindit columns struck hard, distracting blows at the Japanese, and once more Wingate's men displayed wonderful courage and endurance.*

But Wingate's larger ideas—running the whole campaign on long-range-penetration lines, right into Indo-China and Siam—were unrealistic. It just wasn't possible to defeat the main body of the Japanese Army with lightly equipped raiding columns.

Three weeks after the fly-in, Wingate was killed in an air crash. His death was a blow to the whole operation. And the strain on the Chindits themselves, wonderfully gallant as they were, became terrible as their campaign continued. When we finally pulled them out, we found that over 50 per cent of them were medically unfit for any more active service. The Chindits had done an incredibly courageous job, but this was a high price to pay.

Wingate did not live to see the final outcome of his experiment. Perhaps it was just as well for his reputation that his career ended at the height of his fame. When he came to see me on my arrival in Delhi, he had a temperature of 104 degrees. I sometimes wonder whether he ever really recovered. In my opinion he was a sick man in a hurry.

*Wingate's successor was Brigadier Lentaigne, and under him the Chindits carried on their fight with mixed fortunes. But now the focus of attention shifted north. Early in March Mountbatten was visiting General Stilwell's front. On his return, driving his own jeep, a front wheel passed over a bamboo stump, which then flew up and hit him on the left eye with tremendous force. When Mountbatten arrived at an American field hospital it seemed likely that he would lose his eye.*

This accident could hardly have come at a worse time. I had to spend five days in the American forward hospital, with both eyes bandaged, in complete blindness. And just at that moment the Japanese attacked again. They quickly cut off our IV Corps in the Imphal plain, and a very serious situation developed.

*This was the beginning of the Battle of Imphal. General Mutaguchi told his troops:*
'*The Army has now reached the stage of invincibility, and the day when the Rising Sun will proclaim our definite victory in India is not far off.*'

I persuaded the doctor to unbandage my eyes, and let me out of hospital. I immediately flew to Army Air Headquarters, and there took one of the most serious decisions of my whole time as Supreme Commander.

On my own responsibility, I took thirty American transport aircraft off the China supply route, and used them to fly an infantry division into Imphal. This was dead against President Roosevelt's explicit instructions, and although the division was vitally important in the Battle of Imphal, it was even more important not to lose the President's trust. So this time I was really sticking my neck out. But Roosevelt was a man of vision, and he accepted the situation.

*The Japanese attack on Imphal began on March 8th 1944. Three Japanese divisions and a division of the renegade Indian National Army took part. An Order of the Day of the Indian National Army proclaimed:*

*'Let there be but one slogan: Onward to Delhi! Victory will certainly be ours!'*

*Once again the Japanese attempted encirclement: encirclement of the 17th Indian Division, isolated at Tiddim; encirclement of General Scoones's IV Corps Headquarters at Imphal; most serious of all, a thrust at Kohima, cutting the only life-line with the bases back in India, and threatening communications with Stilwell and the Ledo Road to China.*

*The sternest battle of the Burma Campaign had now begun. The Japanese displayed their highest fighting qualities—mobility, aggressiveness and endurance. They had practically no air support; their supplies were slender. Once again they counted on capturing what was needed from the British.*

*As the battle developed, Mutaguchi's army was outnumbered by three to one. Despite this, the Japanese surrounded Imphal and Kohima, and the British/Indian defence was tested to the limit. The battle of attrition at Imphal was always grim; the situation was often serious—but it was never desperate. From the moment of Mountbatten's decision to fly in the 5th Indian Division from Arakan, a new factor had come into play—a significant development in the history of war: this was the first time a large, normal formation had been transported from one battlefield to another by air, and it was decisive.*

Much the biggest part of my Air Transport was American. The American pilots and their C 47s (the famous Dakotas) did a marvellous job. My Allied Air Commander in Burma was a great American, General George E. Stratemeyer. In the end I had 61,000 American air and ground crew in my command, out of a total of 176,000 airmen, and I just don't know what we would have done without them.

At Imphal, air reinforcement, air evacuation, air supply and air support steadily counteracted all the Japanese advantages. Instead of our army dwindling under attack, we were able to build up its strength.

*Kohima was defended obstinately. At Imphal the British and Indian forces conducted a resolute offensive-defence. And a new Corps, the XXXIII, brought in from India, steadily fought its way forward to relieve the garrison.*

*For Mutaguchi, the writing was on the wall; his losses were crippling. One Japanese commander told his men to 'regard death as something lighter than a feather'. Another ordered: 'When you are killed you will fight on with your spirit!' General Slim said: 'I know of no army that could have equalled them.'*

*But they were beaten men. After seventy-four days of battle, Imphal was relieved. Japanese remnants struggled back to Burma, starving, diseased, disorganised. Their casualties were over 53,000. The Fourteenth Army had lost less than 17,000.*

This complete defeat at Kohima and Imphal came as another very unpleasant shock to the Japanese. Their 15th Army had taken a fearful battering: we counted very nearly as many Japanese dead on the battlefield as our own total casualties, and we captured 100 guns.

We also had something else in store for them. I wrote in my despatch:

'Having expected that we would obey the rules, and stop fighting during the monsoon when he stopped, the enemy had hoped to bring in reinforcements and rehabilitate his army to meet our post-monsoon offensive.'

But I did not intend him to have an army to rehabilitate. This is where the next of my 'Three M's' came in: Morale, *Monsoon*, Malaria. I had concluded, even before I had arrived out in South East Asia, that the 'stop-go' which the monsoon always imposed on fighting just would not do. I told my commanders, back in October 1943, that I meant to fight on *all through the monsoon*. This was the hell of a thing for a newly arrived Supreme Commander to come along and say to a lot of experienced soldiers and airmen!

*North Burma, battle-ground of the Fourteenth Army, is the wettest country in the world. As much as 800 inches of rain have been recorded in a year. It falls during the period of the north-west monsoon, from May to October. Mountbatten's decision to fight through the monsoon, imparted to a group of senior officers a fortnight after his arrival in Delhi, was taken in the teeth of all practical experience.*

*Yet now, without a pause, without permitting the Japanese any respite, the Fourteenth Army passed to the offensive. Mountbatten wrote in his report:*

*'Our first objective was the crossing of the Chindwin. . . . On our way to the Chindwin, our object would be not so much to occupy towns or particular areas, but to destroy the Japanese Army wherever it could be found.'*

*Japanese rearguards still resisted stubbornly, but the real enemy, now, was the monsoon. At its nearest point, the River Chindwin is less than sixty miles from Imphal, but the only road for motor vehicles stretched to over 150 miles. A despatch rider took sixteen hours on a journey of eighteen miles. Half a company took ten hours to carry two stretcher cases four miles. Two miles a day was good progress for large units with transport.*

It is not difficult to appreciate what the monsoon means to forces on the ground in Burma : it means five months of wretched discomfort, five months of heart-breaking difficulties. There is a tendency to refer to the Burma Campaign as a land campaign, but really it was every bit as much an air campaign.

We couldn't have held the 'box' in Arakan without Air Power. We could never have held Kohima and Imphal without Air Power, and we certainly couldn't have dreamt of advancing through the monsoon without Air Power. It is hard to recall just what that meant with the aircraft of 1944.

During the monsoon you get formations of cumulo-nimbus cloud which start down in the valleys and can in some cases rise to 30,000 feet—cloudbanks six miles thick. Inside these clouds an aeroplane could be hurled about and smashed to pieces. Often you couldn't fly over them. In the mountains it was extremely dangerous to try to fly under them. And sometimes you couldn't fly round them. I often flew with our Air Forces during the monsoon, and I can remember very few more frightening experiences.

After the monsoon, the Army's speeded-up advance meant a continual lengthening of our supply lines. I realise that we could only keep this up by doubling our air lift. In fact, if we couldn't do this, the Army might even have to withdraw—which would have been a disaster.

I couldn't get more transport aircraft, so I called on the Air Forces to work twice their normal hours. In theory, this was only possible in a short burst, but *our* air and ground crews—British and American—worked at this fantastic rate day after day, week after week, month after month—and achieved the virtually impossible.

*A net was now closing round the Japanese in Burma. While Slim's Fourteenth Army kept up its pressure in the centre, Stilwell's Chinese and American forces captured Myitkyina, with its important airfield. In December the XV Corps joined in with a new offensive in Arakan. Communiqués reported victory on every sector of the front.*

We had won another kind of victory also—no less important than these successes in the field. This was the last of my 'Three M's'. We had won the victory of Morale, we had beaten the Monsoon, and now we had beaten Malaria. If we had not done that, I can't see how we could even have *fought* our battles against the Japanese, let alone have won them.

*'Doctors may not be able to win the war for me,' said Mountbatten, 'but they could easily lose it.' Back in London in September 1943, he set up a Medical Advisory Division, consisting of one senior medical officer each from the Navy, Army and Air Force, and one American. All were hygienists, and all had special knowledge of tropical medicine.*

*'The prevention of tropical diseases', wrote Field Marshal Slim, 'had advanced immensely within the last few years, and one of the first steps of the new Supreme Commander had been to get to South East Asia some of the most brilliant research workers in this field. Working closely with medical officers who had experience of practical conditions, they introduced new techniques, drugs, and methods of treatment. Gradually the new remedies became available, although for long we lagged behind in their supply. Sulphonamide compounds, penicillin, mepacrine, and DDT all appeared later than we liked but still in time to save innumerable lives. Without research and its results we could not survive as an army.'*[1]

My Medical Advisory Division did a truly magnificent job. The bulk of our medical supplies and 90 per cent of our medical units were provided by India Command, so this was just one more thing that we had to be grateful to them for.

I have no hesitation in saying that the medical discipline developed in SEAC was second to none. The figures speak for themselves: in 1943 we had 120 sick for every battle casualty; in 1944

[1] Slim: *Defeat into Victory*: Cassell: 1956.

we had twenty sick for every battle casualty; in 1945 we were down to ten sick for every battle casualty, and the proportion was still decreasing.

*The promise of victory opened up new horizons. In October Mountbatten received a new Directive from the Combined Chiefs of Staff:*

*'Your object is the destruction and expulsion of all Japanese forces in Burma at the earliest possible date.'*

*After that it was agreed that the earliest possible capture of Singapore came next in importance. Singapore . . . and it was only just over six months since the Japanese had set forth on the 'march to Delhi'! But Burma would not be taken by Directives. 'The re-conquest of Burma', wrote Mountbatten, 'promised to be a long and arduous enterprise.'*

*It now became apparent that the Japanese were not going to fight in front of the Irrawaddy River; they were falling back behind it. And to bring them to battle, Slim would have to pass his army across the river—somehow.*

The Irrawaddy is one of the great rivers of the world. It is 1,300 miles long, and navigable for 1,000 miles. It is a tremendous natural obstacle. Its average width is well over a mile, and at one place, where the Chindwin joins it, over two miles.

But it wasn't the width, or the current, or the always shifting sandbanks that gave Slim his worst headache in 1945. It was the sheer absence of any type of craft to cross with. He really had to start from scratch.

*This problem had been foreseen. Two months earlier, Slim had taken his Chief Engineer for a short walk along the banks of the Chindwin. 'Billy,' said Slim, 'there's the river—and there are the trees . . .'*

*The Fourteenth Army then went into boat-building. Several hundred barges were constructed from teak logs. 'They were not graceful craft', wrote Slim, 'but they floated, and carried ten tons each. Three of these lashed together and decked could carry anything up to a Sherman tank.'*

*Outboard engines and marine petrol engines were flown in. Small motor tugs arrived in sections, and were reassembled. Japanese landing-craft, small steamers, tugs and lighters were salvaged from the river and repaired. So the river ports came back to life, and new traffic appeared on the waterways of Burma.*

I sometimes wonder if *General* Slim didn't miss his vocation : perhaps he should have been an admiral. Not content with building the hundreds of boats and rafts that the Fourteenth Army needed to cross the Irrawaddy, he actually presented me with a second Navy.

He built two 'do-it-yourself' gunboats for fighting on the rivers. They were manned by naval crews, and flew the White Ensign, so they were definitely Navy. Slim claims to be the only general who ever built, christened, launched and commissioned ships for the Royal Navy.

The christening almost got him into trouble. He called one of these strange craft H.M.S. *Oona*, after his own daughter, and the other—rather graciously, I thought—H.M.S. *Pamela*, after my younger one. Their Lordships of the Admiralty then pointed out to him that only they were permitted to suggest names for His Majesty's ships. But I don't think Slim was too worried!

*On January 14th 1945 the 19th Indian Division, commanded by Major-General 'Pete' Rees, crossed the Irrawaddy at two points north of Mandalay. This was designed as a diversionary attack. It succeeded brilliantly, as the Japanese hurried reinforcements up to liquidate the 19th Division bridgeheads. When they were well committed Slim displayed his real hand. On February 12th the 20th Division went in, west of Mandalay. The next day, much further to the west, the main assault took place, aimed at the vital rail and road junction of Meiktila.*

I crossed the river myself just behind this attack on February 16th. I wrote in my diary :

'I was fascinated to see what a beach-head looks like in a river crossing, and found that it bore a fairly close resemblance to a beach-head in an amphibious assault, except that the soldiers run all the craft themselves. The Irrawaddy is now in the process of being crossed at four widely separated points, though some of the crossings have not started yet. The casualties in the crossing have, up to date, been surprisingly light.'

*The advance to Meiktila had begun. Once out of the jungle, the British held a big advantage: now they could make full use of their armour and mechanised mobility. The new Japanese commander, General Kimura, was determined to hold the Irrawaddy line, but no amount of obstinate devotion on the part of his troops could halt the British/Indian offensive. Meiktila fell on March 5th.*

*Three days later, eighty miles away, the battle for Manadaly began. There was hand-to-hand fighting up the steep, pagoda-sprinkled slopes of Mandalay Hill. The Japanese made their final stubborn stand in the vast walled enclosure of Fort Dufferin. The walls of Fort Dufferin were twenty feet high; their base, backed by earth embankments, was seventy feet thick. The moat was 200 feet wide.*

*Attack after attack failed. Medium artillery, at a range of only 500 yards, could make no empression. Five-hundred-pound boms did little better. Finally the walls were breached by Mitchell bombers, using the moat for skip-bombing with 2,000-pounders. But there was no need to carry out an assault. By the night of March 19th the Japanese had had enough. On the 20th General Rees hoisted the Union Jack again in Fort Dufferin.*

It was on March 22nd that I entered Fort Dufferin. We had announced that Mandalay had been cleared of the enemy the day before, but it turned out that there were still a few Japanese snipers lurking about while I was making my inspection.

They didn't matter; what mattered was that the capture of Mandalay marked the climax of the Burma Campaign. In my despatch I paid this tribute to General Slim:

'His plan was as brilliant in its conception as in its subsequent successful execution.'

The Meiktila-Mandalay operation was a superb achievement by Slim and his Army. Personally, I consider that Slim was the finest general that the Second World War produced.

Anyway, the Japanese never recovered from this blow. And now a distant prospect became an immediate reality: the liberation of Burma.

# 7
## The March to Victory

---

'Come you back, you British soldier; come you back to Mandalay!'
wrote Kipling.

In March 1945 the British soldier was back in Mandalay—and a
lot else was happening.

Two days after our Fourteenth Army recaptured Mandalay we
heard that the Second Army had crossed the Rhine. Victory was in
sight at last. You could feel it in the air, in Burma as well as in
Europe. It was obvious that Germany was on her last legs, ground
down between the Russians on one side and General Eisenhower's
armies on the other. We knew that Japan was beaten too—though
we also knew that hard fighting would have to be done before she
would admit it!

*The double victory of Meiktila-Mandalay in March 1945 marked
the climax of the fighting in Burma. The Japanese Burma Army
never recovered from this blow.*

*Now the whole of South East Asia Command, from the Supreme
Commander downwards—above all the Fourteenth Army, commanded by General Slim—felt a sense of exhilaration. Rangoon, the
capital of Burma, was still over three hundred miles away—yet felt
as though it lay just behind the next hill. The advance to Rangoon
would be a race with time, to get there before the 1945 monsoon
turned the dusty roads of Central Burma into quagmires again. All
through April the Fourteenth Army pressed forward, knowing the
need for speed.*

*The month of May came in with peals of victory. On the 1st, the
German armies in Italy surrendered to Field Marshal Alexander. On
the 2nd the Russians entered Berlin. Adolf Hitler lay dead in the*

*dismal bunker which was all that remained of his Reich. On May 7th Germany submitted in 'Unconditional Surrender' to General Eisenhower. May 8th 1945 was V.E. Day. After five and a half weary years of war, victory in Europe had been won.*

Victory in Europe was wonderful news for every one of us, a marvellous tonic. Mussolini was dead; Hitler was dead: two of the most sinister figures who have ever threatened European civilisation.

But our war was not yet over; we still had to defeat Imperial Japan. The Fourteenth Army was nearing Rangoon, but the monsoon was also approaching, and it was a toss-up which would win.

We had another card up our sleeves, however: a long-prepared double assault by sea and air. As our main forces closed in, up the Rangoon River, we wondered what was going to happen. The Japanese generally defended places to the last man; if they did that now it would mean a battle through the streets—a very nasty business. On May 4th our forces landed just outside Rangoon and advanced on the city.

For once we couldn't complain if our own successes were somewhat overlooked. It was really bad management to capture Rangoon in the middle of a week so crowded with vast events. But the monsoon was upon us now, and we had to act fast.

The first entry into Ragoon was made by amphibious forces— a major combined operation in SEAC at last. And ironically I was in bed with dysentery when it happened, following its progress with my Commanders-in-Chief at my bedside.

The prisoners of war in Rangoon jail had written on the roof: 'Japs gone. Exdigitate.' But in spite of this obviously R.A.F.-inspired exhortation to take our fingers out we hardly dared to hope that it was really true, so we carried on with the full-dress landing. Yet it *was* true, much to everybody's relief, and Rangoon was reoccupied by us without having to be bombed or fought over. This may have been part of the reason for the tremendous reception we got from the Burmese population.

*Rangoon was a mile-post in the march to victory. The Japanese were completely defeated in Burma: only remnants fought on, trying to make their escape through the encircling British forces.*

*Yet in May 1945 it appeared that there was still heavy work ahead in the SEAC area: Malaya, Singapore, Siam and Sumatra all remained in Japanese occupation. They also occupied the rest of the Dutch East Indies, Borneo and Indo-China. At SEAC headquarters new plans were prepared for new advances.*

We did find time for one celebration, however. On June 14th we held our Fourteenth Army Victory Parade in Rangoon, followed by a Naval Review.

The monsoon was well upon us by now, but I don't think the men minded that. In fact, they rather relished the rain; I hear that they said to themselves:

'We *fought* through the bloody rain, it's only right that the bull should take place in the bloody rain.'

Anyway, they put on a splendid show—but they were splendid troops! These men had marched and fought for a thousand miles across some of the worst terrain in the world. They had beaten the Japanese hands down; they had overcome the monsoon and they had overcome malaria. Their morale was superb. And, of course, it was a comfort for them to know that the end of the war in Europe meant that their families were safe at last from bombs and V-2 rockets.

Victory in Europe seemed to promise strong reinforcements at last, landing craft, shipping, aircraft—all the things that were needed to finish off the war. We were already planning a big amphibious operation—'Zipper'—to capture Malaya and Singapore. But once again all our hopes were dashed.

To my amazement, the Secretary of State for War announced an accelerated scheme for demobilisation without even consulting us in SEAC, as though our war were over too. The promises of early repatriation made to the men made an absolute nonsense of our plans. And when you make promises to soldiers and then break them this does more harm to morale than anything.

So SEAC had once more to water down its plans, but with this unpleasant irony, that this time we were a case of poverty amidst plenty. Still we had to get on with it; and I had another serious matter to deal with at the same time—a preview of things to come, as it turned out.

*In 1942,. when the British evacuated Burma, the Government had left with the Army. It set itself up in Simla as a government-in-exile, headed by Sir Reginald Dorman-Smith, the ex-Governor.*

*Now, with Burma reoccupied, this government expected to return and resume its pre-war authority.*

*But Burmese nationalism now emerged as a force to reckon with. The Japanese had made an empty gesture of liberation from colonial rule to the Burmese. They had set up a puppet Provisional Government, and in addition they had raised and trained a Burma National Army, to fight against 'British Imperialism'. The Commander-in-Chief of this Burma National Army was Major-General Aung San, who now became a key personality.*

*By March 1945, Aung San had realised that Burma's real enemy was not British, but Japanese Imperialism. On March 28th—a week after the capture of Mandalay—the Burma National Army turned against the Japanese. For Mountbatten, this act posed a deeply significant question.*

I knew perfectly well that the Burma National Army had supported the Japanese. I also knew that some of them had committed some atrocities at that time. But I knew too that they were the only people in Burma with any popular backing in 1945. They could either help us—as they were doing by rising against the Japanese— or they could hinder us. And if they did hinder us my military advice was that it would take two divisions to hold them down. I considered the whole idea to be unthinkable.

We had come back here into Burma as rescuers. At that time we had the goodwill of most Burmese; I certainly didn't want to throw that away. The Burmese showed signs of trusting us and General Slim, who had met Aung San in May, told me that we could trust him.

So in June I issued a Directive which said:

'The guiding principle which I am determined shall be observed is that no person shall suffer on account of political opinions honestly held, whether now or in the past, even if these may have been anti-British, but only on account of proven crimes against the criminal law, or actions repugnant to humanity. This principle is no more than an elementary point of British justice.'

*Mountbatten's policy did not endear him to the officials of the old Government of Burma, and was, indeed, misunderstood by many of his own Civil Affairs officers. Nor was it correctly interpreted by the Burmese themselves; some of their leaders had tasted the sweets of executive power, and it seemed to them that their prospects of real liberation would be better if Burma returned quickly to Civil Rule. They failed to anticipate the frame of mind of the returning Civil authorities who expected to find, in 1945, the Burma they had left in 1942.*

I was shocked and alarmed when, only a few months later, Aung San and his people came and told me that they would prefer to have Civil Government back in Rangoon, instead of my Military Administration. I was afraid they didn't understand the implications of what they were asking for—and, as a matter of fact, Aung San admitted as much to me later on. But since they had asked for it, I felt I had to give way, and I allowed the pre-war Civil Government to come back and take over from me in October 1945.

I now think this was a mistake because I knew this Civil Government didn't share my views. I should have tried harder to convince the Burmese or at least to have delayed matters. And then, according to my Burmese friends, there would have been a good chance of Burma remaining inside the Commonwealth. But what's done is done.

*The war against Japan came to its crescendo. In October 1944 General Douglas MacArthur's forces made their promised return to the Philippines. The General waded back ashore through the surf—a symbolic gesture to wash away the black memories of surrender in 1942. In February 1945 the Americans re-entered Manila.*

*Later that month they attacked the island of Iwo Jima. The attack went in under cover of a bombardment of 6,800 tons of bombs from the air and 22,000 shells from the great naval guns. Even so, the capture of Iwo Jima cost the Americans a third of their landing force. Out of 20,000 Japanese, only 216 survived—as prisoners. This was the grim pattern of the Pacific war.*

*In April 1945 America and her Allies suffered a grievous loss. The President, Franklin Delano Roosevelt, in his third term of office, died, with the victories which he had done so much to bring about in sight at last.*

It had been a great thrill to me to meet Roosevelt at various times during the war. I had admired him ever since he was first elected President. I was a strong supporter of his New Deal policy. And the support and help he gave us when we stood alone, before Russia or America came into the war, were things we could never forget.

We became personal friends in 1942 when I stayed with him at the White House. But as Supreme Allied Commander I stood in a special relationship to him. He had made that quite clear to me at Quebec, when I was appointed.

'General Eisenhower,' he told me, 'is as much a servant of your King as of me. I trust you will feel the same way about me in South East Asia.'

I promised him I would be a good American, and he laughed and thanked me. I had done my best to keep this promise, and he in turn had given me splendid backing, even when I had been forced to disregard his Directives. I felt I had lost a good friend and an understanding Chief.

*Already General MacArthur's forces were committed to the next stage of their advance towards the home islands of Japan: Philippines . . . Iwo Jima . . . Okinawa . . .*

*The assault on Okinawa went in on April 1st—another mighty display of amphibious power. The Japanese were now driven to methods of desperation. These were the days of the 'Kamikaze'. The name means 'the Divine Wind'—the typhoon which destroyed the fleet of Kublai Khan, attacking Japan in A.D. 1281.*

*In 1945 'Kamikaze' meant suicide attacks by young Japanese pilots, devoted to the Emperor, and contemptuous of death, who tried to crash their planes with full bomb loads on the decks of American and British ships. In all, in the Battle of Okinawa, the Japanese flew 1,900 suicide sorties; they sank 26 ships, and damaged 164.*

*In return, the cities of Japan were being rocked to their foundations by the attacks of American aircraft—B.29s, the Super-Fortresses. The Allies were closing for the kill.*

As long as SEAC had been mainly concerned with fighting all the way down from the top end of Burma, there wasn't much opportunity, or indeed need, of close co-operation with General MacArthur. But now that we were in Rangoon, and all set to make a jump into Malaya and Singapore, we could obviously help each other more. So I decided to go and see MacArthur at his headquarters in Manila. I was keen to do this anyhow, because he was such an outstanding figure, and I wanted to get to know him. I wasn't disappointed. He was a terrific man. He had a splendid background, he had won tremendous prestige, and he just oozed personality.

His methods were quite unlike mine; he was absolutely autocratic; he never really consulted his Army, Air or Fleet Commanders. He made up his own mind, and told them what to do. But although he was twenty years older than me, we got on well together, and we had no trouble in agreeing about future plans. Neither of us knew at that stage that all our ideas were going to have to be very drastically revised.

*On July 17th 1945, a week after Mountbatten's meeting with General MacArthur, took place the last of the great inter-Allied Conferences of the war—Potsdam.*

*On the day before the Conference the British Prime Minister, Mr. Winston Churchill, toured the ruins of nearby Berlin—and was cheered by some of the unfortunate citizens whose defeat was so much his doing. 'My hate', he wrote, 'had died with their surrender and I was much moved by their demonstrations, and also by their haggard looks and threadbare clothes.' Also at Potsdam was America's new President, Mr. Harry S. Truman. 'I was impressed', said Churchill, 'with his gay, precise, sparkling manner and obvious power of decision.'*

*Churchill summoned Mountbatten, who was on his way to England for other consultations, to attend the Potsdam Conference*

I was only present at Potsdam for a short time, but it is hard to think of any similar span of time so packed with significance. I met the new American President, Mr. Truman, making his first big appearance on the world stage.

I met Stalin—that was an experience. I remembered as a boy visiting my uncle, the Tsar of Russia. In those days to meet the autocrat you had to pass through a line of Cossacks and some police. To meet Stalin you had to pass through an outer line of sentries, then another line, then an inner line, and there were police and security men everywhere—much more protection than my uncle ever had.

Stalin was very polite; there was no hanging about, waiting. Conversation flowed along very well, thanks to his brilliant interpreter,

Pavlov, who could interpret as you talked if you made frequent short pauses.

Stalin was very gay, full of optimism, as well he might be at that time. We were all wondering whether he was going to enter the war against Japan, so I told him about the plans I had agreed with General MacArthur, and how we thought the Russians could fit in. I told him about what we had been doing in SEAC, which seemed to interest him.

Immense decisions were taken at Potsdam, decisions which have affected the whole world ever since. It was at Potsdam, for instance, that I first learned that the boundaries of my Command were going to be very greatly extended. This was not as flattering as it may sound. It was an inevitable reshuffle of responsibilities, in the light of the heavy defeats which Japan had already suffered.

Vastly more important were the decisions about the way in which Japan was to be finished off. The Allied leaders at Potsdam took it for granted that Japan, like Germany, must accept 'Unconditional Surrender'. This was President Roosevelt's phrase, which he had rather sprung on us at the Casablanca Conference in June 1943. Then, of course, it applied to the war in Europe—we were not discussing Japan.

The Chiefs of Staff had doubts about it as soon as we heard it. We feared that insisting on our enemies throwing themselves entirely on our mercy might harden their resistance, and so prolong the war. But the policy was adopted, and 'Unconditional Surrender' was enforced in Europe. Now, in July 1945, the same policy was to be applied to Japan.

Japan was a military Empire. The traditions of the samurai—the warrior class—were built into the Japanese way of life. It was obviously important to knock these on the head. But there was another side to it. In the eyes of the overwhelming numbers of Japanese, the Emperor was 'the Son of Heaven'—in fact, a god. And gods do not perform unconditional surrender.

So our demand struck not only at Japanese politics, but at their religion too. Inevitably, they rejected it. And inevitably, that meant that the Allies would have to use the utmost force against them. I now discovered the appalling implications of that.

It was at Potsdam that I was told the most closely guarded secret of the war: the story of the development of the atomic bomb. The

American Chiefs of Staff, General Marshall and General Arnold, now informed me that an atomic bomb was about to be dropped on Japan. Mr. Churchill and President Truman confirmed this to me.

There was no time for philosophical reflections. The dropping of the bomb was less than a fortnight off, when I was told. So here we were, almost at the end of July, and I was being told to expect the Japanese to surrender in mid-August.

Churchill told me to warn my staff in SEAC—but I was forbidden to give any sort of explanation. I said they would think I was mad if I just told them to prepare for an immediate Japanese surrender, without any explanation at all. But Churchill insisted, and so my SEAC staff had to rush forward all our plans for landing in Malaya and Singapore, and just take my word for it that there would be no opposition. It was a fantastic thought, that this race of stubborn soldiers, who scarcely knew the meaning of fear, would be brought to their knees by one single, dreadful weapon.

Another great leader was now about to depart from the scene. At the Potsdam Conference three men seemed to hold the world in the palms of their hands: Stalin, Truman and Churchill. But on July 25th Winston Churchill flew off to London to hear the results of the 1945 General Election. I don't think he had any premonition of what was coming. But to my great regret I had seen the last of him as my wartime chief.

When the results came through I was in London, and I took my staff down to Broadlands to work while we awaited instructions. I must say I was less surprised than some at what happened. I had sensed from the mood of the troops in SEAC that people wanted a change. Winston Churchill and the Conservatives were swept out of office, and the Labour Party, headed by Clem Attlee, came in with a landslide victory.

It was sad to see Winston go. I had known him since boyhood, and I had enormously admired his stand against Appeasement in the thirties. Then I had spent two exciting years, working very closely with him, when I was on the Chiefs of Staff Committee.

He was never the easiest of men to work with. He nearly drove the Chiefs of Staff mad at times, with his endless flow of ingenious schemes. But he kept us up to the mark all the time. His whole mind was concentrated on winning the war; that is why he was such a wonderful leader. That, and his human touch: he knew how to inspire us, when to make us weep, when to make us laugh.

I was extremely fond of him, and I know he was fond of me—but perhaps for the wrong reasons. I suspect he thought of me as being more of a swashbuckler than I really am. In war he was splendid, but I was already worried about how we would get on in peace.

Now Winston had gone, and Mr. Attleee became Prime Minister. The first thing he had to do was to take over at a major inter-Allied Conference in mid-stream. I could see no possible difficulty in working with Mr. Attlee. I'd had some dealings with him when he was Deputy Prime Minister. I had respect and liking for him. I knew how businesslike he was, and of course he had the advantage of full background knowledge of all the current situations.

Already my job was becoming more political than military. When I reported to Mr. Attlee I explained to him the line I proposed to take with the liberated territories when we had driven the Japanese out of South East Asia—now an imminent prospect. I was delighted to find that I had his full backing—I had a feeling that I was going to need it.

*Japan recoiled from unconditional surrender; she knew she was beaten, but could find no way of obtaining peace.*

*The town of Hiroshima—the seventh largest in Japan—contained an arsenal, oil refineries, factories, a large garrison of soldiers. It was a 'military target'. It also contained 343,000 people.*

*At nine minutes past seven on the morning of August 6th 1945 four American B.29s appeared in the cloudless sky above Hiroshima. The air raid sirens sounded. Twenty-two minutes later the planes had gone; the All Clear was heard; people emerged from their shelters and went about their lives. But there was a fifth plane in the sky that day.*

*A Japanese journalist tells what followed:*

*Suddenly a glaring whitish, pinkish light appeared in the sky accompanied by an unnatural tremor which was followed almost immediately by a wave of suffocating heat and a wind which swept away everything in its path. Within a few seconds the thousands of people in the streets in the centre of the town were scorched by a wave of searing heat. Many were killed instantly, others lay writhing on the ground, screaming in agony from the intolerable pain of their burns. Everything standing upright in the way of the blast—walls, houses, factories and other buildings—was annihilated . . . Hiroshima had ceased to exist.'*

*The first atomic bomb had done its work.*

My reactions to the dropping of the bomb were somewhat mixed. It was all part of the war; it happened in a war context, which was very different from the context in which it has been talked about ever since.

To begin with, I was appalled at the Japanese being given a chance to surrender before being completely defeated in the field. I was confident of our ability to clear them out of South East Asia, because they were on the run everywhere. But now the visible demonstration of their defeat outside Japan would be missing, and it seemed to me that this was rather dangerous for the future. 'Face' means a lot in Asia; I was afraid this would give the Japanese the chance to 'save face'.

On the other hand, one has to reckon this against the great saving of human life—yes, *saving* of life—that was made possible. I don't just mean Allied lives. Okinawa was very fresh in all our minds.

It took eighty-two days to capture Okinawa. It cost 50,000 American casualties, a quarter of whom were killed. But the Japanese army of over 100,000 was practically wiped out.

They absolutely would not surrender. The soldiers would hold hand grenades to their stomachs and blow themselves up rather than give in; the generals committed ceremonial hara-kiri—they disembowelled themselves. As the American Official History says:

'There was only one kind of Japanese casualty—the dead. Those that were wounded either died of their wounds or returned to the front line to be killed. The Japanese soldier gave his all.'

Since they defended outlying islands like this, we had to ask ourselves what they were likely to do in their homeland. More Japanese died at Okinawa than at Hiroshima. How many Okinawas did we want?

That was really how we thought about the bomb: as a means of ending this terrible war as quickly as possible. Even so, it took a second bomb three days later, on Nagasaki, to make Japan sue for peace.

This was what civilisation had come to.

*On August 14th Japan submitted in unconditional surrender. The Emperor proclaimed to his people:*

*'It is our desire to initiate an era of peace for future generations by tolerating the intolerable, and enduring the unendurable.'*

*The surrender was signed in Tokio Bay, aboard the American battleship* Missouri, *on Sunday, September 2nd 1945. General Mac-Arthur was designated to accept the Japanese submission on behalf of the Allied Powers.*

*When the time came for him to sign the document, General MacArthur called forward Lieutenant-General A. E. Percival, who had signed the British surrender to the Japanese in Singapore on February 15th 1942, and Lieutenant-General Jonathan Wainwright, who had surrendered the fortress of Corregidor in the Philippines on May 6th of that year. The presence of these two witnesses, liberated from their Japanese prison, was another symbolic gesture.*

Well, the surrender ceremony in Tokio Bay was very impressive, but for me it was absolutely maddening. It seriously delayed us getting to Singapore. General MacArthur had issued orders that no individual surrenders, and no reoccupation of Japanese-held territory were to take place until after the big surrender at Tokio. This meant a delay of ultimately nineteen days—which was appalling.

I already had a large fleet at sea, making for Malaya. There were lots of landing craft on the way, and we couldn't turn them back, because they were not designed to head into the south-west monsoon, and I was afraid that some of them might even sink. Also, the civilian population of the whole territory had to remain under the Japanese for nearly three more weeks. But by far the worst thing was the tens of thousands of prisoners of war who were waiting to be liberated—some of them in such a weak state that they might die before we could reach them.

*It was not until September 5th that Mountbatten's forces reoccupied Singapore, and the city emerged from its long nightmare of occupation and oppression. Mountbatten's own arrival, with General Sir William Slim, Allied Land Forces Commander, marked the beginning of a moment of triumph for both men, which they savoured.*

*In October 1943 in Delhi, Mountbatten had flown in to lift up the hearts of discouraged men with the promise of victory. Here, in Singapore, they were at last able to taste the victory which he had promised them. And the tasting was in the Mountbatten style. If he—and they—felt cheated at all by the eternal deferments of what was to be their military masterpiece; if they were impatient at the long wait, while General MacArthur played out his part in Tokio, the surrender ceremony in Singapore would wipe those thoughts away. This was to be a moment of victory which everyone could recognise. It was an occasion of panoply: Mountbatten saw to that.*

*On September 12th, in the Council Chamber of Singapore Town Hall, flanked by his senior officers, and in the presence of military representatives of the United States, India, Australia, China, France and Holland, Mountbatten accepted the surrender of 680,879 Japanese in South East Asia.*

I had rather different ideas from General MacArthur about how the Japanese should surrender. He thought the Japanese officers should not give up their samurai swords, because it would mean such loss of face that they would no longer be able to control their men.

I was determined that they *should* lose face, and I was prepared to take the risk of their losing control. So I insisted on senior commanders' swords being handed over in Singapore, and in all other appropriate places under my command.

I don't think there was any doubt in the minds of those who witnessed the Japanese surrenders whether the Japanese were beaten or not.

*Only one actor was missing from the high drama in Singapore. Mountbatten's opposite number, Field Marshal Terauchi, the Japanese Supreme Commander, was suffering from a stroke, and could not make his surrender personally on September 12th.*

*Typically, Mountbatten sent a medical officer to verify that Terauchi was really ill. And, typically, he did not forget Terauchi. In Singapore General Slim took the sword of General Kimura, Commander of the Japanese Burma Army; it stands on his mantelpiece, where he always intended it to be. In Saigon, a few months later, Mountbatten accepted from Marshal Terauchi not one ceremonial sword, but two: one he presented to the King; the other he took home with him to add to his collection at Broadlands.*

I was immensely proud of the achievements of South East Asia Command. It wasn't simply the fact of our victory over the Japanese; it was what we had had to contend with, in order to obtain victory—the jungle, the monsoon, malaria, and perhaps, above all, being so low down in the priority list that we never had enough of anything we needed.

Looking back on it all now, one can see something which could not be seen at the time. Our campaign was the swan-song of the British Empire in the Far East. It was not an unworthy one.

Speaking for my own Service, I would say that the Navy came out of World War II with great credit—far greater credit than from World War I. In 1914 we were the greatest naval power in the world—but although the Navy did well, you could not say that it did brilliantly.

In 1939 we enjoyed no such supremacy—but there were many brilliant exploits, and some very fine commanders came to the top. I can only mention a few: Sir Dudley Pound, as First Sea Lord; Sir Andrew Cunningham, who became famous in the Mediterranean; Sir Bruce Fraser, who was my Naval C.-in-C. in SEAC and then commanded the British Pacific Fleet; Sir Arthur John Power, his very worthy successor in SEAC; Sir Philip Vian, a tremendously dashing leader—and there were many others.

We had had our bad moments, of course; mistakes were made, and there were sad losses of ships and men. But I think we showed that we had done a good deal of our homework well between the wars; our ships were good, our officers knew what they were about, and our men were well trained and as brave as ever.

So now the war was over and all the Services could feel that they had won through. Everyone—and not least our long-suffering forces in SEAC—felt entitled to suppose that the fighting was over. But it was not. I now found myself faced with an entirely new, and in some ways an even more bewildering dimension of Supreme Command.

# 8

# *The Meaning of Victory*

---

At the end of the war, as the saying goes, 'to the victor the spoils'.

I'm afraid we did not collect many spoils from the Japanese in South East Asia in 1945. Their legacy to us, when they laid down their arms, could be summed up in one word: chaos.

Without any interval—no time for cheering, scarcely time to draw breath, in fact—we had to take over and try to sort it all out. The work began immediately: very hard work indeed, of a kind I had never done before, dealing with a situation which had never existed before—a new force in world history.

*Liberation came to Singapore and Malaya on September 12th 1945. It was already a fact in Burma. Liberation, to South East Asia, meant more than the defeat of Japan; it meant the unleashing of a surge of hope, the stimulation of dreams of nationhood, a new future.*

*All these ideas entered the realm of possibility on the day the Japanese forces made their surrender to the Supreme Allied Commander, Admiral Lord Louis Mountbatten.*

I now found myself in a totally new rôle. At the end of the surrender ceremony in Singapore I ceased to be a fighting commander. The problems I had to deal with now were political and human problems on a terrifying scale. And it was impossible to disentangle them from each other. It was as urgent to bring these people food and medicine, or, for instance, to repair the drainage system, as it was to work out a system of administration which would meet the needs of the future.

I was just forty-five years old when I took on this great responsi-

bility. Now, from Government House, Singapore, I found myself
ruling over an enormous area.

Before the Potsdam Conference I had been responsible for Burma,
Malaya and Singapore, Siam and Sumatra. Now I was also responsible for all the rest of the Dutch East Indies and French Indo-China
(but only up to the Sixteenth Parallel); later I had to add Borneo, and
Dutch New Guinea as well, but fortunately not for long.

The original SEAC area was 1 million square miles; now it was $1\frac{1}{2}$
million. It contained 128 million people. There were still nearly
three-quarters of a million Japanese at large in it. There were
123,000 Allied prisoners of war and internees.

The whole of this vast area was in a state of utter administrative
chaos, and much of it was facing imminent starvation. The reports
which poured into my headquarters every day were more and more
depressing.

*The presence of the Japanese was one of the most depressing factors
throughout Mountbatten's command area. With the world shipping
shortage of 1945, nothing like enough was available to carry these
defeated armies back to Japan. And so they remained in South East
Asia, unwanted guests.*

*Uses were found for them. They were put to work, repairing dam-
age, clearing away the distasteful reminders of the time of occupation when they had been the masters. But there were other uses for
the Japanese that were less agreeable—in fact, grimly ironic.*

*Everywhere the Japanese had destroyed the colonial administra-
tions—British, French and Dutch. They had also bitterly antagon-
ised the local populations, who formed resistance groups and guer-
illa forces. These now expected to take power. Lawless elements—
bandits and dacoits—also perceived their opportunities for loot.*

*Until the British could arrive—and this was no easy matter—the
only means of preserving any sort of law and order was the distasteful one of using the Japanese themselves. This was not good
for the Allied 'image'.*

I knew quite well that the spectacle of Japanese troops and our own
apparently co-operating was likely to sap confidence in our intentions, and I didn't like it at all. But there was another reason why I
disliked this. It is hard to express how we who had fought the
Japanese came to loathe them. British troops are not good haters,

and I am quite sure they never felt like this about the Italians or even the Germans—though I dare say the Poles and Russians did.

We came to associate the Japanese with sheer inhumanity towards the wounded, towards prisoners and towards helpless civilians. There were far to many cases of brutality and murder. The Japanese had a habit of bayoneting their captives, and somehow this seemed to make the atrocity worse. When we discovered, in such places as Singapore's notorious Changi jail, or the torture rooms of Outram Road prison, what they had done to the prisoners they didn't kill we were even more horrified and revolted. On the very day they agreed to unconditional surrender the Japanese massacred 152 civilians in Singapore. It was cruelties such as these that caused a number of their leaders to be branded as war criminals.

*The rescue of prisoners of war and civilian internees from the Japanese prisons and prison camps was the most urgent task of the liberating forces. There were nearly 250 of these camps. The first need was to locate them; the second, to rush in medical supplies and food; the third, to get the men out.*

*Thousands had already died, of starvation, disease and brutal treatment. By the Japanese military code, a soldier who surrendered had lost his honour, and his life was therefore worthless. The Japanese were not concerned with keeping their prisoners alive.*

*Conditions in the prison camps were always bad—in certain areas, terrible. From Sumatra, Lady Mountbatten reported to the Red Cross and St. John:*

*'There is no doubt that had the war gone on a few more weeks there would have been no prisoners of war in these areas left alive at all. They were absolutely at their last gasp. . . .'*

Edwina was Superintendent-in-Chief of the St. John Ambulance Brigade and chairman of its Joint War organisation with the Red Cross. She had already had a large hand in the recovery of Allied prisoners of war from Germany, so it would be fair to call her an expert on the problem. When I was in London after the Potsdam Conference I asked her to come out and deal with it in our part of the world. I really don't know what we would have done in South East Asia without her.

I gave her a letter, stating who she was, and that she was in charge of the advanced arrangements for the recovery of prisoners of war and internees. Armed only with this, she went off everywhere, with just a small personal staff, met the Japanese commanders—who kowtowed and did whatever she told them.

*Together, whenever that was possible, the Mountbattens would visit the camps where men waited for repatriation—their deepest desire The compassion of Lord and Lady Louis was visible; their sympathy was utterly practical; their impact was unforgettable.*

It was hard to think what to say to these men. Sometimes, seeing the condition they were in, I could hardly say anything at all. They certainly didn't want to be bothered with formal inspections and a lot of rhetoric.

So quite often I would just gather them round me, and tell them what had been happening, and what was going on. After all, they had been cut off from all civilisation for years, and they needed to be put back in touch with things as much as they needed medicine and food. Anyway, they seemed to appreciate this. I hope they did.

As for Edwina, I am sure that she saved countless lives by her tireless personal activity, and although I am speaking of my own wife, I must add that I consider it was a heroic effort.

*In 1942, when Japan completed her vast conquest in South East Asia and the Pacific, she called these conquered lands 'The Greater East Asia Co-Prosperity Sphere'. This was the beginning, she proclaimed, of a 'New Order in Asia'. In fact, 'Co-Prosperity' had meant something very different.*

*The march of Japan had meant destruction: destruction of natural resources, destruction of productive capacity; destruction of communications, and with them trade and peoples' livings; destruction of shrines and monuments; death and wounds for the civilian populations.*

*Japan's conquests were lands in ruin; 'Co-Prosperity' meant poverty, sickness, subjection and fear. The 'New Order' had not brought independence—but had greatly increased the desire for it. When Japan collapsed, Asian Nationalism surged into new life. But for the time being, this could only mean added disorder.*

It is very difficult to convey the impact of all this at the time. The

*Above:* After the victory of Imphal, the Supreme Allied Commander leads the Viceroy of India, Field-Marshal Lord Wavell, past the four Lieutenant-Generals (Slim, Christison, Scoones and Stopford).

*Below:* Mountbatten visits one of his Chinese armies in action on the northern front: General Sun Li-Jen points out Japanese positions.

'*The bulk of my forces were Indian. . . .*' The Supremo with Lieutenant-Colonel Balwant Singh, commanding 1/Patiala Infantry at Imphal, February, 1944. Major-General Roberts, commanding 23rd Indian Division, on left.

*Above:* Communications in Assam, February, 1944. A new Bailey bridge doubling the Tehri bridge over the Manipur River. The Supreme Commander in foreground with Lieutenant-General Scoones, IV Corps Commander.

*Right:* 'The worst terrain in the world . . .' Looking back with Major-General Pick (U.S. Army Engineers) from the top of the Pangsau Pass, on the India/Burma frontier down the Ledo Road.

*Above:* Mountbatten with the Chindit Commander, Major-General Orde Wingate, and Brigadier-General Merrill (U.S. Army), leader of 'Merrill's Marauders', January, 1944.

*Below:* Chindits of Brigadier Fergusson's 16th Long Range Penetration Brigade being addressed by the Supremo, after completing their operation behind the Japanese lines, May, 1944.

*Above:* Indian troops at Seyura village during the drive on Meiktila, March, 1945. [*Alan Campbell-Johnson Ltd.*]

*Below:* The Supremo had to fly to Ledo for hospital treatment to his injured eye. Here he talks to Lieutenant-Colonel Wilson (Commanding 'V' Force) at Taihpa Ga before taking off.

Mountbatten with Generalissimo Chiang Kai-shek and Madame Chiang Kai-shek visit Chinese troops at Ranchi on their return from the Cairo Conference, November, 1943.

River crossing, February, 1945. Carrying supplies ashore for the capture of Myitson. [*Alan Campbell-Johnson Ltd.*]

Irrawaddy Crossing, February, 1945. Follow-up forces, supplies and ammunition of the 7th Indian Division crossing the mile-wide river near Nyaungu. [*Allan Campbell-Johnson Ltd.*]

Saigon, 1945. The Supreme Commander, Japanese Expeditionary Forces, Southern Region, Field-Marshal Count Terauchi, surrendering his ceremonial ancestral sword, forged in 1292, in its case (a special mark of respect) to the Supreme Allied Commander, South East Asia. (Possibly the last time a sword will be submitted as token of surrender.)

Survivors of the Japanese prisoner-of-war camps. They were brutally treated, given no medical supplies and only just enough food to keep alive. [*Imperial War Museum*]

The Mountbattens at the Shwe Dagon Pagoda, Rangoon, during their
state visit in 1948 to the land from which Lord Louis takes his title,
Earl Mountbatten of Burma.

*Above:* Visit to Katmandu, Nepal, May, 1946. Behind the throne, Lord Brabourne, then A.D.C. to Mountbatten, later his son-in-law.

*Below:* Official visit to Bangkok, 21 January, 1946. Lord Mountbatten, wearing the Star of the White Elephant, talking to the King of Siam at the garden party.

*Above:* Singapore, 19 March, 1946. Lord Mountbatten drives with Pandit Jawaharlal Nehru from Government House to the Indian Y.M.C.A.

*Right:* Allied Control Commission in Saigon. General Leclerc (nearest camera), C.-in-C. French Forces of the Extreme Orient, on his arrival at Saigon, October, 1945. Major-General Gracey, Head of Allied Control Commission in Saigon, is on the left. [*Imperial War Museum*]

The upsurge of Asian nationalism.

*Above:* Slogans in Batavia (Jakarta), October, 1945. [*Imperial War Museum*]

*Below:* Sourabaya, November, 1945. Refugees from the fighting carry their possessions into British lines. [*Imperial War Museum*]

Hanoi, March, 1946.

*Above:* President Ho Chi Minh of the Democratic Republic of Vietnam outside his headquarters. [*Imperial War Museum*]

*Below:* An Independence meeting, demonstrating against French colonialism. [*Imperial War Museum*]

June, 1946. Admiral Mountbatten and his Army Commander, General Slim, receive honorary degrees at Cambridge University.

main point is that these conditions amounted to a complete break-down—and they existed, to a greater or lesser extent, in every one of the territories for which I was responsible. And they all had to be tackled immediately and simultaneously. I can make a list of the problems, and discuss them one by one; but we couldn't deal with them one by one. Everything was happening at once.

The other important thing to remember was that the force at my disposal, upon which our whole position in South East Asia ulti-mately rested, was steadily getting weaker. British units were being systematically demobilised, and they asked for nothing better than to get home. Indian forces—by far the largest component in SEAC—could not be used indefinitely to implement British policy of which Indian opinion often disapproved. So the time factor was all important; we had to do many things, all at once, and very fast.

*Singapore itself, seat of Mountbatten's SEAC headquarters, was in a restless mood in 1945, its population divided and disturbed.*

Today the island of Singapore is independent of the mainland of Malaya. In 1945 both came under my military administration, and our problems were political and racial.

There were 5,000,000 people in the area at that time: 43 per cent of them Chinese, 41 per cent Malays, and a large number of Indians. The Japanese had been playing one community off against another, and the Chinese had been the chief sufferers.

The Chinese, with their strong commercial instinct, were the wealthiest community. They were also the most politically con-scious, and the best organised. It was they who had taken the lead in the resistance to the Japanese. But the most effective section of the Chinese resistance had undoubtedly been the Communist Party—which regarded the expulsion of the Japanese as only a stage towards the expulsion of the British. So we could expect trouble—and we got it.

In Singapore the showdown came in January and February 1946. The Communists tried to subvert the administration by strikes and mass demonstrations. They failed. The administration stood firm, which I think surprised them. But it was a very un-pleasant situation, and I had to take some difficult decisions.

My policy here was on the same lines as it had been in Burma. I had to restore order, but I was against anything that looked like repression by the British. I was determined to err, *if* I erred, on the side of leniency.

I was criticised for this. I probably still am. Some people, including some of my senior officers, thought I was being too lenient. Well, the subsequent history of the area has not been an entirely happy one. All I can say is that while I was responsible what I was trying to do was to promote goodwill and not ill will. And I would do the same again.

*In 1945 Siam was technically an enemy. Her territory had been necessary to the Japanese as a strategic springboard; her rice crop had been necessary to uphold the myth of 'Co-Prosperity'. In 1941 Japanese forces landed. Siamese resistance was slight, and soon the country was under Japanese domination. In 1942 the Japanese forced Siam to declare war on Britain and America.*

*When this 'technical state of war' ended in January 1946 Mountbatten went to Bangkok to attend the peace celebrations. The young King of Siam, brother of the present ruler, welcomed him, and together they reviewed a great parade of Allied troops. Mountbatten had pressed for the retention of the monarchy, believing that this institution was the best means of preserving stability. His friendship with the Siamese royal house dates from this occasion.*

In 1945–6 the Siamese fell over themselves to be friendly and hospitable to our troops, and to wipe out the unfortunate memory of having been technically at war with us. But unfortunately all was not plain sailing in our relations with the Siamese Government at that time.

Under Japanese occupation food production all over South East Asia had declined—above all, rice, which was the staple food. Starvation was an imminent threat—and there is no sharper spur to revolution than starvation. Siam was the largest rice producer in the area. We needed Siam's rice supplies very badly. But it took quite a while to get an adequate flow going again into the starving area.

*In all the countries of Mountbatten's vast domain angry nationalism, spurred by hunger, became a formidable force to reckon with. Each day, each week, threw up new problems.*

The French and Dutch territories were our worst headache by far.

They presented a double problem. First, we were pledged to hand back their overseas possessions to our French and Dutch allies, without really knowing what their policies for these areas were going to be, or how these areas were going to receive them. There was always the disagreeable possibility that SEAC forces might be involved in backing up attitudes and policies which were counter to the Atlantic Charter. And secondly, neither the French nor the Dutch had the resources available to take over immediately themselves. So there was a power vacuum in which Communism, Nationalist extremism and sheer brigandage flourished.

*In French Indo-China—containing the states now known as Laos, Cambodia and Vietnam—the power vacuum produced a situation of complex danger.*

*In 1945 the Japanese had overthrown the last vestiges of Vichy French authority. Now there was a contest for power. The French tried to reassert themselves—but their forces were very weak.*

*The nationalist leader was Ho Chi Minh, who had set up the Viet Minh—the League for the Independence of Vietnam—in exile in China in 1941. Now Ho Chi Minh had returned to end French rule. He was known to be a Communist, but he received American backing as an anti-colonialist.*

*The British, on the other hand, felt obliged to support their French allies and at least keep order until French policy clarified. A further complication was China, under Generalissimo Chiang Kai-shek, who also had a stake in Vietnam. At the Potsdam Conference in July 1945 Chiang Kai-Shek had been made responsible for the country north of the Sixteenth Parallel, while Mountbatten assumed responsibility to the south of it. Now, as fighting broke out between the French and the Vietnamese insurgents, this unhappy division, which prevented any unified settlement, proved to be the origin of the long and bitter wars in Vietnam.*

One could see tragedy building up all the time. Yet I could not leave French Indo-China to anarchy, which was what seemed to be the most likely thing in 1945.

I sent in our troops, under General Gracey, who took a firm grip on the situation straight away, and tried to calm things down. This cost us quite a few casualties, I am afraid.

But after a time Free French troops arrived, with up-to date equipment, and commanded by their famous General Le Clerc. Bit by bit, they took over from us, for which I was thankful: Vietnam was their problem now.

Even so, the division of the country along the Sixteenth Parallel decreed at Potsdam was already revealed as a disaster, for which the whole word was to suffer for so many years. We could not see that far into the future at the time; to us, the Dutch East Indies seemed to be a much worse problem.

*To the Dutch East Indies, Japan had brought promises of independence—and a little more. The Dutch had begun their rule over this empire of 3,000 islands in the sixteenth century. Their form of colonialism had been oppressive. Dr. Achmed Sukarno, the nationalist leader, was interned, and released from Dutch imprisonment by Japanese. Under his leadership, Japan set up an Indonesian Central Advisory Council, to prepare for independence. The Japanese gave the Indonesians arms, and trained them as soldiers.*

*One week before they surrendered, the Japanese warned Sukarno of what they were about to do, and advised him that now was his time. On August 17th 1945, two days after the Japanese surrender, he proclaimed a Republic of Indonesia. By the time Mountbatten's forces and the representatives of the Dutch Government arrived in Java, the new Republic had had a month to organise, and prepare, if necessary, to fight. Mountbatten's troops had two objects: to remove the Japanese, and to evacute the many thousands of Allied prisoners of war and the internees, mostly Dutch. At once they found their task complicated by the bitter conflict which deleveped between the Indonesians and the returning Dutch.*

*The Indonesians began to use the internees as hostages. Conditions in some camps in the interior were very bad, but now an even worse danger arose: massacre, either in the camps or in the course of evacuation.*

*The conflict between colonialism and nationalism became tense. For Mountbatten, the chief consideration was to prevent British and Indian troops being involved on one side or the other. But this was not always possible.*

Indonesia caused us more worry and unhappiness than any other area. At bottom, our troubles were due to lack of information; neither General MacArthur's intelligence staff nor my own Dutch

staff had given me any idea of the strength of the Nationalist movement. I suppose they didn't know themselves. Edwina was really the
first person to give me an inkling of what was going on.

Everything that I had done my best to avoid in the British territories—Malaya and Burma—seemed to happen in Indonesia. Every
attitude seemed to be displayed in its worst aspect. There were
horrible mutilations and massacres and ugly deeds on both sides.

Neither the British nor the Indian troops liked the difficult and
dangerous job they were called on to do—and neither did I. We had
over 2,000 British and Indian casualties in Indonesia in one of the
most thankless tasks our troops have ever had to carry out. It was
really sickening.

*Not until July 1946 was the British task in Indonesia completed.
British strength in South East Asia was now steadily running down,
as the British and Indian forces returned to their homes and the
demobilisation they had earned so well. Civil administrations were
taking over throughout the SEAC area.*

A special Commissioner for South East Asia was now appointed at
my request, and Lord Killearn arrived in Singapore in March. He
immediately became very much involved in the food problem,
which was still acute, because there was a world food shortage at
that time.

In that same month we had another important arrival. Pandit
Nehru, the most distinguished figure in the Indian Interim Government, came to Singapore to study the conditions of the large Indian
community there and meet the Indian forces.

It would be hard to think of a more fateful meeting. It could
easily have gone terribly wrong. Nehru had just been in prison for
opposing our war effort; one of the things in his programme was to
lay a wreath on the memorial to the Indian National Army who had
fought against the Allies.

In fact, his whole visit could have developed into a vast anti
British demonstration. That was not very nice to think about, when
you considered that the bulk of our forces in Singapore and Malaya
were Indian. And yet if the original plans made by the local authorities—in my absence—had been followed I feel sure this was exactly
what would have happened.

The local authorities wanted to cold-shoulder Nehru, to hamper his movements, and to restrict his contacts with the Indian community. I thought this would be disastrous. This man was clearly going to be Prime Minister of India. How fatal for future Anglo-Indian relations to treat him like that!

The local authorities had not even arranged to let Nehru have a car, so I lent him mine. We brought hundreds of Indians into Singapore in army trucks in order to be able to see him. I received him immediately at Government House, and then drove with him through the streets, where he had a fantastic welcome.

At the Indian Red Cross Recreation Centre Edwina was waiting to meet him. The enthusiasm inside was so overwhelming that Edwina was knocked over in the rush and Nehru and I had to rescue her together. That night I invited him to dinner with us; it was a very happy little party. I was able to persuade him not to lay the wreath on the pro-Japanese Indian National Army Memorial and in fact his whole nine-day visit passed off very well, without any unpleasantness of any description, or any disturbances.

This was really a stroke of fate; it was the beginning of a deep friendship between Jawaharlal Nehru and Edwina and myself. How important this was going to be, of course, I couldn't possibly guess, but the value of establishing this link was obvious enough.

It was not merely of value as a matter of British policy—it was valuable to Nehru too. It helped to prevent him adopting extreme attitudes which could not have failed to make things difficult for him later as Prime Minister. It helped to wipe out the bitterness of the past. But what I value above all is the lasting friendship we formed.

*The Mountbatten talent for friendship soon found other outlets. A few days after meeting Nehru, Lord and Lady Mountbatten visited Australia and New Zealand at the invitation of the Governments of those countries. The purpose of the visit was very similar to that of an earlier occasion—the Prince of Wales's tour in 1920, a goodwill tour, when Mountbatten witnessed the enthusiastic welcome of the Prince. Now he was the recipient of such a welcome—he and Lady Louis; for as one Australian newspaper proclaimed in banner headlines:* HE'S A BEAUT SHE'S EVEN MORE OF A BEAUT.'

*Australians would be slow to forget the work that Lady Louis had done for their prisoners of war in the Japanese camps. The visit, in both countries, was a triumph.*

*But Mountbatten was still Supreme Allied Commander, South East Asia. He had business to do with the Australian leaders, and his method of doing it impressed them. There were even rumours that he might become Governor-General, keeping that post in the family by succeeding his cousin, the Duke of Gloucester. But this was not to be.*

*Now his period of command was drawing to an end. In May 1946 the Rt. Hon. Malcolm MacDonald, also at Mountbatten's request, arrived as Governor-General of Malaya and Singapore, and Mountbatten proudly handed over to him a fully functioning administration. In June he was summoned back to London to take part in the Victory Parade; he did not return to South East Asia.*

*In the second half of 1946 the time came when the returning warrior receives his due reward—for one who had done so much the rewards were many. In London's Guildhall Mountbatten was presented with a Sword of Honour and the Freedom of the City. London's honours were followed by other valued Freedoms, by Honorary Degrees, Presidencies of distinguished organisations.*

*Allied countries also added their accolades. At the Invalides in Paris, with full panoply, Mountbatten was invested with the Grand Cross of the Legion of Honour by France's famous fighting soldier, Mashal Juin. The Dutch gave him the Grand Cross of the Order of the Lion of the Netherlands.*

*In October the Mountbattens celebrated an event of different gratification—the marriage of their eldest daughter. The Honourable Patrica Mountbatten was twenty-two years old; now she married her father's A.D.C., Sir John Knatchbull, 7th Baron Brabourne, whose father had been Governor of Bombay and Bengal, and temporary Viceroy of India for six months in 1938. Once more a Mountbatten wedding, attended by the King and Queen, and with Princess Elizabeth as bridesmaid, brightened the social scene.*

*Mountbatten himself now had a new title, commemorating the great campaign conducted under him: Mountbatten of Burma. And a secret ambition was shortly to be fulfilled. The King conferred upon him the most coveted award of all: with ancient ceremony Mountbatten became a Knight of the Order of the Garter, his banner hanging in illustrious company in St. George's Chapel, Windsor.*

It was wonderful to be home again; it was wonderful to be honoured in all these ways. I have always got a tremendous kick out of such things.

I know every commander says that his honours are as much a tribute to his men as to himself—in my case this was true in a special way. My men had to go on fighting when their comrades in Europe had stopped—and then carry on even further, in what should have been 'peace'. To carry on like that, *after* a war, risking their lives all over again, a long way from home, for obscure causes, was a much harder thing than fighting the war itself.

I am not very good at philosophising—it is not a thing I normally do. Yet, obviously, the policies I believed in must have sprung from a philosophy of life. I was quite sure, in 1945, that it was no good fighting against the new tide of Asian Nationalism; I was sure that the thing to do was to try and make the Nationalists our friends. This was easier for me than for some, because I liked many of them personally, and their countries excited me.

Nevertheless, much as I have come to love the East, it was with a sense of relief that I handed over my responsibilities and came home. I was just on forty-six years old. I was still in the Royal Navy. I had just been promoted from the substantive rank of Captain to Rear-Admiral. And I very badly wanted to get back to sea.

# 9

# The Last Viceroy

In March 1947, I came back to India. Less than a year after leaving the East, which already meant so much to me, I was back again—back in the highest position an Englishman could hold: Viceroy of India.

It should have been the most marvellous moment—and in some ways, indeed, it was. But this was a critical time for India, and for Englishmen who loved India. It was not simply the fact that British rule was going to end that worried us—it was the manner of its ending: the awful doubt whether Indian unity might not disintegrate with it. The job I was about to undertake could not fail to be hard, and might well be thankless too; yet I remember feeling full of optimism.

*India 1947: a sub-continent, containing four hundred million people, speaking twenty-three languages and two hundred dialects; living under direct British rule—and in more than five hundred semi-independent States, dating from antiquity; four hundred million people, divided by diversity of race, and by the existence of three thousand castes differing for occupational, territorial, tribal, racial and religious reasons; two hundred and fifty million of them Hindus, ninety million Muslims, six million Sikhs, and in addition Buddhists and Christians and numberless sects; united by the British Raj, and the desire for freedom.*

It was to be my job, now, to bring the people of India the freedom they desired. I suppose, unconsciously, I had been preparing for this task for the last three years.

I had begun to acquire an up-to-date insight into Indian affairs in

1944, as Supreme Commander South East Asia. Then, in 1945 and 1946, I found myself face to face with the new tide of Asian Nationalism, and I had to work out an attitude towards it.

In Burma, in Singapore and in Malaya I had adopted the policy of trying to make the Nationalists our friends, instead of trying to suppress them. I hoped that people in India would remember this, and that now they would at least give me a chance of attempting the same treatment with Indian Nationalism.

The Second World War had brought the issue of Indian Independence to a head. Throughout the whole of my South East Asia campaign the bulk of my forces were always Indian; without the Indian Army there wouldn't have been a campaign.

By the end of the war two million Indians had joined the Services —and the Indian Services themselves had been totally transformed. It was a mechanised war, at times you might almost have called it a technicians' war. Thousands of Indians had to learn to become technicians.

The Indian Air Force and the Indian Navy developed enormously —both of them very technical services. The Indian Medical Corps was especially valuable to me in Burma. Indian women also played their part as nurses and in the Auxiliary Services. All these things helped to transform traditional attitudes and prepare India for a new, independent rôle in the twentienth century.

*India spoke with divided voices. There were Indians who waged war on the side of Britain; there were many who opposed the war. The Indian National Congress—the Congress Party—was born in 1885. All through the twentieth century the Congress Party had been the most powerful agent of the Independence movement. By 1939 it was not only the largest political party in India but its opposition to British rule had become absolute*

*Under the inspiration of Mahatma Gandhi direct action by Congress had generally been non-violent—but not always. New leaders had emerged, most prominent among them Jawaharlal Nehru. Nehru came from a wealthy and talented family; he was educated at Harrow and Cambridge. But he was a man of the Left, the idol of the younger members of the Congress Party. He preached Non-co-operation with the British.*

*In 1939 this meant opposition to the war, and non-participation in government. For the unity of India this was fatal. The Congress*

*Party had always been an all-Indian Party. It was predominantly
Hindu, because Hinduism was the religion of the largest number of
Indians. But a quarter of India's population belonged to the Muslim
religion.*

*Congress had always claimed to speak for Muslim India too. But
in 1940 Congress opposition to the war was matched by Muslim
Opposition to Congress. Mohammed Ali Jinnah, once a believer
in Muslim co-operation with Congress, was now denouncing Hindu
domination and 'Hinduisation'. The Muslim League—founded in
1906—had detached itself from Congress. Jinnah had become its
leader, and now, in 1940, he came out with the open demand for a
separate Muslim state—Pakistan.*

*With Congress weakened by its opposition to the war, the power
of the Muslim League grew. Indian Nationalism perceived its opportunity in 1942 when British Imperialism in the Far East was being
rocked by the onslaught of Japan. Gandhi proclaimed his 'Quit
India' policy—open rebellion, which might well coincide with a
Japanese advance. There were riots and disturbances, which cost
about a thousand lives. The Government acted promptly. Gandhi,
Nehru and the Congress Leaders were arrested, along with 60,000
of their followers.*

This was the situation which Field-Marshal Lord Wavell inherited
when he became Viceroy in October, 1943—the month in which I
arrived in Delhi as Supreme Allied Commander, South East Asia.

In 1945 the Congress Leaders were released, but the elections of
1945 revealed a new situation. Congress remained India's largest
and most powerful party—but it no longer spoke for the Muslims.
These now gave their overwhelming support to the Muslim League
and Mr. Jinnah.

And so the concept of Pakistan steadily became more real—but
that, inevitably, meant Partition. Partition was anathema to Congress, dreaded by many non-Congress Indians, and unacceptable to
the British, for we boasted that we had given India her first real
unity. But there could be no Pakistan without Partition.

*In 1946 Britain's new Labour Government made yet another attempt
to preserve Indian unity. A Cabinet Mission was sent out, headed by
Lord Pethwick Lawrence, who was supported by Sir Stafford Cripps
and Mr. A. V. Alexander. Negotiations dragged on in sweltering heat*

*for three months. They appeared to have achieved some success, but agreement broke down in the atmosphere of mounting distrust between the Congress Party and the Muslim League.*

*With the failure of the Cabinet Mission plan, India faced civil war. The British Prime Minister, Mr. Attlee, concluded that only a completely fresh approach could avert disaster. Lord Wavell's sincerity and goodwill were not enough. There would have to be, said Attlee, 'a change of bowling'. He invited Mountbatten to be Viceroy.*

When Mr. Attlee asked me to take on this job he rather took my breath away. This was not something that could be settled straight off, and in fact we had several meetings about it.

I asked to see the King; as King-Emperor he kept very close touch with Indian affairs. I pointed out to him that the chances of complete failure were very great indeed, and it would be bad for him to have a member of his family fail. He replied :

'But think how good it will be for the monarchy if you succeed!'

And he then asked me formally to accept the appointment.

*This acceptance marked the beginning of the most intensive period of activity of Mountbatten's whole life—a life always conducted at a high pitch of intensity. He now had to turn himself into an expert on the whole complex Indian political scene—and he had just a month to do it in. He wasted no time; work, constant and urgent, began at once. Meeting people became a vital element—and that began in London.*

I knew that the possibilities of failure which I had mentioned to the King were terribly real. There had been appalling riots in Calcutta back in August 1946, with 5,000 dead and 15,000 injured. This was followed by other horrible massacres in other places.

Now, in March 1947, as I was preparing to set out, there was virtual civil war in the Punjab. Faced with such facts as these, the sense of urgency took hold of me at once and never left me.

*Mountbatten arrived in Delhi on March 22nd. The occasion was marked by ceremonial dating back through nearly one hundred years of Viceregal pomp.*

*At the top of the long flight of steps leading up to the Viceroy's house the Viceroy-to-be was greeted by the Viceroy in office. The formalities of the occasion denoted that for one more day Lord Wavell, as the personification of the King-Emperor, held the status of a monarch in that house.*

*When Wavell departed it was with the sadness of leaving a great task unfinished, but with the knowledge of having once again done his utmost in the service of his country.*

*On March 24th Mountbatten was sworn in. Now all India's hopes and all her complexities lay in his keeping.*

It was a very splendid ceremony, very impressive—but very brief; someone who timed it said it was all over in fifteen minutes. It was sobering to think of the responsibility I was assuming in that short space of time. I sat on the throne, with Edwina beside me, and thought that now I had to guide the destinies of one-fifth of humanity.

What I had to do in 1947 was to wind up the British Raj and to bring India into independence. I played my part in all the ceremonies, knowing that I would be the last Viceroy to do so—the last of a line of British rulers going back to Clive and Warren Hastings.

I wondered how to prevent the break with the past, when it came, from being absolute. Would anything survive of the historic links between Britain and India?—links that went back to the East India Company?—then to Imperial India, when my great-grandmother, Queen Victoria, became Queen-Empress?—links that had been forged even stronger on the battlefields of two world wars—and on many other battlefields besides? Would all this be swept away? The thought appalled me.

But one thing was sure, if any of this *was* to survive it could only be by the restoration of goodwill—the goodwill of all Indians.

And so I became Viceroy, and work started in earnest. I opened my first despatch box, and took out a paper which had been sent to me for an immediate decision. It was a death sentence for murder, requiring my confirmation. I read through the case carefully—there was no doubt about it, I'm afraid—and so I sadly signed the sentence. The realities had quickly overtaken me.

The British Government had agreed to give me a time limit: Indian Independence was to be achieved by June 1948—that was only fifteen months off. Fifteen months, then, seemed a very short time for the transfer of imperial power. And the question, the enormous question to which I had to find an answer as rapidly as possible, was: *to whom* could we transfer our power?

Our one desire was to preserve a united India. Could we do it? And if so who would be its rulers? If the leaders of the Indian communities really could not resolve their differences then there would have to be Partition—a hated thought. And how was *that* to be carried out? The realities really did have a bleak look in March 1947.

*Characteristically, Mountbatten had taken certain precautions. He had stipulated to Mr. Attlee that he should have authority to act independently of the India Office in London, where traditionally all the affairs of a sub-continent had been decided.*

Mr. Attlee was distinctly taken aback: 'You are asking for plenipotentiary powers. No one has been given those in this century!'

There was a long silence and then he said: 'All right, you have them.'

It shows his imagination and largeness of mind that he was prepared to accept this too. But it was absolutely essential. I had to be able to make up my mind on the spot; and—even more important—it was essential that the Indian leaders should feel that at last their affairs were being decided here in India, not in London. It made all the difference.

*In April 1947 British administration in India was under tremendous and increasing strain. There had been no recruitment for the Indian Civil Service since 1939, with the result that that body was both understaffed and exhausted. With the growth of the likelihood of Pakistan, Indian officials found themselves faced with divided loyalties. The same dilemma applied to the Police, and, to a lesser extent, the Armed Services. Meanwhile, British troops were rapidly leaving India. The mere day-to-day conduct of government was becoming increasingly difficult, and the threat of civil war was very real.*

*As in South East Asia in October 1943 Mountbatten's rôle was to grip a crumbling situation, to give the ship of state in India the sense of being steered again. This he performed. His presence was felt from the moment he arrived. Every waking minute of every day—and Mountbatten could manage with very little sleep—the Viceroy was tirelessly at work.*

*As in South East Asia, the immediate task was to establish contact with people—the key figures of Indian politics—and through them with the people of India.*

Once again I could see that everything was going to depend upon personal relationships. If I could build up an atmosphere of trust and understanding with the key figures I might succeed. If I could not do that I knew I hadn't got a hope. And, of course, all this had to be done in such a way that none of them could think that he others were being privileged or getting away with backstairs methods.

Far and away the most outstanding man in India—a world figure and (although a Hindu) revered by hundreds of millions of his fellow-countrymen, Muslims and Hindus alike—was Mahatma Gandhi, known affectionately and reverently to them as Gandhiji.

At my first meeting with Gandhi we didn't talk any business at all. We just chatted. I told him how the Prince of Wales and I had tried to meet him when we were here in 1921, and how we were not allowed to—he was really interested in that. Then I got him to tell me about his early life, his political beginnings in South Africa, and how he built up the non-violent Independence movement. We spent two hours talking in this way, and the Press could hardly believe that we had not been deciding the fate of India. Well, perhaps we had—indirectly.

Gandhi's purely political power was on the wane. He was a modern-day saint, really, and saints cannot thrive for ever in a political atmosphere. It was characteristic of Gandhi that at our very next meeting, the next day, he proposed as a solution to India's problems that I should ask Jinnah to form an administration. He really meant it, even though he must have realised that this would give the Muslims virtual control—anything rather than see India divided, or have a civil war.

Of course, it was quite impractical. I told him he must first get the support of the Congress Party, and this he naturally failed to get. But that was Gandhi! His personal popularity and influence were enormous. We might not be able always to take Gandhi along with us—but we would get nowhere if he came out against us.

When he started calling Edwina and me his 'dear friends' I began to have the feeling that we were half-way home.

Pandit Nehru was already a friend, of course. My first meeting with him had been almost a year before, when he visited Singapore whilst I was still Supreme Commander South East Asia. He knew now that he would get a fair deal from me. With Nehru the trust that I was trying to build up with the leaders was already there—and more than trust: friendship.

This was not only between him and me, but it existed with Edwina and my daughters Pamela and Patricia too. He believed that our whole family loved India, and would try to do what was right for India.

Nehru was a great statesman. He had a brilliant mind—he was quite amazingly quick to grasp a point, and very sensitive to situations. I had an early indication of his acuteness. Not long after I arrived he said to me:

'Have you, by some miracle, been given plenipotentiary powers?'

'Why do you ask?'

'Because you behave quite differently from any other Viceroy. One has the feeling that what you say goes.'

'Well, what if I have?'

'In that case you will succeed,' said Nehru.

Sardar Vallabhbhai Patel was another tremendously important figure. Inside the Congress Party he was just about as eminent as Nehru. Patel concentrated on internal politics. He was the man who dispensed patronage in the Party—as Home Minister, that meant that he controlled the jobs.

Patel could be really tough. Perhaps he did not have Nehru's mass-appeal, but he could wield great influence. It was he who had done most to end the mutiny in the Indian Navy in February 1946—a very ugly moment.

Patel could be a great force for moderation—if he so decided; but if he did not he could be most dangerous. At one of our very early meetings Sardar Patel and I had a stand-up row. He was used to getting his own way, and on this occasion I didn't like his manner of going about it.

He was astonished—not to say shocked—to find that he had to give way to me; but he did. From then onwards our relationship improved, until in the end we also became firm friends. Here again the alternative would have been disastrous: we could never have hoped to make any headway against Patel's opposition.

In this case I owe a lot to the late V. P. Menon, who subsequently wrote the history of these events. He was a member of my staff, but he was also very close to Sardar Patel, and he did a great deal to smooth the way, and help us to understand each other.

The man whom I had real difficulty in getting through to was Mr. Jinnah, the Quaid y-Azam (the Great Leader) as his followers called him. If it could be said that any single man held the future of India in the palm of his hand in 1947 that man was Mohammed Ali Jinnah.

To all intents and purposes Jinnah *was* the Muslim League and if the dream of Pakistan—the separate Muslim state—ever did come true it would be Jinnah who brought it to life and fashioned it.

I tried the same technique with him that I had used with Gandhi —no business at the first meeting, just talk, to get to know each other. He was very surprised by this, but after a while he softened up a bit, and we got on well enough. But after that interview I said:

'My God, he was cold!'

*It was not very long after his arrival in India that Mountbatten began to feel that his time limit—Independence by June 1948—so far from being too short, was much too remote. Each succeeding event reinforced his sense of desperate urgency. In mid-April he called a conference of Governors of the Indian Provinces. Each one of them had a gloomy tale to tell. A new trouble centre came into the news: the North-West Frontier Province.*

*On April 28th the Mountbattens flew to Peshawar. No sooner had they arrived than they were told that a huge crowd of Muslims, estimated at 70,000, was about to march on Government House. Mountbatten's Press Officer, Alan Campbell-Johnson, describes what happened:*

*'Mountbatten thereupon drove off to the demonstration, Lady Mountbatten, with great courage, insisting on going with him. The crowd confronting us was certainly formidable. We climbed up the railway embankment close to the historic Fort Bala Hissar, and looked down upon a vast concourse gathered in Cunningham Park and stretching away into distant fields. There was much gesticulation and the waving of innumerable but illegal green flags with the*

*white crescent of Pakistan, accompanied by the steady chant of
"Pakistan Zindabad!"*

'Within a few moments of our arrival, however, the brooding
tension lifted. The slogan changed: "Mountbatten Zindabad!" could
be heard and cheers were raised. Sullen faces smiled. For nearly
half an hour Mountbatten, in his khaki bush shirt, and Lady Mountbatten, also in a bush shirt, stood waving to the crowd, which had a
surprisingly large number of women and children in its midst. Any
sort of speech was out of the question. But the impact of their
friendly, confident personalities on that fanatical assembly had to
be seen to be believed.*

'As we swarmed down the embankment and drove back to a well-
earned lunch, the relief of the Governor and local officials could not
be concealed. They told us that it would have been quite beyond
the resources of the local police and military to have deflected the
crowd peaceably if they had made up their collective mind to invade Government House. As it was, after seeing the Mountbattens
they struck camp and returned to their homes.'[1]*

*Under his cheerful and reassuring manner Mountbatten now
came to a frightening conclusion. Now he had had time to sense
and appreciate India's mood: the sullen intransigence which, day
by day, made it more and more impossible for Hindus and Muslims
to live together. He realised that what had seemed urgent before was
now twice as urgent—that even the cherished goal of a united India
in the future might have to give way to present harsh realities.*

This was a realisation that had been growing on me almost from
the moment I came out here. I could sense a real tragedy just round
the corner if we didn't act very fast—civil war in its worst form.
Beside that, Partition, much as so many of us hated it, seemed a
much lesser evil. I could see no alternative.

So there it was: our dream of handing on a united India had
vanished. Now there would have to be two Indias—and they would
have to come into being long before June 1948.

*It was Jinnah who, more than any other man had made the idea of
Partition real—and yet when it came to practical matters made the
bargaining so difficult that he almost defeated his own ends. The*

[1] Alan Campbell-Johnson: *Mission With Mountbatten*; Robert Hale, 1951.

*argument over the two key provinces, Bengal and the Punjab,*
*seemed to be insurmountable.*

He argued there must be Partition, otherwise as a minority community the Muslims would be swamped in Hindu India.

'Right,' I said. 'Then, by the same argument, the two provinces
you want in Pakistan, with large non-Muslim minorities, will also
have to be partitioned.'

'Oh, no, you can't do that. Punjabi unity and Bengali unity are
much more important than Hindu-Muslim differences!'

'In that case,' I said, 'surely *Indian* unity is much more important
than Hindu-Muslim differences?'

'Oh, no,' said Jinnah, 'we must have Pakistan.'

And so it went on, a circular argument—round and round the
mulberry bush. I never met anybody who could say 'No' so per-
sistently and so effectively.

*Perversity was not all on one side. At one stage Gandhi—the man*
*of peace—even urged that Indian unity should be maintained by*
*force!*

*Yet a plan had to be produced, and a plan was produced in just*
*six weeks—six weeks of pure Mountbatten. On May 3rd it was*
*submitted to the British Government.*

I was up in Simla, taking a short rest—though in fact the most
important single piece of business of all happened there. Nehru was
staying with me when the British Government's amended version of
our plan arrived.

I decided to back a hunch: since Nehru was there with me, I
would show it straight away to him in confidence. Of course, I could
never have thought of such a thing if we hadn't already been such
good friends. This was something I could not possibly have done
except on the basis of complete mutual trust.

Nehru turned the new draft down flat. He said it would lead to
the balkanisation of India, and he would have nothing to do with
it. And he doubted if any party would! If I had not shown it to
him, and he and the other leaders had been forced to say that in
public, what fools we should all have looked! As it was, there
was still a chance. V. P. Menon was with me in Simla, and he came

to the rescue again. We all of us worked at full pressure to find a new formula.

*By indefatigable industry and inexhaustible tact, Mountbatten won the agreement of the Indian leaders to a new plan—the Plan. On June 3rd, at a historic and dramatic meeting, this agreement was put to the test. Right up to the last moment there remained the chance that another clash of personality might wreck everything. But Mountbatten's grip did not falter; he firmly steered the Indian leaders towards acceptance of the Plan—and with it acceptance of the responsibilities of power.*

*On the same day Mr. Attlee announced the Plan in the House of Commons.*

Our plan amounted to this: there were to be two Independent Dominions, remaining within the Commonwealth—thank goodness!—India, predominantly Hindu, in the middle, and—because the Muslims were concentrated into widely separated areas—there would be a divided Pakistan, West and East. Jinnah wanted a corridor between the two parts, but we talked him out of that!

The princely states—over 500 of them all told—would in theory now become independent, but I urged them to accede to one or other of the two new Dominions.

All governmental assets, including the Armed Forces, the Civil Service and the Police, would be divided between them. In disputed areas a Boundary Commission would draw the actual frontiers—it was predictable that there would be areas which would be bitterly disputed, and there was bound to be trouble.

But we had to have a plan, and act on it; the only alternative was chaos.

*On June 4th Mountbatten held a memorable Press Conference in Delhi to expound his solution for India. Alan Campbell-Johnson wrote:*

'Viceroy's House, New Delhi, Wednesday, 4th June 1947.

'This morning, to an audience of some three hundred representatives of the Indian and World Press in the Legislative Assembly, Mountbatten has given the most brilliant performance I have ever witnessed at a major Press Conference. He began without note or loss of word, expounding for some three quarters of an hour a

*political plan of the utmost complexity both in its detail and im-*
*plication. It was a speech which must have cleared many lurking*
*doubts among that audience of professional sceptics, about the*
*plan's substance and purpose. . . . During the Conference he gave*
*the first informal indications that 15th August would be the likely*
*date for the actual transfer of power to the two new Dominions.'[1]*

The August deadline was really dictated to me by my whole experience since I arrived in India, and above all by the virtual breakdown
of normal government. The Viceroy's Executive Council contained
nine members who always voted on the Congress side, and five
Muslim League members. With Partition now in sight, they pulled
in completely opposite directions, and it was no use bringing disputed points to the vote, because the Congress always won, by nine
to five. So the Executive Council in effect broke down.

I tried the expedient of setting up two 'Shadow Cabinets', one for
each future Dominion, but even this eventually broke down.

Direct Rule I considered impossible; the British administration
was no longer capable of carrying it out, and in any case it was a
thoroughly bad solution. The Indian leaders had opted for Partition : they must be the ones to carry it out, and not the British.

*There remained one section of the Indian popultion to be per-*
*suaded to accept the Mountbatten plan: the princes—maharajahs,*
*rajahs, nawabs, khans and petty rulers over more than 500 king-*
*doms, principalities and dependencies.*

*Some of these princes were important potentates, with their own*
*armies of varying size and efficiency. In both world wars contin-*
*gents from the States had served beside the British and Indian armies.*
*sharing their defeats and victories. The lands from which they came*
*sometimes covered large areas; other States were no larger than a*
*fort, a town or a parish.*

*The degrees of independent rule which the princes enjoyed under*
*the British Raj were various, but each of them was indeed a prince,*
*with a stake in India handed down through centuries.*

The princes of India were in a pathetic situation. They belonged to the
past—a remote past—and most of them had no idea of how to conduct themselves towards the people who were going to be India's new

[1] *Mission With Mountbatten.*

rulers. They were disunited, proud, frightened, some of them angry, and all of them uncertain. At my first official reception, one of them was described as 'wandering around like a letter without a stamp'.

As the King-Emperor's personal representative, I had a special duty towards them all, for they were all in treaty relations with His Imperial Majesty. Fortunately, I knew a number of them well— some of them had been friends since 1921, when they had been A.D.C.s with me to the Prince of Wales.

I saw the principal rulers separately, then I summoned a full-scale meeting of the Chamber of Princes. I told them that I wanted to make the best bargain that I could for them, but that after the 15th August I wouldn't be in a position to mediate for them any more, so they must make up their minds now.

I warned them solemnly against any thought of resorting to arms. I told them they could not run away from the new Dominion governments which were going to be their neighbours. They would have to live with them.

*With Independence now in sight, the pace of work for all concerned, already exhausting, became even swifter. The date which Mountbatten had mentioned so seemingly casually, August 15th 1947, was now a target. On a special calendar in Mountbatten's office each successive day was crossed off, bringing India nearer to transfer of power.*

*August 13th 1947 arrived: only two days remained before India achieved her Independence. But by the nature of the plan accepted, Independence would mean two things, and the focus of attention would be in two places. For this was going to mean an independent India and an independent Pakistan. And so, on August 13th, the Viceroy was not in Delhi, but in Karachi.*

It was a great day for the Muslim League, and a great day for Mr. Jinnah, whose dreams had now come true. Not only had he obtained Pakistan, but now he was to be installed as her first Governor-General.

This was not to everybody's liking. It was disconcerting, to say the least, to be aware all through the ceremonies in Karachi that there was a Sikh plot to throw a bomb at Jinnah as he drove back in State from the swearing-in.

In fact, I tried to persuade him from going through with the

State drive altogether—but he insisted on doing it. So I said I would accompany him. He then tried very hard to dissuade me, and it was my turn to insist. Anyway, there we both were, trying to look happy as the vast crowds cheered us and cried out 'Zindabad!'— knowing all the time that somewhere among them there was at least one man with a bomb.

For some reason he did not throw it, so we got back to Government House safely, and Jinnah, in a moment of rare emotion, laid his hand on my knee and said:

'Thank God I've brought you back alive!'

I thought this was a bit much, so I replied:

'Thank God I've brought *you* back alive!'

*Delhi August 14th 1947. Pandit Nehru addressed the Indian Constituent Assembly.*

'*Long years ago we made a tryst with Destiny, and now the time comes when we shall redeem our pledge. . . . At the stroke of the midnight hour, when the world sleeps, India will awake to life and freedom. A moment comes, which comes but rarely in history, when we step out from the old to the new, when an age ends, and when the soul of a nation, long suppressed, finds utterance. . . .*'

Mission accomplished. It was not exactly the mission I had come out to perform; I had come out to see if there was a last chance of handing over a united India. It turned out that there wasn't even a remote chance. We had had to accept that—but it was a sad reflection. So I could not look on this day's achievement with completely undiluted pleasure.

And then, too, there was the sense of the end of an epoch: two hundred years of British rule in India, with all the tremendous memories that that implied. But all through this whole business I had tried to think of the future more than the past.

I had been Viceroy for less than five months, but it seemed like five years—or perhaps like five minutes. On the day that I was installed I said to Nehru:

'I want you to regard me not as the last Viceroy winding up the British Raj but as the first to lead the way to a new India.'

So now, now that it had all happened, that was the way I mostly felt about it: it was not an end, but a beginning—an unbelievably happy beginning.

# 10

# Fresh Fields

August 15th 1947 was one of the great days in world history. One-fifth of the population of the world gained its independence on that day.

It was a day of enormous rejoicing—the fulfilment of millions of dreams. It was a day of unbelievable goodwill. All the animosities between Indians and British which had grown up over decades seemed to melt away. It was wonderful to be carried along on the new tide of friendship.

*In Delhi Mountbatten prepared for the opening of India's greatest day: August 15th 1947, the day of Independence. As midnight on the 14th approached, he was at his desk, signing the last telegrams from a Viceroy to a Secretary of State for India.*

*When the hour struck he cleared his desk to await the Indian leaders, Pandit Nehru and Rajendra Prasad, President of the Constituent Assembly. Prasad told Mountbatten that the wish of the Assembly was that he should be India's first Governor-General. Mountbatten replied:*

*'I am proud of the honour, and I will do my best to carry out your advice in a constitutional manner.'*

*At 8.30 a.m., amid viceregal pageantry, Mountbatten was sworn in as the first Constitutional Head of the new India.*

There was nothing sudden or hasty about my decision to accept this extraordinary honour. As a matter of fact, I had had the greatest trepidations about it, and I had taken all the advice I could get. Edwina, for one, was against it.

One idea, which both sides appeared to favour, had been that I should become the Governor-General of the two new Dominions—Pakistan and India—simultaneously. I did not like this much, but it would clearly have strengthened the co-operation between them which was so essential.

And then we all assumed that Nehru and Jinnah would be the respective Prime Ministers, with effective power. All that fell to the ground when Mr. Jinnah suddenly announced that he would *not* be the first Prime Minister of Pakistan, but the Governor-General.

Supporters of Pakistan suggested later that when Jinnah made this announcement I should have refused to stay on as Governor-General of India. But almost in the same breath as telling me that he would become the Governor-General of Pakistan, Mr. Jinnah said that he particularly hoped that I would accept the Governor-Generalship of India. So what finally decided me to accept the invitation to become Governor-General of India after Partition was the clearly stated general view that I could best help the Indian sub-continent as a whole by so doing.

*Mountbatten's first day in office as Governor-General was tumultuous with excitement. His first act was to address the Constituent Assembly; then a drive back to Government House amid delirious crowds shouting 'Mountbatten Ki Jai!'*

*After that the Mountbatten family spent the afternoon amid 5,000 school children, celebrating the day with India's traditional amusements—snake-charmers, dancing bears and so forth.*

*This informality was in keeping with many occasions and many acts which had already made Mountbatten himself, Lady Mountbatten and their younger daughter, Lady Pamela, known as friends to large numbers of Indians. These moments counted for more than the ceremonial unfurling of India's flag, which followed, or the great state banquet that evening.*

*August 15th, in Delhi and all over India, was a day of rejoicing. But the rejoicing was not unmixed, for August 15th was not only Independence Day—it was also the day of Partition.*

*The sun had not long risen on August 15th 1947 when the meaning of Partition was made clear. To divide a sub-continent, not along natural or historic frontiers, but according to religion; to create, out of well-mixed populations, a Muslim Pakistan, and a predominantly Hindu India, was a task which appalled, by its sheer difficulty, and by the suffering which it must cause.*

*In Calcutta, traditional storm centre of Indian politics, where violence was always expected, one man stood in the path of fanaticism and massacre: Mahatma Gandhi. Gandhi began a fast which he threatened to continue till death if the communities did not end their strife. The miracle worked. Gandhi's presence in Bengal, said Mountbatten, was worth four divisions of soldiers.*

*In the Punjab the story was sadly different. There, despite all the efforts of the 55,000-strong Punjab Boundary force, and men of goodwill of all races, massacres of Hindus by Muslims, Muslims by Hindus, generally headed by the warrior caste of Sikhs, were producing horrible loss of life and dreadful destruction.*

*They also produced a new problem, born of fear: the refugees— Muslims trying to escape to Pakistan, Hindus and Sikhs escaping to India, on foot, by any vehicle, crowding the trains—all of them natural objects of attack and plunder. By August 27th Mountbatten calculated that some ten million people were on the move.*

*By the beginning of September the crisis in the Punjab had become accute. Delhi, India's capital, all too close to the region of disturbance, was almost in a state of siege. Mountbatten was in Simla; he received a telephone call urging him to return to Delhi. Prompted by Mountbatten, the Indian Government, headed by Pandit Nehru and Sardar Vallabhbhai Patel, set up an Emergency Committee. It was unanimously decided to invite Mountbatten to be its Chairman.*

Once again, I had my doubts. I was being asked, within three weeks of the transfer of power, to assume more direct power as Constitutional Governor-General than any Viceroy had ever wielded. I could see the dangers in this—the danger of my motives being misinterpreted if I accepted, and the even more serious danger that the new Indian Government might undermine its own authority by delegating in this way. But Nehru and Patel were sure they wanted me, and in the tragic atmosphere of the times I simply could not say 'No'.

Delhi itself, the seat of government, was right next to the trouble-torn Punjab and in imminent danger. The very existence of the new Dominion appeared to be at stake. It was a terrible situation. It would have seemed sheer callousness not to do all I could. So I plunged in with my staff, and my wife, and we set to work to tackle what was practically a military operation—with this conviction all the way, that the measure of our success would be how quickly we could phase our Emergency Committee out of existence and hand back to the constitutional authorities.

*Once more, in a time of danger and difficulty, Mountbatten found at his side an incalculable support. While he struggled to avert further perils, Lady Mountbatten bent her astonishing energies to mending the damage already done—as far as that was possible. It was during this period, when she devoted herself to untiring work for the refugees from Partition, that Lady Mountbatten earned the undying love of the people of India.*

*Slowly, as the Emergency Committee gripped its task under Mountbatten's guidance, the communal crisis was brought under control—leaving an inevitable legacy of hate and destruction behind.*

*Other crises were already in full development. The princes of India —once the supreme rulers of their States—had been urged by Mountbatten to accept a new future by acceding either to Pakistan or to India. All but three out of over five hundred had taken his advice. This meant that they would no longer be rulers; now they asked themselves what they would be?*

All the Indian princes, whose whole way of life—their power, their status, their fortunes, their traditions—were at stake, had had to make difficult decisions. Most of them had made their adjustments. But it was predictable that there was going to be a tragedy in Kashmir.

Kashmir was a predominantly Muslim State with a Hindu ruler, who simply could not make up his mind how to act. He did not want to subject himself to Muslim Pakistan, but he was afraid of losing his ruling powers in democratic India. So, despite my repeated urging, he let things slide.

At first the Indian Government did not particularly mind which dominion Kashmir acceded to. But then things hotted up. On October 24th Muslim tribesmen from Pakistan entered Kashmir and marched on Srinagar, the capital. Three days later Indian troops were flown in.

We had to act fast, because winter was now coming on. But I had argued strongly that Kashmir must first accede, since otherwise this action by India would be illegal. The Maharajah, in a panic, agreed just in time. But from the moment Indian troops arrived, tempers in Pakistan and in India became steadily worse. There seemed to be no meeting of minds at any point on Kashmir; normally reasonable men ceased to be reasonable on this issue.

The result was a running sore—a permanent disastrous quarrel between India and Pakistan. This was terribly disappointing to me, as I felt particularly responsible for all matters affecting the princes. Yet I don't easily see what more I could have done.

*Slowly the new Dominions settled down. The cost of Partition was high—but has been greatly exaggerated. H. V. Hodson, the most recent and comprehensive historian of the transfer of power, wrote:*

*'It is impossible to be sure, even within a wide margin, how many people were killed in the communal war of August to November 1947. In the earlier stages there was no effective civil authority to report the widespread deaths; with the vast refugee movement, local records were destroyed or rendered useless. The figure of a million was popularly bandied about. The truth was probably around 200,000 men, women and children, a terrible enough total.'[1]*

*Although 200,000 is a relatively small number, as against India's population of 400,000,000 (one in two thousand), this killing left a legacy of bitterness, to which Kashmir and other disputes between India and Pakistan added further fuel.*

*On November 20th 1947, public duties, for the Mountbattens, became intervoven with private affairs in the most pleasant manner. Their nephew, Philip Mountbatten, now created Duke of Edinburgh, was married on that day to Princess Elizabeth, the heir to the British throne.*

This was a great moment in the history of our family—yet such was the state of affairs in India in November 1947 that I had grave doubts whether I ought to go back to London for the wedding or not. Of course, I wanted to very badly—and the Indian Government settled the matter for me by saying that if I didn't that would make

---

[1] H. V. Hodson in his forthcoming book, *The Great Divide*. Sir Penderel Moon, who in 1947 was an official in the Punjab with first-hand experience of the tragedy, comes to the same conclusion in his book *Divide and Quit* (Chatto & Windus, 1964).

the atmosphere of crisis in India appear even worse. So home we went.

Prince Philip, of course, was more like a son than a nephew to Edwina and to me. I was pleased to see how well he was doing in the Navy. I firmly believe that a naval training is the best possible training for royal duties, which he would now have to perform.

Princess Elizabeth herself was very close to our family. In age she comes just in between our two daughters, and it was less than a year since she had been a bridesmaid at Patricia's wedding.

When this great occasion was over, to our delight, the Princess and Philip accepted our invitation to spend their honeymoon at our house, Broadlands, where Edwina and I had so happily spent part of ours.

For most people in Britain the royal wedding provided a marvellous, cheering splash of colour in the midst of austerity. For me it was a splendid interlude in the midst of the hardest work I have ever done in my life. And then it was back to India, where the crisis atmosphere was still intense.

*Contrary to the hopes of idealists, the sub-continent of India, at the opening of the new year, remained bitterly divided. Pakistan and the new India glowered at each other in hostility; communal tension remained high on both sides of the border. In India the Muslims found a new and unexpected champion—Gandhi.*

*Once again Gandhi threatened a fast to the death, to induce the Government of India to deal fairly with Pakistan, and to reduce communal violence. Once again Gandhi's 'miracle' worked; he ended his fast on January 18th, 1948. But only twelve days later the Mahatma was killed by the bullet of a Hindu fanatic in the grounds of Birla House, Delhi.*

I had just returned from Madras that afternoon. First I heard that there had been an attempt on Gandhi's life, and then, very soon afterwards, that he was dead.

To say that I was appalled conveys nothing—I was absolutely numbed and petrified. I went round at once to Birla House. There was a large crowd round the house already, and inside it most of the members of the Government—everyone in tears.

Gandhi looked very peaceful in death, but I dreaded what his death might bring.

As I went into the house where his body was lying, someone in the crowd shouted out:

'It was a Muslim who did it!'

I turned immediately and said:

'You fool, don't you know it was a Hindu?'

Of course, I didn't know—no one knew at that stage; but I did know this: if it was a Muslim, we were lost. There would be civil war without fail. Thank God it wasn't! It turned out to be a Hindu extremist.

What terrified me most now was the thought that these people might strike again—at Nehru, or Sardar Patel. There had been a growing coolness between these two great men. I took this opportunity, then and there, in front of Gandhi's body, of bringing them together again, as I knew he would have wished. They embraced each other in tears. I felt this act was a symbol of Gandhi's power, even after death. You still feel it strongly in India today.

*India, for which he had striven to hard, held one more disappointment for Mountbatten. Hyderabad, largest of the princely states, contained a population of seventeen millions—85 per cent of them Hindu—and lay in the midst of Hindu India. But the Nizam of Hyderabad was a Muslim, influenced by religious extremists. His British Constitutional Adviser, Sir Walter Monckton, tried to persuade him that the future of Hyderabad could only lie with India. But the Nizam could not bring himself to accept this. Indian patience wore thin, and Mountbatten sensed the possibility of another tragedy. Then, at last, to his delight, Monckton told him that Hyderabad was prepared to put forward proposals which, although not what India wanted, might just prove acceptable.*

Shortly before I left India I went to say goodbye to Sardar Patel, Minister in charge of the States. He made a wonderful gesture. He said I could ask him for anything in his power to give me. So I pulled out the latest Hyderabad proposals, and I asked him to initial them. He was very shaken by this, but he stuck to his promise.

So here was settlement at last—the Nizam's own proposals agreed to by India. Walter Monckton was absolutely astounded and delighted. But—would you believe it? When he took them back to Hyderabad the Muslim extremists now rejected them—their own proposals!

Walter Monckton and I left India that month with heavy hearts; we had done all we could, more than either of us could have hoped to do, but the Hyderabad extremists had defeated us. When India, later, after I had left, invaded Hyderabad, I found there were people who blamed me for this! I thought that most unfair, after all that I had done to avoid such an outcome.

*Fifteen months of the most strenuous and intense activity of even Mountbatten's strenuous career now drew to an end. On June 21st 1948 he handed over the office of Governor-General to C. Rajago-palachari, now, with the death of Ghandi, the most venerable of India's statesmen, a fitting figure to be the first Indian Governor-General of free India.*

*In those last days the people of India made their feelings towards Mountbatten and towards his family unmistakably clear. Everywhere the Mountbattens went they received tremendous ovations. In the words of an Indian politician at the time of Independence:*

*'At last, after two hundred years, the British have conquered India.'*

I loved India, and I had always done my best to serve the people of the whole sub-continent. It had been a great disappointment to find, in 1947, that there was no way of keeping it united. Partition was a blow to every lover of India.

On the other hand, I was glad to have played a part in bringing about Independence, and proud of the affection which the people of the new India showed for me and my family. I was also very relieved and happy that, even with Partition, both the new Dominions had decided to remain in the Commonwealth. This was very important to me, and—although they did not seem to realise it—a reason why I had tried my best to serve the interests of Pakistanis too.

I had to accept misunderstanding, in India and at home. One could not take part in such vast events as these without making some enemies. But I could look into my own conscience without dismay. From first to last I had done my utmost to serve the true interests of Britain and India—the whole of India.

*Perhaps the greatest tribute to Mountbatten's work was paid by Pandit Nehru at the farewell banquet given to the Mountbattens just before they left India in June 1948. Nehru said:*

'You came here, sir, with a high reputation, but many a reputation has foundered in India. You lived here a during period of great difficulty and crisis, and yet your reputation has not foundered. That is a remarkable feat. Many of us who came into contact with you from day to day in these days of crisis learned much from you. We gathered confidence when sometimes we were rather shaken, and I have no doubt that the many lessons we have learned from you will endure, and will help us in our work in the future.'

Mountbatten returned to England, to be greeted at Northolt by the Duke of Edinburgh and the Prime Minister, Mr. Attlee, whose name would always be linked with his in the telling of his achievement in India.

He now discovered that there was more than one way of regarding what he had done. The Conservative Press, and many members of the Conservative Party, who had begun by congratulating him, now blamed him for the disorder and loss of life which had followed Partition. Old friends now turned against him; he found himself being cut dead by people he knew well; his whole family became the target of spiteful attacks. Most hurtful of all, Winston Churchill, whom he had known all his life, accused him of breaking up the Empire and refused to speak to him.

Mountbatten's outward reaction to all this was to disregard it, saying 'History will be the judge'. Yet these were not good auspices for the reshaping of his life at the age of forty-eight, the new beginning which he was determined to make.

He had extracted a promise from the Prime Minister, Mr. Attlee, that he should be allowed to return—at last—to the Navy. So now, in October 1948, the ex-Supremo, ex-Viceroy, ex-Governor-General, stepped down to the rank of Rear-Admiral, commanding the 1st Cruiser Squadron in Malta.

In the island he was thirteenth in the order of social precedence. In the Fleet he was under the command of officers who had served under him in South East Asia. He thought this was a very good thing.

There is a saying that power corrupts and absolute power corrupts absolutely. Well, very few people had argued with me when I was a Supreme Commander, and when I was Viceroy more and more people kept telling me that I was always right. I had begun to believe it myself. And I recognised that this was a symptom of

The Viceroy and Vicereine at the Investiture in the Durbar Hall of the
Viceroy's house, Delhi, 1947.

*Left:* March, 1947. Lord Mountbatten greeted on his arrival in India by the retiring Viceroy, Lord Wavell.

*Below:* The Governor-General of India and his personal staff in 1948. [*Rear Admiral Howes*]

*Above right:* The Mountbattens with Prime Minister Nehru in the howdah of a state elephant at the Mela, 1948.

*Below right:* The Prime Minister practises Yoga at the swimming pool of Viceroy's House, 1947.

*Above:* Devastation in Amritsar during the Punjab disturbances, March, 1947.

*Below:* Lady Pamela Mountbatten attends one of Mahatma Gandhi's prayer meetings with Rajkumari Amrit Kaur. [*Rear Admiral Howes*]

*Above:* Lady Mountbatten displays her unfailing sympathy and affection for the people of India.

*Below left:* Mountbatten and Mohammed Ali Jinnah during the State Drive in Karachi, which was threatened with a bomb attack, 13 August, 1947. [*Rear Admiral Howes*]

*Below right:* Lord and Lady Mountbatten, with Lady Pamela, attend a Children's Celebration as part of the festivities in Old Delhi, 15 August, 1947.

*Above:* 15 August, 1947. Independence Day. 'Mountbatten Ki Jai!' The Mountbattens greeted by the people of free India.

*Left:* The Governor-General and Lieutenant-General His Highness Maharaja Sri Sadul Singhji Bahadur at Bikaner, January, 1948.

*Above:* The Farewell Banquet, 19 June, 1948. Rajkumari Amrit
Kaur (Minister of Health) between the outgoing and incoming
Governors-General, Mountbatten and C. Rajagopalachari.

*Below:* Return home of Mountbatten, 23 June, 1948. The
Prime Minister, Mr. Attlee, welcomes the retiring Governor-General
and the Indian Finance Minister, Mr. Chetty, at London Airport.

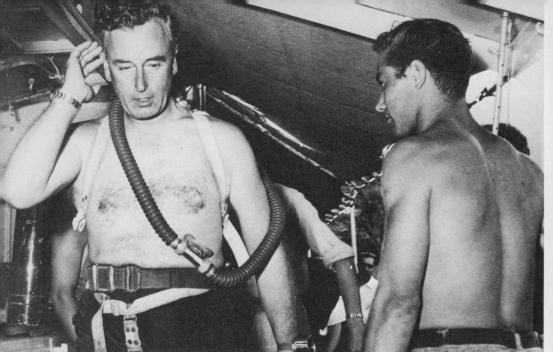

*Above:* Mountbatten, C.-in-C. Allied Forces Mediterranean, tests
his aqualung equipment before doing a dive with Italian Naval divers
at Leghorn, June, 1952.

*Below:* The C.-in-C., Mediterranean Fleet, pays a visit to President Tito
of Yugoslavia (left) at Brioni, June, 1952.

*Above:* The Mountbattens with Prince Charles and Princess Anne on the occasion of the Royal visit to Malta, 1954.

*Below:* Six Admirals, representing the Commander-in-Chief of the six Allied Navies in his Command, pull the Admiral's Galley, taking Mountbatten to H.M.S. *Suprise* when he relinquished his appointment as the first Commander-in-Chief of the Allied Forces, Mediterranean. December, 1954. [*Admiralty*]

A contrast in styles.

*Above:* Rear-Admiral Prince Louis of Battenberg (2nd from left), commanding the 2nd Cruiser Squadron, pays his official call on the U.S. Naval Academy, Annapolis, 1905.

*Below:* Admiral of the Fleet the Earl Mountbatten of Burma, First Sea Lord, pays his official call on the Supreme Commander, Atlantic, at Norfolk, Virginia, 1958.

*Above:* The Chief of the Defence Staff visits a jungle airport in Borneo during the Indonesian 'Confrontation' Operations in February, 1965.

*Below:* A unique ceremony for Lord Mountbatten on completing exactly 49 years' active service. On the day of his retirement as Chief of the Defence Staff, Guards of Honour from the Royal Navy, the Life Guards, the Royal Air Force and the massed bands of the Royal Marines saluted him at the Ministry of Defence on his departure.

*Above:* The Commonwealth
Chiefs of Naval Staffs
Conference organised by the
First Sea Lord in 1957 at the
R.N. College, Greenwich.
(*Left*) The Queen visits the
Conference Exhibition. (*Right*)
The Duke of Edinburgh is
conducted by the First Sea Lord
to the Conference Hall.

*Below:* Mountbatten signs the
Freedom Book in West Berlin,
when calling on the Mayor,
Herr Willy Brandt, after a tour
of inspection of British Forces,
March, 1960.

*Above:* Mountbatten, founder and President of the Royal Naval Film Corporation, at their dinner on board H.M.S. *Victorious* in 1959. On his right, Jack Hawkins; on his left, Kenneth More and the new First Sea Lord, Admiral Sir Charles Lambe.

*Below:* The funeral of Pandit Nehru, 1964. Left to right, Dean Rusk, U.S. Secretary of State, Lady Pamela Hicks, Lord Mountbatten, and the President of India (Dr. Radhakrishnan).

"Soon as he's passed, start leaving at five-minute intervals to avoid suspicion!"

*Above:* The Prison Escapes and Security Enquiry, 1966—one of Mountbatten's post-permanent tasks. [Cartoon by Jak in the London *Evening Standard*].

*Below:* Lord Mountbatten on the Home Farm at Broadlands.

*Above:* Filming in Jaipur, 1967. Production conference with Peter Morley (producer, centre) and John Terraine at the Old City Palace.

*Below right:* Sitting bare-footed in the Jama Masjid, Delhi, India's Mountbatten learns his lines with characteristic concentration.

*Above:* Earl Mountbatten of Burma's coffin borne on a naval gun carriage from St. James's Palace to Westminster Abbey, followed by members of the family, Prince Charles and Prince Philip. [*Keystone*]

*Below:* Prince Charles reads the lesson during the funeral service for Earl Mountbatten. [*Keystone*]

megalomania. I was disturbed by it. I decided the only thing to do was this precise process of stepping down to a position where I could have my backside kicked again!

*The Navy is a jealous Service, proud of its own proficiency, demanding dedication from those who serve it. Was there something faintly disapproving in the Navy's official annotation of Mountbatten during his fifteen months in India? 'Rear-Admiral, etc., lent for temporary duty as Viceroy . . .'? Certainly in 1949 he had to make his mark all over again in the much changed post-war fleet.*

It is not easy to step back into a profession after a gap of several years. I had a lot to pick up. I was given the chance of showing what I could do in the Combined Fleet manœuvres of 1949. Thanks to Sir Arthur Power, who had been one of my subordinates in South East Asia, and who was the umpire for the manœuvres, I was lucky enough to be given command of the Mediterranean Fleet against the Home Fleet.

I am afraid I pulled a fast one. I slipped my warrant telegraphist ashore at Gibraltar, on the pretext that he had a broken arm. Nobody paid much attention to him, and he was able to get right into the other side's headquarters, and discover the movements of their ships. Then he relayed these to me on a portable transmitter. This was regarded in some circles as fearfully unfair. Well, possibly. I may still have had a lot to re-learn about handling ships, but I did know one thing about war: you can't always expect the enemy to play the game by Queensberry Rules.

*It was not all hard work, however, in Malta in 1949. Mountbatten found time to enjoy himself, as he had done as a young officer in the Mediterranean Fleet in the twenties and thirties.*

It was in 1949 that I discovered a new thrill. This almost displaced polo in my affections. It was skin-diving, with an aqualung, a system perfected by Cousteau. Until you have done it you cannot imagine the thrill of deep diving—it opens up an entirely new world to you. It is wonderful to be weightless under the sea, to find that it is no more effort to swim up than it is to swim down, or, if you like, that you can just remain still and, as it were, hover.

You see fish that you have never met in your life! The first time that you see a big octopus, or a shark, or a large stingray, or any other of the creatures that you meet face to face under the sea, it is wildly exciting. Or you can float out in the sea over the edge of a precipice—a wonderful sensation. You look down, and you see the new bottom a long way down below you. If you feel like it, you can plunge right down to it.

I suppose that during this time in the Mediterranean I must have spent many hundreds of happy hours beneath the surface of the sea.

*Once more, Mountbatten was on a ladder, and once more his climb was swift. In 1949 he was promoted to Vice-Admiral. In 1950 the Commander-in-Chief, Mediterranean, wrote in his confidential report:*

*'Ordinary men may climb up with distinction; only extraordinary men can climb down without some loss of distinction. He has achieved the latter.'*

*In that year Mountbatten was appointed Fourth Sea Lord of the Admiralty. The appointment was not glamorous—it was concerned with what the Navy calls 'the nuts and bolts'. But it was a challenge, which Mountbatten accepted, and part of his professional education for still higher posts.*

*In May 1952 he returned to the Mediterranean as Commander-in-Chief. At the end of that year he assumed a double rôle. The North Atlantic Treaty Organisation was setting up its chain of commands, and Mountbatten became Commander-in-Chief, Allied Forces, Mediterranean—in effect a Supreme Allied Commander once again.*

It is hard to recall the tense atmosphere of the period when I held that command at Admiralty House in Malta. Here we were, so soon after the end of the war, faced with the task of setting up a large inter-Allied command all over again.

Every command in NATO had intractable problems, and mine was certainly no exception. I had to co-ordinate the work of six navies—six very different and outwardly ill-assorted navies at that.

The Italians had ended the war as co-belligerents, but before that they had been our enemies. Their fleet had been pretty heavily knocked about by our Mediterranean fleet. In fact, the last appearance of the Italians in Malta was in 1943, on the occasion when Admiral Cunningham sent his famous signal to the Admiralty :

'Be pleased to inform their Lordships that the Italian Fleet now lies at anchor under the guns of the Fortress of Malta.'

Now Italy, and such fleet as we had left her, was an ally. And there was France. Many Frenchmen had not yet forgiven us for the damage we did to their fleet at Oran in 1940. Then there were the Greeks—and the Turks. When I first came to the Mediterranean they were at war with each other. They were only brought together now by sheer necessity. In fact the only strong naval forces in the Mediterranean were the British Fleet and the American Sixth Fleet, which was not under me at all, though some American units were at my disposal.

With this unlikely mixture I had to devise practical plans to meet a possible Russian threat to our sea communications through the Mediterranean. First of all, as in the case of all Allied commands, I had to arrange to get people to work together. I had to iron out possible clashes of national policy and Allied policy. I thought that the best way of doing this would be to divide the command into areas—a French area for which the French C.-in-C. would be responsible, an Italian area under the Italian C.-in-C., and so forth. In that way every national commander would also be a NATO commander, and would in fact wear two hats; and his Number 2 would be with me in Malta the whole time, to act as a liaison officer. This system really worked very well.

What is more, I made sure that it worked with the smallest possible number of people at my headquarters. I never had more than 250 officers and men in my NATO headquarters—some NATO staffs ran into thousands!

As soon as the organisation was established, and the plans were made, the next thing was training, training, training, and devising a *system* of training which would hold good for all contingents, no matter what their language or what their national habits or customs might be.

*Mountbatten's tour of duty in the Mediterranean—the period of his return to the Fleet—ended in December 1954, on a note of splendour. The six admirals representing the Allied Commanders-in-Chief under him formed a crew, and rowed him to his flagship. It was a fitting tribute to his happy and triumphant return to the sea.*

These had been satisfying years. I had always enjoyed serving in the

Mediterranean—it was a wonderful place for combining the pleasures of work and play—except during the war, of course!

The Mediterranean Fleet had always prided itself on being a crack fleet. It was that in my father's day; it had won great renown during the war under Sir Andrew Cunningham; I think I can claim that I left it as efficient as it had ever been.

In six years I had come up from junior Rear-Admiral to Commander-in-Chief, as well as being the C.-in-C. of the NATO Navies in the Mediterranean. I felt that I had really justified myself professionally. But there was still one ambition unfulfilled—one more job that I particularly wanted to do.

## 11

# *Full circle*

---

When I was born, in 1900, my great-grandmother, Queen Victoria, was still on the throne. Since then, I had lived through the reigns of four kings.

In the aftermath of two world wars almost every vestige of Victorian Britain had been swept away. I have seen enormous changes in my lifetime—in fact, I have had quite a lot to do with some of them. But one thing, I am happy to say, has not changed. When I reached the last phase of my career, and fulfilled ambitions which I had hardly dared to admit even to myself, a new Queen was on the throne, and the British monarchy was as strong and well loved as it was when I was born.

*Queen Elizabeth II was summoned suddenly to her throne. With the Duke of Edinburgh she had been on her way to tour Australia and New Zealand. The unexpected news of her father's death reached her in East Africa, and she flew home at once. It was a sad moment for all her family.*

King George VI—my cousin Bertie—was a very old friend. In fact, our friendship went back even further than my friendship with his brother, the Duke of Windsor.

We were both sailors; we had been in the Grand Fleet together during the First World War, and being a few years older than me, he had been at the Battle of Jutland, which I just missed. We saw a lot of each other at Cambridge in 1919. And I knew only too well how distressed he was when he had the responsibilities of kingship thrust upon him.

George VI never had the immediate charm or ease of manner of his brother David. As Duke of York, he struggled to overcome his natural diffidence. Later, as King, he even overcame the stammer which had always made his life difficult.

He became a fine king, very much loved and admired. He had enormous common sense, which I feel sure his Prime Ministers found a great source of strength. I consider that his reign was a great demonstration of the value of constitutional monarchy, under a sensible, high-minded king.

Strangely enough, I felt even closer to our new Queen than to either her father or her uncle, though both were my contemporaries and friends. She and her sister, Princess Margaret, were playmates of our daughters Patricia and Pamela, and so we got to know them well as children. And then, after her marriage, when my nephew Philip was serving in the Mediterranean Fleet, they shared house with us in Malta. I look back on that as one of the happiest times of my life. Young as she was, I was quite certain that she would make a superlative queen.

*In Westminster Abbey ceremonial returned in a blaze of light and colour. The pageant of the Coronation, in June 1953, brightened the austerities of the post-war British scene. In the crowded London streets not even drenching rain could diminish the enthusiasm as the young Queen drove past.*

*And London's crowds had something else to cheer about; it was on Coronation Day itself that Britain learned that Sir Edmund Hillary and the Sherpa Tensing had succeeded in their quest—they were the first men to climb the world's highest mountain, Everest. It seemed a good omen for the opening of the new reign; and more good news soon followed.*

*Further East, at Panmunjom, an armistice was signed which brought peace in Korea. A hard war, dangerous to the peace of the world, ended in July, one month after the Coronation.*

*In the next year there came an interval in another Eastern drama. Ever since the liberation of Indo-China by Mountbatten's forces in 1945 the French had tried to hold their colony by force of arms. In May 1954, at Dien Bien Phu, they suffered disaster at the hands of the Vietnamese Communists under Ho Chi Minh. French imperialism was compelled to accept defeat in Vietnam. Two months later an armistice was signed in Geneva which confirmed the Communist*

*hold on North Vietnam, but established the independence of the
remaining states of Indo-China.*

*At the Geneva Conference the outstanding mediator was the
British Foreign Secretary, Anthony Eden. Less than a year later,
Sir Winston Churchill, whose second Ministry had lasted four years,
resigned. He was succeeded by Eden on April 6th 1955, amid general
acclaimation, with his Geneva laurels still fresh upon him.*

Twelve days after Anthony Eden became Prime Minister my life's
ambition was fulfilled. I became First Sea Lord. Actually, it was
Winston Churchill who was responsible for the appointment, one
of his last acts in high office. That made him the only man to have
appointed a father and son to the post of First Sea Lord. It also
meant that he had got over his hard feelings about what I had done
in India. I was glad about that.

So there I was, on the Board of Admiralty, the First Sea Lord, the
professional head of the Royal Navy. Now, dotted across my life
there had been many occasions when I had found myself more or
less at loggerheads with the Board

As a junior officer I used to enjoy the jokes that circulated about
the Board of Admiralty: we used to call their Lordships 'their Block-
ships'. Pointing to a board drifting by on the tide, someone would
say: 'What's the difference between that board and the Board of
Admiralty?' answer: 'That board is moving.' And so on. And now
it was my turned to be the target of the jokes!

I hope I wasn't a 'Blockship'. In fact, my rôle—like my father's,
and like Admiral Fisher before him, when I was still a small boy—
was to be a reformer. And I reached this conclusion: when we were
the greatest naval power in the world change did not benefit us—
quite the opposite—and so the Admiralty became instinctively conservative, and opposed to change.

That was one thing; secondly, as a committee, it was naturally
slow-moving—most committees are. But whenever anything good
was done there was a tendency for the Navy to credit it to one
particular officer, while if something unpopular happened the
Board as a whole was blamed. This wasn't really fair, because the
final approval for everything had to come from the Board.

There is nothing like being at the receiving end to help you see
the other point of view!

*In 1955, ten years after the Second World War, Britain possessed unchallenged Great Power status. Anthony Eden's diplomatic skill, the patience and persistence which he brought to difficult negotiations, his prestige as Churchill's heir, the apparent permanence of Commonwealth ties—all contributed to uphold the tradition of greatness.*

*Yet significant changes were already at work, closely affecting Mountbatten and the other Chiefs of Staff. Ever present in their minds was the new dilemma: the Cold War—the bitter clash between the Soviet Union and her wartime Western allies. The cost of defence in the nuclear age reached figures which had never been dreamt of in peacetime:*

*£1,000 million in 1951.*

*£1,500 million in 1955.*

*Britain was firmly committed to a nuclear policy—an 'Independent Deterrent'—which swallowed up much of the Defence budget. At the same time she maintained large conventional Services, which now had all too much of a Second World War look about them. Conscription was still in force, but increasingly unpopular. Equipment, in all the Services—much of it dating from 1945—badly needed bringing up to date.*

I was pretty clear in my mind about what I intended to do if I should be fortunate enough to occupy the post of First Sea Lord. The Navy in 1955, I considered, was in a dangerously bloated condition. During the war, shore establishments of every kind had proliferated, and many of these were still being kept on, although their numbers were now uneconomic.

It was time to do some drastic streamlining, both for the sake of the national economy and for the benefit of the Service itself. So I set up a committee, the 'Way Ahead Committee', with myself in the chair, and most of my colleagues on the Board as members, to review the whole situation. And then things started to move.

In the end we were able to cut down personnel by about 30,000, uniformed and civilians, and save about £15,000,000 a year, without losing a single ship from the sea-going fleet.

I went round to all our fleets—Home, Mediterranean, Far East, East Indies—tub-thumping and explaining. I also took this opportunity of having a look at the navies of the Commonwealth—our old associates of two world wars, Australia, New Zealand and

Canada—and the young navies of new independent countries, India, Malaya, Ceylon.

Naval morale, which had been drooping a bit, began to revive. But both the Navy and the Commonwealth were now about to undergo a very severe trial.

In June 1956 Colonel Nasser, the firebrand of Egyptian politics, became President of the Republic of Egypt. Egypt's economy was backward, her poverty chronic. To remedy this, Colonel Nasser sought backing for a new irrigation scheme—the Aswan High Dam.

Britain and America informed him, in July, that they would not finance this project. One week after this Anglo-American decision, Nasser announced the nationalisation of the Suez Canal. The Suez Crisis of 1956 had begun.

For three months, negotiations—in London, in Cairo, in the United Nations—dragged on. But from beginning to end there was the clear indication that the British and French Governments (the chief shareholders) might use force if they remained dissatisfied with other solutions. As First Sea Lord, Mountbatten would have to find the means of applying such force, which could only be by yet another large Combined Operation.

By October, Anglo-French dissatisfaction was obvious, and an Anglo-French build-up in the Middle East was nearly completed. A further factor was the long-standing quarrel between Egypt and Israel. On October 29th Israeli troops invaded Sinai.

On November 5th, in the teeth of world disapproval, and with the Commonwealth sharply divided, British and French forces attacked Port Said. Britain herself was also divided; Anthony Eden firmly believed that this act was a matter of stopping aggression on the dangerous model of the thirties—in other words, a 'police action'. Hugh Gaitskell, Leader of the Opposition, took an exactly contrary view.

As the British and French entered Port Said, world reactions sharpened. The United States, Canada and India condemned their actions with words; the Soviet Union threatened to use rockets.

In forty-eight hours the British and French made excellent progress, but at the end of that time the pressures of world opinion, and the great stress imposed on the British economy, compelled the Government to accept the United Nations' insistence on a cease-fire. On November 15th a United Nations Peace-Keeping Force *arrived in the Suez area, and shortly afterwards the British and French withdrew. The dispute over this fiasco has never died away.*

As we all know there have been recriminations about the very motivation of the Suez policy, about collusion with Israel, about the breakdown of relations with America and the United Nations, about our military preparedness, about going thus far, and then suddenly stopping short of our objective.

As an ex-Chief of Staff, I am not permitted to comment on these matters. But those who have followed my story so far will realise that the Suez policy was inspired by very different ideas from those which I had tried to work out in South East Asia in 1945 and 1946, and in India in 1947 and 1948. I carried out my duties, but it would be foolish to pretend that I did not have very grave doubts about the whole thing.

And I would like to say one other thing. In the summer of 1956, when most of Britain was on holiday, but the Services had to try to mobilise, we found ourselves in the extraordinary position of being neither at war nor at peace.

Nothing could be less satisfactory from the Services' point of view. The Navy, with its inherent 'instant readiness', found this less awkward than the others. The Army and the R.A.F. had great difficulties to contend with. But once the Combined Force was assembled, and got off the mark, the operation went forward with great efficiency. The Services did not let the country down, I am sure of that.

*On January 9th 1957 ill health compelled Anthony Eden to resign. He was succeeded as Prime Minister by Harold Macmillan, and in the new Ministry Duncan Sandys took over the office of Defence. His appointment marked the beginning of a series of searching re-examinations of British defence policy which continued through the rest of Mountbatten's career.*

*In April 1957 the new Minister of Defence produced a White Paper which contained some startling statements. Once again there was heavy emphasis on the nuclear deterrent. With the Russian rocket threat still fresh in mind, people learned from Mr. Sandys:*

'It must be frankly recognised that there is at present no means of providing adequate protection for the people of this country against the consequences of an attack with nuclear weapons. This *makes it more than ever clear that the overriding consideration must be to prevent war rather than to prepare for it.'*

*With this in mind, Duncan Sandys concluded:*

*'The only existing safeguard against major aggression is the power to threaten retaliation.'*

For the time being, the V-bombers of the R.A.F. remained Britain's deterrent weapon. But the old dilemma continued; the White Paper reaffirmed that:

*'The frontiers of the free world, particularly in Europe, must be firmly defended on the ground.'*

That would be the Army's rôle. Then came a statement which disconcerted the Admiralty:

*'The rôle of naval forces in total war is somewhat uncertain. It may well be that the initial nuclear bombardment and counter-bombardment by aircraft and rockets would be so crippling as to bring the war to an end within a few weeks, or even days, in which case naval operations would not play any significant part.'*

Duncan Sandys was in fact challenging the assumption that the war at sea might continue after the war on land had collapsed. This he regarded as unrealistic. But to some, at the time, he seemed to be casting deeper doubts upon the Navy's rôle. Naval officers were alarmed, among them Mountbatten himself.

Nevertheless, together Duncan Sandys and Mountbatten now set about the reshaping of the Navy of the fifties. They laid emphasis on mobility: the creation of Task Forces based on the aircraft-carrier, the development of Commando-carriers for amphibious operations, re-defining the rôle of the Royal Marines, building new ships of revolutionary design.

Perhaps most important of all, this forward-looking programme gave the Navy renewed confidence in its future. And all the time, for all three Services, each year produced its crop of problems.

A State of Emergency had existed in Cyprus since 1955; the quarrel between Greek-Cypriots and Turkish-Cypriots remained intransigent. Cyprus continued for several years to be a strain on British resources.

In July 1957 a revolt in Oman brought a demand for British military aid. In 1958 there was a State of Emergency in Aden, another military commitment. And in the same year paratroops were flown into Jordan at the request of King Hussein.

Between 1945 and 1960 more than fifty incidents called for the *intervention of British forces; there were hurricanes, there were floods, there were earthquakes—but there were also at least seventeen major military operations.*

We found that, United Nations or no United Nations, NATO or no NATO, deterrent or no deterrent, our soldiers, sailors and airmen had plenty to keep them occupied. These tasks had never been easy. As each year went by, in the troubled condition of the world, and against the background of Britain's ever-present economic weakness, they became more difficult and more thankless.

In the years after 1956 it became clear that Britain's status in the world had changed—and I don't think anybody is yet clear what our new position is. Looking back, I can see that the process has been going on all through my life.

When my father was First Sea Lord we were by far the greatest naval power in the world, with by far the largest empire. After 1918 the Empire turned into a Commonwealth, and we could no longer afford to remain pre-eminent at sea.

After 1945 there were even greater changes: as last Viceroy I transferred power in India; I assisted at the birth of Pakistan and at the independence of Ceylon; Burma opted out—to my great regret. Yet right up to 1955, when I ceased to be Commander-in-Chief, Mediterranean, the fleets of the Royal Navy had remained a force to be reckoned with.

But after 1956 it became sadly apparent that power, in the military sense, really lay with the super-states—America and Russia, with China beginning to come forward fast. Our foreign policy has been forced to recognise this more and more; we now have to depend on our alliances.

A 'wind of change', as Harold Macmillan described it, again changed the Commonwealth—and we have not yet seen the end of that process. We have been caught up in an economic revolution—and we have not found the answers to that.

Defence policy has had to be adjusted to all these circumstances. I don't suppose there has ever been such a period of rapid, drastic change, in which all fundamental defence questions have been so difficult to answer. The whole field—our alliances, our commitments, our weapons, our bases, our means of communication—have all had to be re-examined in the most critical manner.

This is very largely due to the quite astonishing and ever-accelerating revolution in technology which has been taking place. The Americans hit the nail on the head when they said 'If it works, it is obsolete'.

Nineteen fifty-nine was an astonishing technological year. The great powers had invented a new 'status symbol'—the Space Race; and in this year the great costly space programmes of the United States and Russia produced remarkable results.

In January the Soviet Union launched the cosmic rocket Lunik I. The Americans sent up an artificial planet, Pioneer IV, in March, and in June we had the British rocket Black Knight. But these achievements were only appetisers. On October 4th, Lunik III succeeded in photographing the Moon—an almost unbelievable extension of human knowledge. Manned flight in space soon followed. Both the Russians and the Americans put up their astronauts, and we became familiar with the names of new pathfinders—Gagarin, Glenn, and their fellows.

Progress was not only happening in Space. I was particularly pleased with the success of a new British invention—the Hovercraft. In July 1959 one of these new craft showed its potential by crossing the Channel.

In the very early days, when the inventor, Cockerell, could find no one to back him, he finally wrote to me—and I was able to get him the Government support he needed. That is why I got such a kick when the new sea-going class of Hovercraft in 1968 was named after me.

I find it exciting, living in an age of technological progress. In fact, quite recently, one of our brighter comedians impersonated me in a skit on television and he had me saying:

'Actually I invented technology.'

Well, anyway, I've never been afraid of it. In the Navy as a wireless officer I specialised in communications. But I've never been able to resist sticking a finger into other pies as well. I invented a number of things—some of them just gadgets, some of them important enough to have patented, and to be adopted by the Admiralty.

There was my sub-focal signalling shutter; my wireless wavelength calculator; my course ruler; the 'M'-type torpedo sight—and the one I am proudest of, my station-keeping device, which would take far too long to explain, but which may be said to have saved my life, because I stood on it when the *Kelly* capsized at Crete, and I had to swim clear of the bridge!

As First Sea Lord, as well as streamlining the Navy, I did my best to fit it to take its part in this age of nuclear power, computers and missiles. The 'County' class guided-missile destroyers were my special babies—beautiful ships, and splendid examples of computerised, electronic efficiency.

I was determined to introduce nuclear propulsion. That was a struggle: first, there was the question of know-how. This I was able to overcome by making friends with Admiral Rickover of the U.S. Navy, the father of nuclear propulsion. He gave us invaluable help.

Then there was the question of cost. When Admiral Fisher started a naval revolution in 1906 with the design of H.M.S. *Dreadnought*, the prototype of all dreadnought battleships, her building took a year and a day, and that great ship cost just under £1,800,000. Our H.M.S. *Dreadnought*, half a century later, our first nuclear-powered submarine, was also revolutionary: but she took nearly three times as long to build, and she cost ten times as much! However, I was able to win over the Chancellor of the Exchequer, and work began on her in 1958.

*In July 1958 Mountbatten was appointed Chief of the Defence Staff. The event marked the inauguration of the most sweeping changes ever to take place in the British Armed Forces—more revolutionary than the Fisher naval reforms and the Haldane army reforms which had transformed the Services before 1914.*

The idea of the reorganisation of defence did not suddenly dawn on me. It was the result of twenty years' experience in war and peace. It was what one might call an intellectual fulfilment, whereas being First Sea Lord was more of a sentimental fulfilment. I could hardly believe my good luck in being able to achieve both these things, because what was happening now was really the conclusion of something which began as far back as 1941, when I went to Combined Operations.

That was when the idea of inter-Service organisation and operations really took hold of me. In Combined Operations Command, we demonstrated that it was possible for Army, Navy and Air Force people to sink their Service identities completely, and work as one outfit.

In SEAC, with its integrated inter-Allied staff, the same thing applied. My SEAC staff, and those of the other Supreme Commanders, showed that *national* identities, as well as Service identities, could be submerged. I was horrified when this structure was abandoned in South East Asia after I had left, in spite of my strongest protests. But NATO brought it to life again, and I was able to organise my Allied Forces headquarters in Malta on similar lines in 1953.

I was certain that this was the only way to wage modern war; Plans, Organisation, Logistics, Operations, all depended on complete co-operation, and this has to be built up in peacetime. You simply cannot rely on working it all up at the last moment.

Once again I knew I would have a terrific struggle, because I would be up against tradition and vested interest—a formidable combination. In fact, one senior officer told me quite frankly when I took over as C.D.S. that he regarded my appointment as 'the greatest disaster' which had befallen the British Defence Services within his memory'. I knew I was going to antagonise a lot of people —but I couldn't help that.

*All through the years of Mountbatten's eminence his image had been coupled with another: Edwina Mountbatten, 'Lady Louis', as she was known to many thousands.*

*Their public lives had come dramatically together during the war, when Lady Mountbatten had risen as swiftly to the top in her own field—the Red Cross and St. John—as her husband in the sphere of high command. In South East Asia they had worked closely together on the rescue and repatriation of prisoners of war. In India, as Vicereine, Lady Mountbatten had made an unforgettable impact— among ordinary people perhaps greater than her husband's.*

*She had been seen and admired at Mountbatten's side when he resumed his naval career in 1948 and climbed the ladder from Rear-Admiral to First Sea Lord. But her work for the St. John Ambulance Brigade never ceased. She gave herself to this without stint, refusing to recognise the clear symptoms of illness through overwork.*

*In February 1960 there was a happy family occasion: the wedding of the Mountbattens' younger daughter Pamela to the interior decorator David Hicks.*

My wife Edwina was on the top of her form at Pamela's wedding. I have never known her more gay, more happy, more lovely in recent years. Everybody remarked on it. As somebody said afterwards, it was like a candle that flares up just before it gutters and goes out.

Four days after the wedding she went away on a tour of the Far East as Superintendent-in-Chief of St. John. She shouldn't have gone, of course, but we couldn't stop her. We tried to get her to cut down her programme, but typically she wouldn't hear of it. She must have been dying on her feet, but her sense of duty drove her on, right to the end.

I found out afterwards that on the last night of her life, after a full day in Borneo, she went to an official party. Two ladies had to support her as far as the door. When she got there she pushed them aside, drew herself erect, and walked in and sparkled, as she always did. That night she went to bed and never woke again.

I heard the news by telephone at about two or three o'clock in the morning. It was a poleaxe blow. I simply couldn't grasp it. I didn't have time to. Because as soon as the news came out the heavens opened.

I received over six thousand telegrams and letters, from Kings, Presidents, Prime Ministers, Governors, but what astonished me most was that at least five thousand of them were from people in all walks of life, from many countries, who said that they were her personal friends. I am sure they were, and yet I had never heard of them.

Edwina had asked in her will to be buried at sea. I was not too sure about this, but I was wrong. The First Sea Lord at once offered a frigate, and not only that, he came down himself, and with him the Commander-in-Chief, Portsmouth, and all his senior officers. The Indian Government insisted that one of their frigates should accompany her as her last Indian escort. I was deeply touched at this unique tribute from two Navies. And it was then, I think, as we committed her to the sea, that the sense of loss really came home to me.

*Mountbatten returned to work, a lonely figure without the brave and brilliant woman who had supported him for so long, but no less dedicated to the work he had set in hand. He was due to retire in 1962, but the Prime Minister, Mr. Harold Macmillan, prevailed on him to stay on and complete the work of integration of defence which he had already begun.*

Our new unified Ministry of Defence Building was not completed until 1964. The very core of the building is the Chiefs of Staff room. I like to think of this room as being symbolic of what I was trying to do. We carried out a work-study, to ensure that it was absolutely functional.

In sessions in this room the Chief of Staff can be linked whenever they wish to the Operations Rooms in the Ministry, or overseas commands. On screens they can be seeing exactly the same maps and teleprinter conversations as an overseas Commander-in-Chief at the very same moment. They can receive information and transmit orders by these means with the minimum of fuss and difficulty.

All this, of course, was planned to meet the demands of our world commitments. Our overseas bases were part of the apparatus for dealing with what we called 'brush fires'—those sudden, dangerous contingencies which have to be dealt with instantly, and of which there never seemed to be any lack.

Bases, of course, are vulnerable, so in addition we also had flexible, amphibious Task Forces ready for instant action. As long as we intended to uphold our alliances, and our Commonwealth ties, a co-ordinating nerve centre like this was vital.

I regard that room and the Operations Rooms which are linked to it as a headquarters rather than the old-fashioned Committee Rooms. We British have always liked to wage war by committee, but during the Second World War we learnt to accept the Supreme Commander principle, and all subsequent experience showed that you cannot do without it.

After I became Chief of Defence Staff, I was able to reintroduce Supreme Command, or Unified Command, as we now call it, in all our overseas theatres. In the Far East, as it turned out, this happened just in time.

*In 1962 British policy was to set up a Malaysian Federation which would add economic and political unity to the fragmented independence of that part of South East Asia. The implementation of this policy put Mountbatten's apparatus to its first test.*

*Indonesia bitterly opposed the concept of Malaysia. Once again, the British defence system faced the threat of escalating war. In December 1962 there were Indonesian-inspired revolts in Brunei and*

*Sarawak, which were quickly crushed with the help of British troops. In 1963 Indonesian irregulars appeared openly in attacks on Malaysian territory. 'Confrontation' had begun.*

*British forces were increasingly drawn in to defend Malaysia. This was a strange war, without pitched battles but constantly imposing great strain on small units, requiring great initiative from junior commanders, skilful Intelligence work, and complete co-operation between all units and Services.*

The new command system, under a unified C.-in-C., who was in effect a Supreme Commander, ensured co-operation as I knew it would. The Services worked splendidly together, and they all had a hard job to do. The Navy's task, besides giving all support to the Army, was really to discourage escalation—to convince the Indonesians that it was impossible to launch a large-scale invasion across the narrow strip of water that separates them from Singapore.

We made a brave show in Eastern waters, and it did the trick. 'Confrontation' ended in 1966. We had won this war quietly, efficiently, and at a very low cost in life.

By this time I had retired from the post of Chief of Defence Staff. It was gratifying to me that the last major enterprise of the Services, in which I was involved, should have had such a happy outcome.

Saying good-bye to the Services, of course, was not so happy. It is a bleak moment when you realise that you have reached the end of something that has occupied almost the whole of your life. I had been in uniform for fifty-two years. I had always been proud of that uniform—proud and happy.

As a young midshipman, I wept when I left my first ship—Admiral Beatty's flagship, the *Lion*. I dare say I thought I would never love another ship so much. But of course I did. The Navy gave me great happiness.

How lucky I am to be an Admiral of the Fleet! An Admiral of the Fleet never retires—so I have never had to think of myself as leaving the Navy. I still belong to it, and the Navy will always be a very big part of me.

And so I came home to Broadlands once again—but this time it was with some trepidation. Until now I had kept myself too busy to realise it, but now I knew that mine was an empty place and I would have to keep house by myself. And I would have to face up to this fact, because there was no longer a job to keep me busy and to occupy every minute of my time.

I had always been used to a very active life. Now I wondered what I would find to be active about! I must confess that I was rather frightened at this lonely prospect.

# Epilogue

## JOHN TERRAINE

My real involvement with the making of the television series on Lord Mountbatten began in early 1966. I approached the project with excitement—and trepidation. I knew a little about him: it would have been very difficult to live through the years 1939–45 without hearing his name mentioned. He was, for many people of my generation (twenty years younger than him), something of a hero. I knew that Noël Coward's skilful and moving film, *In Which We Serve*, was largely based on Mountbatten and his ship, H.M.S. *Kelly*. I remembered wartime newsreel shots of one of the most dashing and handsome personalities ever to wear an Admiral's uniform. I had an inkling of what he had achieved as Supreme Allied Commander in South East Asia. I had absolute sympathy with his policy and its execution in India, as last Viceroy in 1947. The Mountbatten charm was a legend; I understood him to be a man of great informality and affability.

Yet, as I say, I had trepidations. Partly, these arose out of the prospect of being thrust into fairly intimate continuous contact with a great man; the great men I have had to deal with before have nearly all been dead. This was something new and slightly intimidating. Secondly, being a historian, I was aware that there were large gaps in my knowledge of the man—fortunately, I did not know how large they were! Thirdly, trying to be objective, I had to recognise that there were possibilities of disagreement between us, which I did not welcome. An advantage of dealing with dead heroes is that they cannot talk back. I had the feeling that Mountbatten might talk back to some effect. Finally, there was the work itself, which I could not possibly visualise at that stage, but which would predictably be testing. There was plenty to worry about.

There never ceased to be plenty to worry about; but of the four items which were on my mind when I first went to meet Lord Louis, only the last proved to be really valid. The first thing I discovered, within minutes of entering the drawing-room at Broadlands (I think the most beautiful, relaxed room that I have ever been invited to make myself at home in, with the invaluable 'do-it-yourself' Grog Tray at the window for the benefit of disintegrating guests), was that the legend of charm had not been overstated. Formality was brushed aside (was it ever there?), and I found myself plunged, in what I later understood to be the Mountbatten manner, straight into the middle of things. It was 'business' not so much 'as usual' as 'at once and all the time'; it generally was with Lord Louis. It was wearing, but it definitely did not permit the mind to dwell on trifles—such as dress, or address. The capacity for putting people quickly at their ease had served Lord Louis well down the years. I was making an early encounter with an ingredient of greatness.

One of the first things that had to be done was for Lord Louis to tell me (and Peter Morley, the producer of the television series) what he thought to be his story. 'What he thought to be . . .'; disarmingly, he said to us straight away: 'I haven't the faintest idea where to begin. I don't know what you want. I don't know how we are going to do this.' And, less disarmingly, he added: 'Do you?' So it was up to us; we made appropriately professional noises. In fact, of course, we *didn't* know—how could we? And Lord Louis, at that stage, naturally had reservations. He told us, with great emphasis, how reluctant he had been to embark on this project, and how he had allowed himself first to be persuaded, then to be enthused, by his son-in-law, John Brabourne. But now that it was actually beginning, he found himself being 'put on the couch' by people he didn't know, whose judgment he had as yet no means of estimating, to have his life probed by questions which could easily be distasteful, impertinent, or just silly.

We found out something else of cardinal importance at once. When Lord Louis set his hand to the plough he did not turn back. From the beginning—though sometimes with a visible effort—he was astonishingly frank. We found that we could indeed ask him questions which in any other circumstances *would* have been impertinent—and we got some very surprising answers. But this did not always help with the story we had to elucidate. We found— and this was no joke for me—that a great man whose life has been

filled with major events in which he has played a conspicuous part
may have little sense of their continuity, and find it hard to dis-
criminate between them. After all, this is the historian's function.
Lord Louis had never tried to be his own historian. Slowly, stage by
stage, we had to overcome this difficulty. I much regretted the gaps
in my knowledge, which seemed to multiply day by day. What could
scarcely have been foreseen was the patience with which Lord
Louis himself tried to fill them, once he understood the problem.

And then came the disagreements. On matters of substance there
were very few of these. Yet disagreements were bound to arise, even
though they might not be about such great issues as strategy during
the Second World War, post-war politics in Asia and elsewhere, the
integration of defence, and so forth. Mainly, they were disagreements about what to put in, and what to leave out in our narrative.

We then encountered a very surprising fact—at least, it surprised
me. We found ourselves steering a curiously zig-zag course between
the danger areas of Lord Louis's habitual boastfulness (to which he
cheerfully admitted) and his habitual diffidence. We found that the
Admiral of the Fleet, the ex-chief of Defence Staff, the ex-First Sea
Lord, the ex-Viceroy, the ex-Supremo, would constantly slide away
from the immense issues which he had deeply influenced in those
roles, sometimes, indeed, brushing 'all that' aside, and insist on
unique qualities in himself in spheres which bordered upon the
bizarre.

'The great thing about me . . .' he announced one night, after a
long, far-reaching conversation; there was a breathless pause; we sat
up, tense, alert, impatient; Revelation was at hand. 'The really important thing about me is . . .' (unendurable tension) 'that I am the
man who cured lameness in horses.'

We sighed.

He cured lameness in horses.[1] He was the first man to adopt a
zip-fastener instead of fly-buttons. He invented elastic shoelaces to
save time. He went from one ship to another to a dinner party on
water-skis, wearing full evening dress. He wore socks with built-in
suspenders—his own design. He invented tracking headlights which
follow a car's front-wheels round corners. He produced a new paint

---

[1] Indeed, Mr Charles Strong, who has been so successful in curing lame horses
by the use of 'Faradism' designed for humans, freely concedes that it all began
with Lord Louis's insistence that one of his lame polo ponies should be treated
by this method.

for the ships of the Royal Navy: 'Mountbatten Pink'.[1] He designed
jewellery. He 'invented technology'. He was the first man to . . . and
also the first to . . . oh, and also the first . . . And these, he seemed
to be telling us, were the things that *really* mattered. It was
disconcerting.

The other side of the picture was no less so. Lord Louis was
brought up in an aura of great affairs, and in particular great naval
affairs. He worshipped his father, who was also a First Sea Lord and
an Admiral of the Fleet. I think Lord Louis would have agreed that
his father was a profounder thinker than he was himself, because
his own nature was much more of a 'doer'. Yet it would pass belief
that some of the mental quality of a father to whom he was always
very close did not impart itself to the son. And it would also pass
belief that this enlightenment would not help the son in following
the same profession. It took a long time to make this point, but when
made it was very fruitful.

Lord Louis was Chief of Combined Operations at the height of the
Second World War. In that capacity he 'put himself on the map' as
a leader, a candidate for the highest command. The Dardanelles
Expedition ('Gallipoli') was the great Combined Operation of the
First World War.

'But I was only fifteen at the time of Gallipoli! Who on earth
wants to know what a boy of fifteen thought about it?'

'Twenty-six years later you were running Combined Operations.
You must have known something about Gallipoli.'

'Possibly. But at the time I only knew what my father told me.'

'Sir, what *did* your father tell you?'

It turned out that his father had told him a great deal, including
a theory of the application of sea-power derived from his study of
Admiral Mahan. It turned out also that Lord Louis had retained this
very clearly in his mind—but would only talk about it as something
attributable to his father.

Similarly with the Battle of Jutland.

'Who wants to hear a pompous old admiral orating about things
that he didn't take part in, and which happened when he was too
young to form a sensible opinion?'

It turned out, this time, that Lord Louis himself had become an

---

[1] This interesting pigment, which was adopted for use by the Admiralty, was
designed to make destroyers more difficult to see in conditions of low visibility
and mist.

expert on the subject, and had lectured to the Mediterranean Fleet about the Battle of Jutland.

Boastfulness and diffidence . . . it took a long time to balance the mixture. But what was important was that Lord Louis, once he felt that he knew us, once he had decided that we knew what we were about, would almost always yield to our judgment. There were battles; and Lord Louis did not give up easily. But he was a professional, he liked and respected professionalism, he was prepared to concede to the professionalism of others. This is not a common quality. In one whose own capacities ranged so widely it was all the more remarkable.

As the work continued, and as we came to know Lord Louis better, we found reflected in our own experience of him many of the characteristics which carried him to eminence in so many spheres. We had long sessions (weeks at a time)—talking, recording, filming —at Broadlands. We went to Malta. We did an exhausting but invaluable tour of the Far East—Ceylon, Singapore, Siam, Burma, India. One by one, qualities of greatness revealed themselves.

The very technique which we found we had to adopt was significant. Compression was a vital necessity and in order to achieve compression I had to take each part of the story as Lord Louis told it, and retell it in far fewer words, yet leaving out nothing vital. I have never experienced anything quite like that exercise.

Neither, of course, had Lord Louis. And the really remarkable thing was that he accepted this technique at once—indeed, he insisted on it. This was his sense of professionalism at work. But what it meant was gruelling labour for him. Everything I wrote for him had to be gone over, and gone over again, to make absolutely sure that the wording, the sense, the facts, were as right as we could make them. Lord Louis was indefatigable; his patience at this was never exhausted. And then, when that was at last done—he had to learn the whole thing, like an actor learning a part, and perform it before the camera, again like an actor. But he was not an actor; he was an Admiral of the Fleet. Yet he brought to this effort a perseverance, a humility, a capacity for taking pains which had to be seen to be believed. Filming is hard work; the days can seem very long. In the great heat of the East, or Malta, or underground in the old War Cabinet rooms, one learns what exhaustion is. Lord Louis was sixty-seven years old when he undertook this task. He utterly refused to be daunted by it. He was determined to get it right.

Thus, in our very manner of work, we saw important aspects of the character of the man. We saw that scrupulous attention to detail which is so often an ingredient of greatness—has it not been said that 'genius is a capacity for taking infinite pains'? We saw also the qualities of pure industry and application without which so much else of genius is wasted. When, hopefully, Lord Louis would look at Peter Morley and at me, after a succession of exacting 'takes', and catch the flicker of doubt in our eyes, and say at once: 'All right, it was no good. I'll do it again,' that, I submit, was an aspect of greatness. And another, perhaps, was the ability to turn the whole thing into a joke, by picking up an all-too-familiar saying of Peter Morley's:

'That was absolutely marvellous, sir—but I think we ought to do it just once more.'

As time went by, I perceived the truth of something which had occurred to me before, writing about other great men of affairs. To be a great soldier, or sailor, or statesman—truly great; in the first rank—a man must be endowed with an unusual degree of energy. This is very unfair, of course, because it is essentially something that one is born with, and no amount of brain-power can compensate for the lack of it. Laziness is fatal; but even the ordinary human weaknesses of fatigue and mental sagging are impediments to greatness. The great man has to be—or just is—rather inhuman.

Already, from what I have just written, some ideas of Lord Louis's energy may be formed. His normal 'speed', at the age of sixty-seven, was, I should say, about three times the highest speed that I have ever been able to achieve at any time in my life. He was notorious for wearing out his A.D.C.s—one of them, presumably to get his own back, had to become Lord Louis's son-in-law. Lord Ismay, who had many dealings with him when he was a member of the Chiefs of Staff Committee, and who later headed his staff in India, wrote:

'A long flight with Mountbatten was an experience which I was careful not to repeat. The idea of a reasonable degree of comfort never entered his head. Speed was all that mattered.'[1]

I know what Lord Ismay meant. My own strongest impression of

---

[1] *The Memoirs of Lord Ismay*: Heinemann, 1960. When Lord Ismay asked for permission to go home after completing his task for Mounbatten in India he said: 'I know I've only done a short time as your Chief of Staff, but candidly six months with you have exhausted me far more than six years doing the same job for Winston.'

Lord Louis's energy was formed at Broadlands. Our own work with him had opened my eyes, but the occasion I have in mind was produced by the intervention of another television film unit. An American concern was making a film on the Dieppe Raid—one of the most controversial episodes of the Second World War. The Raid was, of course, a Combined Operation, and took place while Lord Louis was Chief of Combined Operations. The American producer wanted Lord Louis to appear in the film, and Lord Louis agreed. There followed a voluminous correspondence, which culminated in the presentation to Lord Louis of a questionnaire containing, I think, thirty-one questions. This arrived at the beginning of a week when we were immersed in our own work every day, all day.

Once more we saw his meticulous attention to detail in operation. Ex-staff officers were consulted in writing and on the telephone; documents and diaries were sought out; the Ministry of Defence was consulted and produced still-restricted material. And every night, after dinner, dismissing the day's previous exertions, Lord Louis would say to me :

'Now come on. I need your help. We've got to get this Dieppe thing straightened out.'

And so we would set to again, thrashing out the questions, trying to establish truths and arrive at correct answers. On the night before the Americans arrived, I crawled upstairs some time after midnight, leaving the ex-Chief of Combined Operations still at his desk, writing out in long-hand his thirty-fourth statement. He had added a few items of his own. And he had still to deal with his normal day's correspondence. I had learned something about energy.

In the Far East we learned something about leadership, too. It happened in Singapore. We had been in the East for about ten days, filming away merrily. Then Peter Morley began to receive reports from London on what we had shot—and the reports were dreadful. As far as we could make out, from cables and half-heard long-distance calls in the middle of the night, just about everything that we had done was useless, for technical reasons which no one seemed able to explain. What was to be done? Many things would have to be done, but the most important was, evidently, a drastic revision of a very tight schedule, in order to re-shoot everything that we had already filmed. This was fearful; and it was not at all an appetising prospect to have to break the news to Lord Louis. His own time-table had been very carefully arranged to enable him to pay the minimal but essential courtesy calls wherever he went, to include a strictly limited number of social events (charity premières, etc.) and to visit his own regiment, the Life Guards, in their Far Eastern stations. A spanner in these delicate works would cause havoc. It would be open to him to ask us whether we really knew what we were doing, whether we had taken all proper precautions before we set out, whether we appreciated what his time meant, etc., etc., all freely sprinkled, perhaps, with some crisp naval language. Peter Morley and I mounted the long drive to the beetling classical portico of the Istana (once Government House, Singapore) with gloomy forebodings.

Our fears were groundless. Lord Louis listened to what we had to tell him almost without interruption. Then his reaction took two forms. First, the 'technological man' asserted himself; he was deeply interested in the reasons for the disaster, deeply puzzled, as we were. 'Let's try to analyse this. As I see it, there are likely to be three possible causes. Let's see if we can work by elimination. Now . . .' It was, in other words, as far as he was concerned, a mutual problem, to be solved (if it *could* be solved) mutually. From this flowed, quite naturally, his second reaction, which was like a healing draught: 'Just tell me what you want me to do. I'm at your disposal. I'll do anything I can.' And he added: 'My God! In SEAC things went wrong all the time—what a bore life would be if they didn't!'

So we discovered how a leader can dismiss despondency, bring encouragement in a black moment, and, by adding a joke or two, restore the pleasure which goes out of work when a situation turns sour. He saw to it that there *was* no sourness. He might have left it at that—this was already quite something. But he knew that not only Peter Morley and I, but the whole team (six other people), who had been working hard but cheerfully up to now, would be feeling depressed. In particular, our cameraman, Michael Rhodes, might be feeling that since it was his film that had gone wrong, fingers might be silently pointing at him. Lord Louis, without fuss, without making any drama of it, quietly let each member of the team know that he, personally, had not lost confidence in any of us, that he was not interested in blame of anyone, but simply in solving the problem. And so we remained 'a happy and efficient ship'.

In part, of course, this display of morale-building can be attributed to something other than Lord Louis's capacity for understanding and leadership: to his deep, genuine concern with technological problems as such. It would be fair to say that one reason why he did not make any kind of scene over our misfortunes was that he could not be bothered to—he was too interested in probing the reasons for them. He really *was* a technological man. He was proud of this, and while he accepted that it created some limitations for him, he was not disposed to pay undue attention to them. He had a fine collection of pictures at Broadlands, but confessed that he was not the one to appreciate them best. He was as pleased with a painting by Vernet of his grandfather's Russian Lancer regiment in *grande tenue* as with a Van Dyck. (Both could be better placed and better lit.) His concealed Hi-Fi apparatus in the drawing-room was as likely to be offering a selection by the band of his other regiment, the Royal Marines, or musical comedy, as anything. He knew the jade collection and the porcelain collection were very fine, but valued the 110 silver cups he won in Polo tournaments up to the age of fifty-four much more, to say nothing of his collection of thirty-six swords (headed by the ceremonial sword of Field Marshal Count Terauchi, forged in 1292). He had a good grounding in basic litera-ture, as taught during the first decades of the century, but he would never pretend to be a literary man. Kipling appealed to him as much as any author (and why not?).

All this was the other side of the passionate interest which Lord Louis always felt in the technological aspects of our age. Communi-cations—across a wide field—had been his business all through his life. Electronics probably gripped him first as an element, a vehicle, of Communication. He became the President of the Institution of Electronic and Radio Engineers (twice) and of the British Computer Society; he founded the National Electronics Council of which he was Chairman. These were no empty titles. I would not care to say what any of those distinguished bodies thought they were getting when they invoked the name of Mountbatten at the head of their lists of officers. What they got—as I know from personal observation —was a day-in, day-out attention to their affairs and promotion of their causes with Viceregal energy, Supremo attack. I mean this quite literally. At the Guildhall, on 18 October 1967, Lord Louis addressed an audience of British businessmen. He told them:

'I had the fortune to take part in the higher direction of the war, so I know at first hand how perilous our position then was, and how magnificently the country responded when at last they realised the danger. Undoubtedly the greatest factor in our ultimate victory was that in those days America was our ally. Now, thirty years later, we are fighting for our economic survival. The situation is just as perilous, or rather, it is more perilous, for now we have no allies, only competitors.

'Yet we are the same people who won through in the war, and we have ever greater technological progress at our hands if we can only make really full use of it. Our first computer ACE was produced in 1946, the same year as the Americans produced ENIAC. Yet they now have 43,000 computers compared to our 2,700; that is four times as many per head of population as we have. And other countries, Switzerland and West Germany, are ahead of us in computers per million population . . .

'I once more find myself in the higher levels of a struggle for survival. I feel I cannot let this cause go by default . . .

'What we have to face and fight is not computers but competitors. Our firms, factories, businesses and professions must all join this fight, and join quickly. Non-combatants cannot expect to survive in the end. The enemy conquered Singapore, Malaya, Burma and North Borneo. When final victory came they were liberated. But no comparable liberation can be looked for by firms that have gone into liquidation.'

In retirement Lord Louis was as adamant against any defeat by our great enemy as he ever was against the human enemies whom he had met and beaten. Head of the Immigration Mission visiting Commonwealth Countries, Enquirer into Prison Security, these were two public duties performed after he ceased to be Chief of the Defence Staff in 1965, over and above this ceaseless work on behalf of computers and electronics—and over and above making our series of twelve one-hour films.

Lord Louis was a great family person. There was one member of his family to whom, as I came to realise, he was not only linked by all the ties of blood which meant so much to him, but who also had the capacity to draw from him a quality of romanticism which was not his normal form. Lord Louis had an immense love and loyalty towards his considerably younger cousin, Her Majesty the Queen.

That special relationship apart, his family was the focal point of his life. His two daughters, Patricia and Pamela, and their vigorous horde of children were very close. His sons-in-law were included in the fold. His astonishing mother, who died in 1950, his much-admired brother Georgie, his sister Louise to whom he was so deeply attached, and his sister Alice were lodged for ever in his affections. This is an old family, from which many distinguished people have sprung; it goes far back beyond the name 'Mountbatten', beyond the name 'Battenberg'; its connections embrace many lands in many centuries. To be of the family was, to Lord Louis, to be something special. The head of the English branch of the family is his forty-nine-year-old nephew David, the 3rd Marquess of Milford Haven. To be the Head of the Family was, in Lord Louis's eyes, an important distinction.

Three years' close contact with this man was, for me, an unforgettable experience. I could wish that it had come to me earlier: the qualities of greatness are easy enough to perceive intellectually, more difficult to appreciate without such a contact. To have met Lord Louis before would have helped me to understand other great figures better. But as matters stand, I am grateful to have encountered the force of a true leader; grateful to have been drawn in, even briefly, to that activity which was so well known to his staff in SEAC, in India, in HAFMed., in the Ministry of Defence—and in film-making: he called it 'the spirit of the hive'. I hope that I have been able to pass on something of the impact of his astounding story upon me.

## POSTSCRIPT: 'SO RARE A PERSON'

Lord Mountbatten was assassinated on 27 August, 1979, in his eightieth year. He was enjoying the annual family holiday at Classiebawn Castle, County Sligo, in the Republic of Ireland; one of the regular rituals of the holiday was sea-fishing from the family's unimposing boat, *Shadow V*. A bomb had been planted which blew *Shadow V* to pieces, killing Lord Mountbatten instantly. With him died the Dowager Lady Brabourne, aged eighty-two, mother of his son-in-law, Lord Brabourne, his fourteen-year-old grandson, one of twins, the Honourable Nicholas Knatchbull, and fifteen-year-old Paul Maxwell, a boy who liked boats and was helping the Mountbattens to sail *Shadow V*. On the same day eighteen British soldiers were killed at Warrenpoint in Ulster by a landmine explosion, and four British Army bandsmen were injured in Brussels by a time-bomb for which the IRA also claimed responsibility. All these people were casualties of the long and tragic war which has wracked Northern Ireland since 1969.

For an Admiral of the Fleet to be killed, instantly, at sea, by his country's enemies, is not the worst way to go. Those who knew and loved Lord Mountbatten will accept that his active, tireless personality was never made for the ultimate feebleness of old age. But no nation can lose such a man without a sense of deep tragedy and dire loss; he was, as the Archbishop of Canterbury said at his funeral service, 'so rare a person'.

Lord Louis was throughout his seventy-nine years, summoned and dedicated to the Public Service; his extraordinary range of talents was always at the nation's disposal. It will not be easy to match.

Yet I believe that what will ultimately be missed most, by his family, by his friends, by those who served with him or under him and those who worked with him on so many projects, large and small, is his good cheer, the lightness of spirit which could ease the burdens of an ordeal (as in Burma) or turn hard duty into pleasure, as the crew of H.M.S. *Kelly* and many others would testify. Few occasions found Lord Louis without a ready joke; the worse the moment, the more his spirits rose to it. It was this happy quality (whose value at different times has been inestimable) that was so superbly caught in the soaring music of his funeral fanfare, exactly as he would have wished.

The funeral itself, on 5 September, 1979, was altogether an occasion after his own heart—indeed, typically, he went to great pains to prepare the pageantry of the procession and the service in Westminster Abbey in the meticulous detail with which he considered every serious matter. Lord Louis wanted a happy funeral, and though September 5 could not fail to be a day of mourning for the whole British people, and for uncounted millions across the world, it was also a day of splendour—a fitting reminder of the greatest days of the Empire into which he was born, and which he so loyally and fruitfully served. With unerring skill, Lord Louis chose and fashioned the way in which he must be remembered: thanks to the reverent precision of the officers and men of the Forces which he had commanded with such distinction, he will remain forever in memory as a paladin of this country in this century.

JOHN TERRAINE
*October 1979*

# Index